3rd Workshop on Computational Modeling of PEople's Opinions, PersonaLity, and Emotions in Social media (PEOPLES 2020)

Held online due to COVID-19

Barcelona, Spain
13 December 2020

ISBN: 978-1-7138-2836-5

PEOPLES 2020

Computational Modeling of PEople's Opinions, PersonaLity, and Emotions in Social media

Proceedings of the Third Workshop

December 13, 2020
Barcelona, Spain (Online)

Preface

Welcome to the third edition of PEOPLES, the Workshop on Computational Modeling of People's Opinions, Personality and Emotions in Social Media, co-located with the 28th International Conference on Computational Linguistics (COLING 2020). PEOPLES 2020 is the continuation of a successful series of workshops that were held at the 26th International Conference on Computational Linguistics (COLING 2016) in Osaka, Japan, and at the 16th Annual Conference of the North American Chapter of the Association for Computational Linguistics: Human Language Technologies (NAACL-HLT 2018), New Orleans, USA, aimed at providing a forum for researchers who share an interest in personality, opinion and emotion detection, as well as the impact of work in this research field on society.

The communities' response, with 32 received submissions coming from 15 different countries from Asia-Pacific, Europe and the USA, and going well beyond typical Natural Language Processing topics, proves again this year that there is wide interest at the intersection of fields studying sentiment analysis, emotion detection, and personality in disciplines such Computational Linguistics, Natural Language Processing, and Computational Social Science, and we are happy to be able to provide a context for exchanging ideas. Also, we deem it important to provide a forum where crucial discussion about ethical aspects related to the research involving the PEOPLES traits can find a place to be, and to grow.

Following the reviewers's advice, 15 papers were selected for inclusion in the proceedings. They cover a wide range of topics related to the three main PEOPLES themes (personality, emotion and opinion), their interaction and the impact of their modelling on social aspects like well-being, inclusion, political preferences and language use. This year, we also noticed that multilinguality is definitely a key issue, with a large variety of languages represented in the research described. Additionally, we had specifically mentioned in the call that we would very much welcome research focusing on how the usual PEOPLES dimensions might have changed or might be changing due to the special COVID-related circumstances. Clearly this is a dominant topic in the community from several viewpoints, with at least four papers specifically discussing pandemic-related research.

We are extremely grateful to David Jurgens from the University of Michigan for giving a keynote talk. His work at the interesection of NLP and Computational Social Science enriches the workshop program.

We would like to thank our program committee consisting of researchers from a variety of backgrounds for their insightful and constructive reviews. Without their support, this workshop would not have been possible. In addition, we thank all authors for submitting papers and making PEOPLES a big success. A big thanks to our publicity and publication chair Esin Durmus, Cornell University, for her endless support and for compiling these proceedings, particularly in these difficult pandemic times.

We thank COLING for hosting us again, this time virtually, and in particular the local organizers for their support. Thanks for all the extra efforts of moving the conference and all workshops online, unlike the original plans. We hope you and your family are all safe. Lastly, we are extremely grateful to our sponsors, CELI Language Technologies, and the Computational Linguistics group of the University of Groningen for their financial support.

We look forward to welcoming you all at this fully virtual edition of PEOPLES 2020!

Malvina, Viviana, Barbara, and Esin

PEOPLES: https://peopleswksh.github.io/

Organisers

Malvina Nissim, University of Groningen, The Netherlands

Viviana Patti, University of Turin, Italy

Barbara Plank, IT University of Copenhagen, Denmark

Esin Durmus, Cornell University, US

Programme Committee

Jeremy Barnes, University of Oslo, Norway

Maria Barrett, IT University of Copenhagen, Denmark

Pierpaolo Basile, University of Bari, Italy

Valerio Basile, University of Turin, Italy

Elisa Bassignana, University of Turin, Italy

Meriem Beloucif, Universität Hamburg, Germany

Laura Bostan, University of Stuttgart, Germany

Erik Cambria, Nanyang Technological University, Singapore

Tommaso Caselli, University of Groningen, The Netherlands

Chloé Clavel, LTCI-CNRS, Telecom-ParisTech, France

Walter Daelemans, University of Antwerp, Belgium

Dipankar Das, Jadavpur University, India

Esin Durmus, Cornell University, US

Komal Florio, University of Torino, Italy

Tommaso Fornaciari, Bocconi University, Italy

Aparna Garimella, University of Michigan, USA

Albert Gatt, University of Malta, Malta

Rob van de Goot, IT University of Copenhagen, Denmark

Mareike Hartmann, University of Copenhagen, Denmark

Delia Irazú Hernández Farías, Universidad de Guanajuato Campus León, Mexico

Aditya Joshi, CSIRO, AU

Svetlana Kiritchenko, NRC-Canada, Canada

Roman Klinger, University of Stuttgart, Germany

Florian Kunneman, Vrije Universiteit Amsterdam, The Netherlands

Fei Liu, Melbourne University, Australia

Nikola Ljubešić, Jožef Stefan Institute, Slovenia

Kim Luyckx, Antwerp University Hospital, Belgium

Gosse Minema, University of Groningen, Netherlands

Dong Nguyen, Utrecht University, The Netherlands

Malvina Nissim, University of Groningen, The Netherlands

Scott Nowson, Artificial Intelligence Lead, PwC Middle East, United Arab Emirates

Debora Nozza , Bocconi University, Italy

Endang Wahyu Pamungkas, University of Turin, Italy

Viviana Patti, University of Turin, Italy

Paola Pietrandrea, Université de Lille, France

Barbara Plank, IT University of Copenhagen, Denmark

Daniel Preotiuc-Pietro, Bloomberg, USA

Paolo Rosso, Technical University of Valencia, Spain

Ingmar Weber, QCRI, Qatar

Charlie Welch, University of Michigan, USA

Sponsors

PEOPLES 2020 is organized with the support of CELI Language Technology (https://www.celi.it/en/) and the Computational Linguistics group of CLCG (http://www.rug.nl/research/clcg/), University of Groningen.

Social Interpretations of Interpersonal Communication
David Jurgens
University of Michigan, US

Table of Contents

Conference Program

Sunday, December 13, 2020

14:00–15:00   Session 1

14:00–14:10   *Opening Remarks*

14:10–14:30   *Inferring Neuroticism of Twitter Users by Utilizing their Following Interests*
Joran Cornelisse

14:30–14:50   *Matching Theory and Data with Personal-ITY: What a Corpus of Italian YouTube Comments Reveals About Personality*
Elisa Bassignana, Malvina Nissim and Viviana Patti

14:50–15:00   *Red Is Open-Minded, Blue Is Conscientious: Predicting User Traits From Instagram Image Data*
Lisa Branz, Patricia Brockmann and Annika Hinze

15:00–16:00   Session 2

15:00–15:20   *Persuasiveness of News Editorials depending on Ideology and Personality*
Roxanne El Baff, Khalid Al Khatib, Benno Stein and Henning Wachsmuth

15:20–15:30   *HopeEDI: A Multilingual Hope Speech Detection Dataset for Equality, Diversity, and Inclusion*
Bharathi Raja Chakravarthi

15:30–15:40   *KanCMD: Kannada CodeMixed Dataset for Sentiment Analysis and Offensive Language Detection*
Adeep Hande, Ruba Priyadharshini and Bharathi Raja Chakravarthi

15:40–15:50   *Contextual Augmentation of Pretrained Language Models for Emotion Recognition in Conversations*
Jonggu Kim, Hyeonmok Ko, seoha song, Saebom Jang and Jiyeon Hong

15:50–16:00   *TWEETEVAL: Unified Benchmark and Comparative Evaluation for Tweet Classification (Findings of EMNLP 2020)*
Francesco Barbieri, Jose Camacho-Collados, Leonardo Neves, Luis Espinosa-Anke

16:00–17:00   Session 3

16:00–16:45   *Keynote: Social Interpretations of Interpersonal Communication*
David Jurgens (University of Michigan, US)

16:45–17:00   Break

17:00–18:00   Session 4

17:00–17:20   *Social Media Unrest Prediction during the COVID-19 Pandemic: Neural Implicit Motive Pattern Recognition as Psychometric Signs of Severe Crises*
Dirk Johannßen and Chris Biemann

17:20–17:30   *Topic and Emotion Development among Dutch COVID-19 Twitter Communities in the early Pandemic*
Boris Marinov, Jennifer Spenader and Tommaso Caselli

17:30–17:50   *Sentiments in Russian Medical Professional Discourse during the Covid-19 Pandemic*
Irina Ovchinnikova, Liana Ermakova and Diana Nurbakova

17:50–18:00   *Multilingual Emoticon Prediction of Tweets about COVID-19*
Stefanos Stoikos and Mike Izbicki

18:00–19:00   Session 5

18:00–18:20   *Experiencers, Stimuli, or Targets: Which Semantic Roles Enable Machine Learning to Infer the Emotions?*
Laura Ana Maria Oberländer, Kevin Reich and Roman Klinger

18:20–18:30   *Learning Emotion from 100 Observations: Unexpected Robustness of Deep Learning under Strong Data Limitations*
Sven Buechel, João Sedoc, H. Andrew Schwartz and Lyle Ungar

18:30–18:50   *Cross-lingual Emotion Intensity Prediction*
Irean Navas Alejo, Toni Badia and Jeremy Barnes

18:50–19:00   *The LiLaH Emotion Lexicon of Croatian, Dutch and Slovene*
Nikola Ljubešić, Ilia Markov, Darja Fišer and Walter Daelemans

19:10–20:00   *Closing Remarks and QA*

Inferring Neuroticism of Twitter Users by Utilizing their Following Interests

Joran Cornelisse
University of Amsterdam
joran.cornelisse@gmail.com

Raoul Grasman
University of Amsterdam
R.P.P.P.Grasman@uva.nl

Abstract

Twitter is a medium where, when used adequately, users' interests can be derived from what he follows. This characteristic can make it attractive for a source of personality derivation. We set out to test the hypothesis that, analogous to the Lexical hypothesis, which posits that word use should reveal personality, following behavior on social media should reveal personality aspects. We used a two-step approach, wherein the first stage, we selected accounts for whom it was possible to infer personality profiles to some extent using available literature on personality and interests. On these accounts, we trained a regression model and segmented the derived features using hierarchical cluster analysis. In the second stage, we obtained a small sample of users' personalities via a questionnaire and tested whether the model from stage 1 correlated with the users from step 2. The the explained variance for the neurotic and neutral neuroticism groups indicated significant results ($R^2 = .131$, $p = .0205$; $R^2 = .22$, $p = .0044$). Confirming the hypothesis that following behavior should be correlated with one's interests and that interests are correlated with the neuroticism personality dimension.

1 Introduction

With the advent of massive data streams of personal online behavior, there has been a surge in interest in relating this behavior to classical constructs in psychology. In particular, the question of whether online behavior can be related to personality profiles obtained from psychometric personality instruments, often the Big Five (Digman, 1990), has led to a field of research that has been coined *Personality computing* (Vinciarelli and Mohammadi, 2014). Studies in this field have found significant correlations between personality scores and lexical elements in written text, such as essays (Mairesse et al., 2006), blogs (Oberlander and Nowson, 2006; Yarkoni, 2010; Minamikawa and Yokoyama, 2011; Iacobelli et al., 2011), self-presentations (Batrinca et al., 2011), emails (Estival et al., 2007), texting (Holtgraves, 2011), and even the choice of email addresses (Back et al., 2008).

The idea that an author's personality is reflected in written or spoken text at all, is referred to as the *Lexical hypothesis* (Pennebaker and King, 1999; Mairesse et al., 2006), and has been confirmed in many studies. As personality involves and influences the interaction with one's environment, it should be expected to influence other facets of linguistic and non-linguistic expression. The rise of social media over the last decade resulted in this interaction being partly transposed to digital platforms. In fact, the current omnipresence of social media have compounded to the availability of records of individual expression and extends well beyond just the textual, and includes Facebook "likes" (Kosinski et al., 2013), sharing behavior (Gou et al., 2014), website visiting behavior, YouTube videos (Biel and Gatica-Perez, 2012; Farnadi et al., 2013), LinkedIn profiles (Faliagka et al., 2012), Instagram pictures (Ferwerda and Tkalcic, 2018), and tweets on Twitter (Golbeck et al., 2011; Chen et al., 2014; Li et al., 2014).

At face value, Facebook, Twitter and other social media platforms seem quite similar. Indeed lexical hypothesis-driven approaches have treated Facebook status updates as more or less equivalent to Twitter tweets. However, there is an essential distinction between the purposes of the two media. Facebook is

Proceedings of the Third Workshop on Computational Modeling of PEople's Opinions, PersonaLity, and Emotions in Social media, pages 1–10
Barcelona, Spain (Online), December 13, 2020.

generally used as a place to keep in touch with friends and acquaintances. Twitter, on the other hand, is a medium that is used for sharing and gaining information related to someone's interests. As a result, to use Twitter adequately and benefit from its full set of features, an active Twitter user is forced to follow his different interests on Twitter. This characteristic of Twitter can make it especially attractive as a source for personality derivation, as preferences of individuals can, to a significant extent, be explained by underlying personality traits (Ozer and Benet-Martinez, 2006).

It has often been contended that the social network(s) that people find themselves embedded in is reflective of many personal characteristics (Kosinski et al., 2013). Social media networks —reflected in the connections users can make to other users, e.g., by 'friending' on Facebook or 'following' on Twitter[1] —have been related to various personal characteristics such as gender, age, ethnicity, sexual orientation, religious and political views (Kosinski et al., 2013). Although it has been observed that various generic network metrics that do not take into account the node characteristics of the connected nodes, including connectedness, node centrality measures, as well as the total number of friends / followers and the number of users followed, are correlated with personality (Quercia et al., 2011; Li et al., 2014), to our knowledge, no research on computational personality has investigated whether the *specific set of accounts* followed by a Twitter user is associated with personality.

In this study we aim to investigate if, and how profiles of accounts followed by a user are related to personality. We do this by deriving a predictive model from Twitter following graph data related to a set of prior chosen interests, and validating this predictive model on a sample of Twitter users from whom we obtained personality profiles using a standardized test. We focused particularly on neuroticism, as it has shown to have a reliable correlation to social media extracted features (Blackwell et al., 2017; Abbasi and Drouin, 2019). The specific interest were chosen on the basis of available literature that relates the interest to personality, and on the requirement that this interest can be relatively easily inferred from Twitter accounts using heuristic methods. We hypothesize that the following of (clusters of) nodes in the Twitter graph (that we coin 'influencer accounts' below) are significantly correlated with personality scores on a standardized personality test.

2 Methods

To build a predictive model that uses the links between nodes, a large sample of users is required as predictor variables within all the possible connections in the following graph data. While it is easy to obtain a large sample of Twitter users and the information regarding their following behavior, it is not easy to obtain their personality profiles by having these users fill out a psychometric test. We therefore developed a two stage approach: In the first stage we select a large sample of Twitter users for whom it was possible to infer personality profiles to some extend by heuristic means from their expressed interests and professions (we detail this below). On this data set, we trained a regression model. In the second stage, we obtained a small sample of Twitter users who were willing to fill out a personality questionnaire (the NEO-FFI) to provide us with a validation sample: We tested whether the predictions by model from stage 1 for the people in our stage 2 sample significantly correlated with personality profiles obtained from the questionnaire they filled out.

2.1 Using specific interests as a personality gauge

In the first stage we used heuristic methods to build a regression model. In particular, we searched for Twitter users who expressed specific interests on their Twitter accounts that have been linked to personality characteristics in previous research. For instance, we searched for Twitter users who expressed interest in *yoga* as people participating in yoga tend to score *lower* on neuroticism than the general population (Venkatesh et al., 1994). Similarly, social interests have been correlated with agreeableness (Costa and McCrae, 1985); interest in self-enhancing or affiliating humor have been found to negatively correlate with neuroticism (Greengross et al., 2012); and entrepreneurial inclinations correlate negatively with neuroticism (Zhao and Seibert, 2006). Twitter users express these specific interests not only in their

---

[1]Note that the difference between 'friending' and 'following' is another difference between Facebook and Twitter, in that the former is a symmetric relation, while the latter is unidirectional.

tweets, but also in the Twitter accounts that they follow. We will coin Twitter accounts followed by a user *influencer accounts*, or *influencers* for short, in line with the use of these terms in the field of marketing. Furthermore, such interests can be expressed in their profile in their occupational denomination, which is either announced in their profile or can possibly be inferred from the influencer accounts that they follow. Research showed that sort-alike interests, such as food consumption, brand-preference, and political preference could all be deducted from following behavior (Abbar et al., 2015; Chu et al., 2016; Golbeck and Hansen, 2014). Correspondingly, neuroticism is negatively associated with the *Enterprising type* of Holland's RIASEC model of occupational interest (Armstrong and Anthoney, 2009; Holland, 1997; Costa Jr and McCrae, 1992; Zhao and Seibert, 2006). This way, an Enterprising-occupational preference can be used as a parameter for the emotional stable group.

Using a set of specific interests and occupations, we collected three large groups of together 6107 Twitter users that we could classify as more likely *neurotic* (NEU+), more likely *emotionally stable* (NEU-), and more likely *neutral* (NEU±) based on the influencers that these accounts follow. In particular, users in the *neurotic group* (NEU+) were found by searching for users interested in *self help information for stress coping* (Saper and Forest, 1987; Kessler et al., 1997), or *artistic profession* (Marchant-Haycox and Wilson, 1992; Gelade, 1997; Nowakowska et al., 2005; Srivastava and Ketter, 2010); users in the *emotionally stable* group (NEU-) where found by searching users who were interested in *entrepreneurial topics* (Zhao and Seibert, 2006; Brandstätter, 2011) or in *self-enhancing humor* (Greengross et al., 2012; Kuiper and Leite, 2010; Mendiburo-Seguel et al., 2015), while users in the *neutral* group were found by searching for users who were interested in topics from both these groups (e.g., both interested in yoga and in entrepreneurial topics). For finding the included Twitter accounts we extracted the followers of accounts resembling these particular interests via the Twitter REST API. The validity of the collection was assessed by verifying a random sample of a small number accounts from each group at face value. Example searches are presented in Table 1. The logic behind the neutral group entails that a user who is interested in both interests for the neurotic and emotional stable group, would be classified as neutral. Similar according to the NEO-FFI. However, this does result for the groups not being mutual exclusive. As a result, users who were in more than one group, were excluded from the data set. In Table 2, some examples of the used influencer accounts are given.

The collection of all these *influencer* accounts constitutes our set of predictors: Each *influencer* account defines a dummy variable that is equal to 1 for users who follow this *influencer*, and 0 for users who do not follow this *influencer*. Because this results in a very large set of dummy variables (over 20,000), we clustered them into a limited set of 100 *influencer clusters* by means of (complete linkage) hierarchical clustering (McQuitty, 1955), and scored each user on these groups by counting the number of accounts in each *influencer clusters* a user followed. Hence, our data set for stage 1 consisted of 18,000 Twitter users, divided over three inferred neuroticism groups, for each of which we had as predictive features their count scores for the 100 different *influencer clusters*.

2.2 Feature selection

Using this first stage data set, we built a regression model in order to determine which of the 100 *influencer* groups count features were important for the prediction of neuroticism. We used multinomial least absolute shrinkage and selection operator (*Lasso*) regression (Tibshirani, 1996) to predict neuroticism group membership from these features. Lasso regression penalizes regression coefficients by adding their absolute values to the least squares criterion, weighted by a regularization strength parameter. This penalty promotes coefficients to be exactly equal to zero that would have been close to zero in normal regression. The non-zero coefficients of the resulting model defines the set of relevant features. This, in effect, automatically selects the features that are relevant for distinguishing between the neuroticism groups. How many coefficients end up at zero depends on the regularization strength parameter. We used 10-fold cross-validation to determine the optimal regularization strength (Friedman et al., 2010).

2.3 Model validation

In order to validate the *influencer* group count features derived from the first stage data set, and in order to test the hypothesis that personality is correlated with Twitter following behavior, we conducted ordinary

Group	Query

Neurotic group	`SELECT * FROM SAMPLE WHERE`
	`user follows >= 3 Stress coping influencers`
	`OR >= 3 Artistic profession influencers`

Emotional stable group	`SELECT * FROM SAMPLE WHERE`
	`user follows >= 5 Enterprising influencers`
	`OR >= 3 self-enhancing humor influencers`
	`OR >= 5 Yoga influencers`

Neutral group	`SELECT * FROM SAMPLE WHERE`
	`user follows >= 3 Enterprising influencers`
	`AND 3 Stress coping influencers`
	`OR >= 3 self-enhancing humor influencers`
	`AND >= 3 Artistic profession influencers`

Table 1: Overview of example queries used in order to create groups reflecting different dimensions of neuroticism.

Group	Influencers
Neurotic influencers	@WakeupPeople, @suicidalwrxck, @sosadtoday, @depressingmsgs,@AgainstSuicide, @depression
Emotional stable influencers	@ondernemer24, @nieuws_4_zzp, @de_ondernemer, @GreenBiz, @MKBNL, @FinancialTimes

Table 2: In this table, we can find some examples of influencers used to generate the three different groups. The neurotic influencers depict anxiety, self-help, and stress-coping accounts, which aim to help people with negativity in their lives.The emotional stable influencers found were mostly connected to entrepreneurship. The word *ondernemer* is dutch for entrepreneur. ZZP an organization connected to freelancing and MKB, stands for middle and small companies, supports entrepreneurial companies. Note that these are just some examples to give a general idea of what kind of accounts were categorized as influencers.

multiple linear regression of neuroticism scores onto the derived features in a new sample of Twitter user participants who we asked to fill out the NEO-FFI.

These participants were recruited through ads on Twitter using targeted campaigns to Dutch nationals with an expressed affinity for scientific research, universities (students or professors) and/or psychology. The reason to target these individuals was to maximize the response rate. The ads were running from November 2018 through January 2019, until $n = 130$ responses were collected. The ad invited Twitter users to participate in research on personality. Users who clicked on the ad were directed to an online survey form.

After a brief explanation of the purpose of the study—relating Twitter activity to personality—they were asked to fill out the Dutch version of the NEO-FFI (Hoekstra et al., 2007). We asked to fill in the personality test truthfully and emphasized that their results would be kept private. The NEO-FFI measures personality based on the Big Five personality dimensions (Costa Jr and McCrae, 1992). The Dutch NEO-FFI has been evaluated and normed(Hoekstra et al., 2007). The manual reports a reliability of 0.89 (Cronbach's alpha) for Neuroticism. In the survey, we also asked participants to share their Twitter account handle. The Twitter account handles of the participants were used to extract their following behavior (*influencer accounts*).

3   Results

3.1   Feature extraction: Clustering and Lasso regression

The database queries yielded a total of 6107 twitter users divided into 2301 NEU+, 1156 NEU±, and 2650 NEU- accounts. All subsequent data processing was conducted in R (R Core Team, 2019). These

6107 Twitter users followed a total number of 669104 unique *influencer* accounts. To reduce this number of potential predictive features, we first removed the *influencer* accounts from that had near zero variance (Kuhn and Johnson, 2013, those that were either followed by less than 1% or not followed by less than 1%). This reduced the set of 669104 *influencer* accounts to 4367 potential predictive features. We then reduced the number of predictive features further by means of agglomerative hierarchical clustering with complete linkage as cluster dissimilarity measure (Venables and Ripley, 2013) on the basis of similar follower patterns across the 6107 Twitter users. The output yielded 100 *influencer* group count clusters of varying sizes, ranging from just a few Twitter accounts to nearly 200. Subsequently, we used multinomial lasso regression (Tibshirani, 1996) to find the *influencer* group count clusters that are most predictive for group membership. Before fitting the multinomial lasso regression model, the *influencer* group count features were standardized to have zero means and unit standard deviations. The lasso-penalty strength was fine tuned with 10-fold cross-validation to optimize the predictive classification accuracy. The cross-validated prediction accuracy of this model was more than 90%, indicating that the NEU+, NEU±, and NEU- groups could be well seperated.[2] Of the 100 *influencer* group count features that entered the multinomial lasso regression, 76 had non-zero coefficients on at least one of the multinomial predictive functions. Only 46 of these we considered of predictive importance: *influencer* features with a regression coefficient of at least 10% of the largest coefficient in absolute value.

3.2   Validation: Multiple linear regression

130 Twitter users filled out the personality questionnaire. Participants were excluded if they did not complete the survey, or had protected Twitter accounts.[3] In total, 98 participants were eligible.

We admitted the *influencer* group count features selected by the multinomial lasso regression to a multiple linear regression analysis in which the NEO derived neuroticism score was used as the dependent variable. We did this separately for each of the three prediction functions for the NEU+, NEU±, and NEU- groups in the previous step. While for the NEU± and NEU- group equations the explained variance was significant at the .05 level, $R^2 = .248$, adjusted $R^2 = .131$, $F(18, 84) = 2.125$, $p = .0205$, and $R^2 = .38$, adj $R^2 = .22$, $F(20, 77) = 2.328$, $p = .0044$, respectively, the explained variance for the NEU+ equation was only marginally significant, $R^2 = .261$, adjusted $R^2 = .104$, $F(17, 80) = 1.66$, $p = .068$. Note that these tests evaluate different predictive equations because they include mostly non-overlapping sets of *influencer* group count features. The influencer Twitter handles (i.e., their '@' names) that are associated with significant coefficients are displayed in Table 3. The significant coefficients for the NEU± and NEU- regressions were mostly negative, indicating that with increasing counts on the corresponding features (i.e., with increasing number of influencer accounts followed within the feature cluster) the neuroticism score decreased. Hence, these regression models are mostly indicative of emotional stability. The only regression coefficient that was significant in the NEU+ equation was positive.

We did various diagnostic checks on these regressions (Fox, 2015; Fox and Weisberg, 2018). Because influence measures indicated some of the cases to be influential, we also ran the regression analyses with these influential cases removed. For all three equations, this only had the effect of making the observed effects larger, and the p-values smaller—indeed rendering the previously marginal significance of the NEU+ regression model highly significant ($R^2 = 0.346$, adjusted $R^2 = 0.207$, $F(16, 75) = 2.48$, $p = .004$), while the NEU± and NEU- models maintained high levels of significance ($R^2 = 0.3$, adjusted $R^2 = 0.184$, $F(13, 79) = 2.6$, $p = 0.0047$, and $R^2 = 0.457$, adjusted $R^2 = 0.306$, $F(20, 72) = 3.025$, $p = 0.0003$, respectively).

Because it has been previously reported that the number of Facebook 'friends' is associated with personality, we verified that adding a total number of following accounts feature did not change any of the models, $\Delta R^2 = 0.01$, $F(1, 79) = 1.134$, $p = .29$ for the NEU+ model, $\Delta R^2 = 0.017$, $F(1, 83) =$

---

[2]Note that this high prediction accuracy indicates that the lasso model has learned the differences between the queries that were used to create our NEU+, NEU± and NEU- groups. By extension, it presumably learns to distinguish between Twitter users that score high, medium, or low on the neuroticism personality axis.

[3]Twitter allows users to make their account private. As a result no information can be extracted for that account by third parties.

$1.957, p = .165$ for the NEU$\pm$ model, $\Delta R^2 = 0.007, F(1, 76) = 0.812, p = .371$ for the NEU-model. Also, a separate regression of the neuroticism score on this feature did not yield a significant explained variance, $F(1, 96) = 0.03061, p = 0.862$. In addition, because the *influencer* accounts that are associated with significant coefficients were mostly related to entrepreneurial interest and self-employment, we checked whether the significant predictive power of the models simply resulted from entrepreneurial interest by adding the count totals of the number of accounts participants followed that were also followed by Twitter users in the NEU- group. This also did not lead to a significant change of models, $\Delta R^2 = .002, F(1, 79) = 0.254, p = .642$ for the NEU+ model, $\Delta R^2 = .01, F(1, 76) = 1.065, p = .305$ for the NEU$\pm$ model, and $\Delta R^2 = .002, F(1, 76) = 0.217, p = .642$ for the NEU-model; nor did a separate simple regression of the neuroticism scores on this feature yield a significant effect ($F(1, 96) = 0.031, p = .861$). Hence, taken together these results indicate that it is not merely the number of account followed, nor merely an entrepreneurial interest that is able to explain the variance in the neuroticism scores, but the specific pattern of *influencer* groups that are followed. A series of similar regressions in which the other personality scores (openness, conscientiousness, extraversion, and agreeableness) were used as dependent variables did not result in significant omnibus tests, which shows that the results are particular to neuroticism for which we constructed our *influencer* group count features.

Group	Relation	(example) Accounts	Cluster Size
Neu+	Positive	@9GAG, @9GAGTweets, @Rosssen, @OhDailyJustin	4
Neu$\pm$	Negative	@JOR_ID, @BoogerdLive, @TeamSunweb, @RobScheepers, @lars_boom	14
Neu$\pm$	Negative	@MINOCW, @Leraar24, @SanderDekker, @LerarenMetLef, @JelleJolles	25
Neu$\pm$	Positive	@bibliotheek, @NPO2extra, @NOGvacatures, @taalmissers, @vangoghmuseum	21
Neu-	Negative	@StephenRCovey, @MarcStijfs, @woutsmelt, @TonyRobbins, @Upgres	17
Neu-	Negative	@Politie_Zeeland, @zeelandzakelijk, @JoAnnesdeBat, @hvzeeland, @PetradeBoevere	22
Neu-	Negative	@OP_Nederland, @KVK_NL, @AccWeek, @Taxence, @BDONederland	32
Neu-	Positive	@Sebastiaan_IMG, @Brandpunt_plus, @nieuwelente, @StudioLizix, @TL_070	19

Table 3: Influencer account handles ('@' names) associated with the *influencer* group count features with significant multiple regression coefficients in the validation data set. *Top row*: Features that predict NEU+ membership. *Middle rows*: Features that predict NEU$\pm$ membership. *Bottom rows*: Features that predict NEU- membership. Only features with significant multiple regression coefficients are displayed. For each cluster, we indicate whether it had a negative (i.e., indicate lower neuroticism score) or positive (i.e., indicate higher neuroticism score) coefficient. We show five arbitrary chosen accounts per cluster.

4   Discussion

We set out to test the hypothesis that, analogous to the Lexical hypothesis which posits that word use should reveal personality, following behavior on social media should reveal aspects of personality. This hypothesis was motivated by the fact that following behavior should be highly correlated with one's interests and occupation, and that interests and occupation are correlated with personality dimensions. In particular, we aimed to test this hypothesis with respect to the degree of neuroticism of an individual. To do so, we introduced a novel technique for constructing predictive independent variables: On the basis of these well established correlations between personality on the one hand, and interests and occupation on the other, we were able to gather a sufficiently large database of Twitter users and their following behavior to extract clusters of *influencer* accounts that discriminate between Twitter users that have a lower or higher propensity to score high on the neuroticism dimension of the Big Five. Using these predictors we were then able to confirm the hypothesis by showing that these predictors were significantly related to neuroticism scores in a relatively small sample of 98 participants recruited to fill out the NEO-FFI.

On the basis of these results we can conclude that it is possible to derive estimates of neuroticism from following behavior. A significant consequence of these findings is that, in contrast to personality profiles extracted on the basis of lexical hypothesis which requires active engagement of social media platform users, our results are purely based on information that is passively conveyed by Twitter users by their following behavior. Hence, a neuroticism score can be obtained even from social media users who do not actively engage in information sharing on these platforms. One might object that the explained variance is rather low and consequently, very imprecise. This is certainly true for assessing specific individuals reliably—that is, our results do not really support the notion that it is possible, e.g., for employers to screen a specific applicant for a job. However, it is sufficient for targeting population segments; e.g., it allows for talent recruiters to target subgroups of the population that are more likely to have certain personality profiles, or for marketeers to target population segments, e.g., in attempts to sway an election.

4.1   Time and Location

A relevant note for this study is that its results are subject to time and location. This is because individual interests can be prevalent during a specific period or at a particular location. For instance, yoga or meditation are rising interests, which are now much more popular than several decades ago. These interests were used as a *neurotic features* (i.e., influencers). However, regarding their rising popularity, they might not be *significant* features in the future, as then *all kinds* of people would be interested in performing yoga or meditation. In respect to location, the interests used are subjective to Dutch nationals, and more or less the Western world. The *neurotic interests* might be different in other parts of the world. Not to mention that personality determination in itself works differently in other parts of the world, for instance, Asia (Markus and Kitayama, 1998). Therefore, the results from this study are dependent of time and location.

4.2   Caveats

It is not clear what population our sample represents, as it is a self-selected group. Also, Twitter suggests a user which accounts to follow based on the accounts the user already follows. This causes accounts to be clustered due to Twitter's recommender system. Furthermore, concerning the choice of interests and occupations for deriving our prediction variables, we limited our database to Twitter users consisting of entrepreneurial or artistic users, or expressed interest in yoga, stress coping, or certain types of humor. Needless to say, this is a minimal set of expressed interests and/or occupations. Although the validation set was not selected on the basis of these criteria and the results should generalize to a broader population of Twitter users, we anticipate that a broader range of topics of interest and/or occupations that have been shown to be correlated with personality aspects will potentially improve and extend personality profiling concerning Twitter following behavior.

4.3   Privacy

Lastly, an interesting point worth mentioning is that more and more aspects of the digital footprint of individuals present pile up to attributing variance in the process of personality computation. This way, it becomes increasingly likely that a complete combination of all an individual's social media activity could be quite an accurate determinator for one's personality. Because of this, it becomes increasingly important to think about the privacy legislation of different media. Twitter provides the opportunity to protect your account, and this way, your shared information cannot be extracted using the Twitter API. Every media should offer the option for a user to make his or her data private. Hence, if it is not in human's interest to have every individual's personality available on the web or in the hands of a few corporations, it will become imperative that legislation forces this option to be mandatory.

References

Sofiane Abbar, Yelena Mejova, and Ingmar Weber. 2015. You tweet what you eat: Studying food consumption through twitter. In *Proceedings of the 33rd Annual ACM Conference on Human Factors in Computing Systems*, pages 3197–3206.

Irum Abbasi and Michelle Drouin. 2019. Neuroticism and facebook addiction: How social media can affect mood? *The American Journal of Family Therapy*, 47(4):199–215.

Patrick Ian Armstrong and Sarah Fetter Anthoney. 2009. Personality facets and riasec interests: An integrated model. *Journal of Vocational Behavior*, 75(3):346–359.

Mitja D Back, Stefan C Schmukle, and Boris Egloff. 2008. How extraverted is honey. bunny77@ hotmail. de? inferring personality from e-mail addresses. *Journal of Research in Personality*, 42(4):1116–1122.

Ligia Maria Batrinca, Nadia Mana, Bruno Lepri, Fabio Pianesi, and Nicu Sebe. 2011. Please, tell me about yourself: automatic personality assessment using short self-presentations. In *Proceedings of the 13th international conference on multimodal interfaces*, pages 255–262. ACM.

Joan-Isaac Biel and Daniel Gatica-Perez. 2012. The youtube lens: Crowdsourced personality impressions and audiovisual analysis of vlogs. *IEEE Transactions on Multimedia*, 15(1):41–55.

David Blackwell, Carrie Leaman, Rose Tramposch, Ciera Osborne, and Miriam Liss. 2017. Extraversion, neuroticism, attachment style and fear of missing out as predictors of social media use and addiction. *Personality and Individual Differences*, 116:69–72.

Hermann Brandstätter. 2011. Personality aspects of entrepreneurship: A look at five meta-analyses. *Personality and individual differences*, 51(3):222–230.

Jilin Chen, Gary Hsieh, Jalal U Mahmud, and Jeffrey Nichols. 2014. Understanding individuals' personal values from social media word use. In *Proceedings of the 17th ACM conference on Computer supported cooperative work & social computing*, pages 405–414. ACM.

Shu-Chuan Chu, Hsuan-Ting Chen, and Yongjun Sung. 2016. Following brands on twitter: An extension of theory of planned behavior. *International Journal of Advertising*, 35(3):421–437.

Paul T Costa and Robert R McCrae. 1985. The neo personality inventory.

Paul T Costa Jr and Robert R McCrae. 1992. Four ways five factors are basic. *Personality and individual differences*, 13(6):653–665.

John M Digman. 1990. Personality structure: Emergence of the five-factor model. *Annual review of psychology*, 41(1):417–440.

Dominique Estival, Tanja Gaustad, Son Bao Pham, Will Radford, and Ben Hutchinson. 2007. Author profiling for english emails. In *Proceedings of the 10th Conference of the Pacific Association for Computational Linguistics*, pages 263–272.

Evanthia Faliagka, Athanasios Tsakalidis, and Giannis Tzimas. 2012. An integrated e-recruitment system for automated personality mining and applicant ranking. *Internet research*, 22(5):551–568.

Golnoosh Farnadi, Susana Zoghbi, Marie-Francine Moens, and Martine De Cock. 2013. Recognising personality traits using facebook status updates. In *Seventh International AAAI Conference on Weblogs and Social Media*.

Bruce Ferwerda and Marko Tkalcic. 2018. Predicting users' personality from instagram pictures: Using visual and/or content features? In *Proceedings of the 26th Conference on User Modeling, Adaptation and Personalization*, pages 157–161. ACM.

John Fox and Sanford Weisberg. 2018. *An R companion to applied regression*. Sage Publications.

John Fox. 2015. *Applied regression analysis and generalized linear models*. Sage Publications.

Jerome Friedman, Trevor Hastie, and Rob Tibshirani. 2010. Regularization paths for generalized linear models via coordinate descent. *Journal of statistical software*, 33(1):1.

Garry A Gelade. 1997. Creativity in conflict: The personality of the commercial creative. *The Journal of genetic psychology*, 158(1):67–78.

Jennifer Golbeck and Derek Hansen. 2014. A method for computing political preference among twitter followers. *Social Networks*, 36:177–184.

Jennifer Golbeck, Cristina Robles, Michon Edmondson, and Karen Turner. 2011. Predicting personality from twitter. In *2011 IEEE third international conference on privacy, security, risk and trust and 2011 IEEE third international conference on social computing*, pages 149–156. IEEE.

Liang Gou, Michelle X Zhou, and Huahai Yang. 2014. Knowme and shareme: understanding automatically discovered personality traits from social media and user sharing preferences. In *Proceedings of the SIGCHI Conference on Human Factors in Computing Systems*, pages 955–964. ACM.

Gil Greengross, Rod A Martin, and Geoffrey Miller. 2012. Personality traits, intelligence, humor styles, and humor production ability of professional stand-up comedians compared to college students. *Psychology of Aesthetics, Creativity, and the Arts*, 6(1):74.

Harold Hoekstra, J. Ormel, and F Fruyt. 2007. Handleiding neo-pi-r en neo-ffi persoonlijkheidsvragenlijsten.

John L Holland. 1997. *Making vocational choices: A theory of vocational personalities and work environments*. Psychological Assessment Resources.

Thomas Holtgraves. 2011. Text messaging, personality, and the social context. *Journal of research in personality*, 45(1):92–99.

Francisco Iacobelli, Alastair J Gill, Scott Nowson, and Jon Oberlander. 2011. Large scale personality classification of bloggers. In *international conference on affective computing and intelligent interaction*, pages 568–577. Springer.

RC Kessler, KD Mickelson, and S Zhao. 1997. Patterns and correlates of self-help group membership. *American Psychologist*, 44(27):27–46.

Michal Kosinski, David Stillwell, and Thore Graepel. 2013. Private traits and attributes are predictable from digital records of human behavior. *Proceedings of the National Academy of Sciences*, 110(15):5802–5805.

Max Kuhn and Kjell Johnson. 2013. *Applied predictive modeling*, volume 26. Springer.

Nicholas A Kuiper and Catherine Leite. 2010. Personality impressions associated with four distinct humor styles. *Scandinavian Journal of Psychology*, 51(2):115–122.

Lin Li, Ang Li, Bibo Hao, Zengda Guan, and Tingshao Zhu. 2014. Predicting active users' personality based on micro-blogging behaviors. *PloS one*, 9(1):e84997.

Franc Mairesse, Marilyn Walker, et al. 2006. Words mark the nerds: Computational models of personality recognition through language. In *Proceedings of the Annual Meeting of the Cognitive Science Society*, volume 28.

Susan E Marchant-Haycox and Glenn D Wilson. 1992. Personality and stress in performing artists. *Personality and individual differences*, 13(10):1061–1068.

Hazel Rose Markus and Shinobu Kitayama. 1998. The cultural psychology of personality. *Journal of cross-cultural psychology*, 29(1):63–87.

Louis L McQuitty. 1955. A method of pattern analysis for isolating typological and dimensional constructs. Technical report, ILLINOIS UNIV AT URBANA TRAINING RESEARCH LAB.

Andrés Mendiburo-Seguel, Darío Páez, and Francisco Martínez-Sánchez. 2015. Humor styles and personality: A meta-analysis of the relation between humor styles and the big five personality traits. *Scandinavian journal of psychology*, 56(3):335–340.

Atsunori Minamikawa and Hiroyuki Yokoyama. 2011. Personality estimation based on weblog text classification. In *International Conference on Industrial, Engineering and Other Applications of Applied Intelligent Systems*, pages 89–97. Springer.

Cecylia Nowakowska, Connie M Strong, Claudia M Santosa, PO W Wang, and Terence A Ketter. 2005. Temperamental commonalities and differences in euthymic mood disorder patients, creative controls, and healthy controls. *Journal of Affective Disorders*, 85(1-2):207–215.

Jon Oberlander and Scott Nowson. 2006. Whose thumb is it anyway? classifying author personality from weblog text. In *Proceedings of the COLING/ACL 2006 Main Conference Poster Sessions*, pages 627–634.

Daniel J Ozer and Veronica Benet-Martinez. 2006. Personality and the prediction of consequential outcomes. *Annu. Rev. Psychol.*, 57:401–421.

James W Pennebaker and Laura A King. 1999. Linguistic styles: Language use as an individual difference. *Journal of personality and social psychology*, 77(6):1296.

Daniele Quercia, Michal Kosinski, David Stillwell, and Jon Crowcroft. 2011. Our twitter profiles, our selves: Predicting personality with twitter. In *2011 IEEE third international conference on privacy, security, risk and trust and 2011 IEEE third international conference on social computing*, pages 180–185. IEEE.

R Core Team, 2019. *R: A Language and Environment for Statistical Computing*. R Foundation for Statistical Computing, Vienna, Austria.

Zalman Saper and James Forest. 1987. Personality variables and interest in self-help books. *Psychological Reports*, 60(2):563–566.

Shefali Srivastava and Terence A Ketter. 2010. The link between bipolar disorders and creativity: evidence from personality and temperament studies. *Current psychiatry reports*, 12(6):522–530.

Robert Tibshirani. 1996. Regression shrinkage and selection via the lasso. *Journal of the Royal Statistical Society: Series B (Methodological)*, 58(1):267–288.

William N Venables and Brian D Ripley. 2013. *Modern applied statistics with S-PLUS*. Springer Science & Business Media.

S Venkatesh, Madan Pal, BS Negi, VK Varma, et al. 1994. A comparative study of yoga practitioners and controls on certain psychological variables. *Indian Journal of Clinical Psychology*.

Alessandro Vinciarelli and Gelareh Mohammadi. 2014. A survey of personality computing. *IEEE Transactions on Affective Computing*, 5(3):273–291.

Tal Yarkoni. 2010. Personality in 100,000 words: A large-scale analysis of personality and word use among bloggers. *Journal of research in personality*, 44(3):363–373.

Hao Zhao and Scott E Seibert. 2006. The big five personality dimensions and entrepreneurial status: A meta-analytical review. *Journal of applied psychology*, 91(2):259.

Matching Theory and Data with Personal-ITY: What a Corpus of Italian YouTube Comments Reveals About Personality

Elisa Bassignana◇♡   **Malvina Nissim**♣   **Viviana Patti**♡
♡Dipartimento di Informatica, Università degli Studi di Torino, Italy
◇Department of Computer Science, IT University of Copenhagen, Denmark
♣ CLCG – Faculty of Arts, University of Groningen, The Netherlands
♡viviana.patti@unito.it, ◇elba@itu.dk
♣m.nissim@rug.nl

Abstract

As a contribution to personality detection in languages other than English, we rely on distant supervision to create Personal-ITY, a novel corpus of YouTube comments in Italian, where authors are labelled with personality traits. The traits are derived from one of the mainstream personality theories in psychology research, named *MBTI*. Using personality prediction experiments, we (i) study the task of personality prediction in itself on our corpus as well as on TwiSTY, a Twitter dataset also annotated with MBTI labels; (ii) carry out an extensive, in-depth analysis of the features used by the classifier, and view them specifically under the light of the original theory that we used to create the corpus in the first place. We observe that no single model is best at personality detection, and that while some traits are easier than others to detect, and also to match back to theory, for other, less frequent traits the picture is much more blurred.

1 Introduction

Human Personality is a psychological construct aimed at explaining the wide variety of human behaviours in terms of a few, stable and measurable individual characteristics (Snyder, 1983; Parks and Guay, 2009; Vinciarelli and Mohammadi, 2014). Research in psychology has formalised these characteristics into what are known as *Trait Models*. Two are the major models widely adopted also outside of purely psychological research (see Section 2.1): *Big Five* (John and Srivastava, 1999) and *Myers-Briggs Type Indicator* (*MBTI*) (Myers and Myers, 1995).

The psychological tests commonly used to detect prevalence of traits include human judgements regarding semantic similarity and relations between adjectives that people use to describe themselves and others. This is because language is believed to be a prime carrier of personality traits (Schwartz et al., 2013). This aspect, together with the progressive increase of available user-generated data from social media, has prompted the task of *Personality Detection*, i.e., the automatic prediction of personality from written texts (Whelan and Davies, 2006; Argamon et al., 2009; Celli et al., 2013; Youyou et al., 2015; Litvinova et al., 2016; Verhoeven et al., 2016). Personality detection can be useful in predicting life outcomes such as substance use, political attitudes and physical health. Other fields of application are marketing, politics, psychological and social assessment and, in the computational domain, dialogue systems (Ma et al., 2020) and chatbots (Qian et al., 2018).

As a contribution to personality detection in languages other than English, we have developed Personal-ITY, a novel corpus of YouTube comments in Italian, which are annotated with MBTI personality traits. The corpus creation methodology, described in detail in (Bassignana et al., 2020), makes use of a Distant Supervision approach that can also serve as a blueprint to develop datasets for other languages. In this work, we use Personal-ITY to cast light not only on the feasibility of personality detection *per se* on this corpus, but also on the relationship between our data and the theory it is based on. More specifically, we want to investigate if our distantly obtained labels are meaningful with respect to the psychological theory they come from, and whether language does indeed reflect the traits that should be associated with such labels. To do this, we run a series of in- and cross-dataset experiments; on top of

Proceedings of the Third Workshop on Computational Modeling of PEople's Opinions, PersonaLity, and Emotions in Social media, pages 11–22
Barcelona, Spain (Online), December 13, 2020.

performance analysis we conduct an in depth study on the relevant features used by the classifiers, and how they might relate to the source psychological theory.

Personal-ITY is available at `https://github.com/elisabassignana/Personal-ITY`.

2 Background

Personality profiling is addressed both from a psychological viewpoint (traits model for the classification of personality) and from a computational perspective in the field of Natural Language Processing. We provide relevant background from both sides, as they are intertwined in our work.

2.1 Psychological models

There are two main personality trait models widely accepted and used by the research community, also outside of psychology: *Big Five* and *Myers-Briggs Type Indicator* (*MBTI*).

Big Five (John and Srivastava, 1999), also know as Five-Factor Model (FFM) or the OCEAN model, was developed from the 1980s onwards. This theory outlines five global dimensions of personality and describes people by assigning a score in a range for each of them. The five traits considered are: OPENNESS TO EXPERIENCE, CONSCIENTIOUSNESS, EXTROVERSION, AGREEABLENESS and NEU-ROTICISM. Thus a person's personality would be defined through five corresponding scores indicating the positive or negative degree to which each dimension is expressed. Interestingly, the Big Five tests usually assign scores on the basis of semantic associations between personality traits and words considering the texts of the users' answers, rather than relying on neuropsychological experiments. The use of the Big Five model in computational approaches to personality began more than one decade ago and it is now widely accepted in academia.

The MBTI (Myers and Myers, 1995) theory is based on the conceptual theory of the Psychological Types proposed by the psychiatrist Carl Jung, who had speculated the main dimensions able to describe how people experience the world. Assessment is based on a self-reported psychological questionnaire that helps researchers to classify people into one personality type out of sixteen. The sixteen labels are the product of binary labels over four different dimensions, as follows: (EXTRAVERT-INTROVERT, INTUITIVE-SENSING, FEELING-THINKING, PERCEIVING-JUDGING). Each person is assumed to have one dominant quality from each category, thus producing sixteen unique types. Examples of full personality types are therefore four letter labels such as ENTJ or ISFP.

The initial intention of the test was to help women who were entering the industrial workforce for the first time during the Second World War to identify the "best, most comfortable and effective" job for them based on their personality type. In later years, MBTI continued to be used in order to predict validity of employees' job performance and to help students in their choice of career or course of study.

Although several studies suggest that the MBTI test lacks convincing validity data for these types of applications as it can measure preferences and not ability, it continues to be popular because it is very easy to administer it and it is not difficult to understand.

2.2 Personality Detection

Most approaches to automatic personality detection are supervised models trained on silver or gold labelled data. In this section, we revise existing datasets and standard methods of personality detection.

Corpora There exist a few datasets annotated for personality traits. For the shared tasks organised within the *Workshop on Computational Personality Recognition* (Celli et al., 2013), four English datasets annotated with the *Big Five* traits have been released. For the 2013 edition, the data contained "Essays" (Pennebaker and King, 2000), which is a large dataset of stream-of-consciousness texts collected between 1997 and 2004, and "myPersonality"[1], a corpus collected from FaceBook including information on user social network structures. For the 2014 edition, the data consisted of the "YouTube Personality Dataset" (Biel and Gatica-Perez, 2013), which contains a collection of behavioural features, speech transcriptions, and personality impression scores for a set of 404 YouTube vloggers, and "Mobile Phones", which is a

---

[1] `http://mypersonality.org`

Corpus	Model	# user	Avg.
PAN2015	Big Five	38	1,258
TwiSTY	MBTI	490	21,343
Personal-ITY	MBTI	1048	10,585

Table 1: Summary of Italian corpora with personality labels. Avg.: average tokens per user.

collection of call logs and proximity data of 53 subjects living in a student residency of a major US university, collected through a special software incorporated in their phones (Staiano et al., 2012).

Schwartz et al. (2013) collected a Big Five annotated dataset of FaceBook comments (700 millions words) written by 136.000 users who shared their status updates. Interesting correlations were observed between word usage and personality traits.

For the 2015 PAN Author Profiling Shared Task (Pardo et al., 2015), personality was added to gender and age in their standard profiling task, with tweets in English, Spanish, Italian and Dutch annotated according to the *Big Five* model assigning a score in a range [-0.5; +0.5] for each trait.

If looking at data labelled with the MBTI traits, we find a corpus of 1.2M English tweets annotated with personality and gender (Plank and Hovy, 2015), and the multilingual dataset TwiSTY (Verhoeven et al., 2016). The latter is a corpus of data collected from Twitter using a Distant Supervision approach. It is annotated with MBTI personality labels and gender for six languages (Dutch, German, French, Italian, Portuguese and Spanish), and includes a total of 18,168 authors.

As we concentrate on Italian, we report in Table 1 an overview of the available Italian corpora labelled with personality traits. We include information on our own Personal-ITY corpus, which is described in Section 3. For TwiSTY, we only report information for the Italian portion.

Computational work exists also on comparing (labels from) the two models (Celli and Lepri, 2018). Furnham et al. (2003) defined some correlations between various dimensions across the two trait models: Big Five Extraversion is correlated with MBTI Extraversion-Introversion, Openness to Experience is correlated with Sensing-Intuition, Agreeableness with Thinking-Feeling and Conscientiousness with Judging-Perceiving. In order to increase the amount of data we could work with, and to obtain a general, usable model, we tried to convert the PAN 2015 Italian data to MBTI annotations. We considered the mid value in the Big Five range as threshold between the opposite poles of MBTI dimensions. This experiments didn't led to any informative results, probably due the the small dimension of the corpus (see Table 1): almost all the few users present have been annotated with the same MBTI label.

Detection Approaches Regarding detection approaches, Mairesse et al. (2007) tested the usefulness of different sets of textual features making use of mostly SVMs. At the PAN 2015 challenge (see above) a variety of algorithms were tested (such as Random Forests, decision trees, logistic regression for classification, and also various regression models), but overall most successful participants used SVMs. Regarding features, participants approached the task with combinations of style-based and content-based features, as well as their combination in *n*-gram models (Pardo et al., 2015).

Experiments on TwiSTY were performed by the corpus creators themselves using a LinearSVM with word (1-2) and character (3-4) *n*-grams. Their results (reported in Table 4a for the Italian portion of the dataset) are obtained through 10-fold cross-validation; the model is compared to a weighted random baseline (WRB) and a majority baseline (MAJ). Let us notice that the model proposed in (Verhoeven et al., 2016) for the Italian language is the only one not reaching any baseline (for all the other languages the model proposed reach at least the weighted random baseline). This also prompted us to work on the Italian language, where there is still ample room for improvement on the development of resources and models for the personality detection task. More in general, our choice has to be seen as an intention of improving the state of the art for languages other than English (Joshi et al., 2020).

Recent computational approaches on personality prediction from texts investigated the use of deep learning (Majumder et al., 2017) and regression models (Akrami et al., 2019).

3   Data

To run experiments on personality detection, we have created a dedicated corpus with MBTI labels, exploiting distant supervision: Personal-ITY (Bassignana et al., 2020). Here, we summarise the choices that we made regarding the source of the data and the theoretical trait model, the procedure followed to construct the corpus, and provide a description of the resulting dataset. In addition, we also partly use the existing TwiSTY (see Section 2.2 and Table 1).

Because we deal with personal data, and because we do believe profiling is a sensitive task in general, we also provide an Ethics Statement.

Ethics Statement

Personality profiling must be carefully evaluated from an ethical point of view. In particular personality detection can involve ethical issues regarding the appropriate use and interpretation of the prediction outcomes (Weiner and Greene, 2017). Also, concerns have been raised regarding the inappropriate use of these tests with respect to invasion of privacy, cultural bias and confidentiality (Mehta et al., 2019).

The data included in the Personal-ITY dataset was publicly available on the YouTube platform at the time of the collection. As we explain in this Section (but see (Bassignana et al., 2020) for details), the information collected consists in comments published under public videos on the YouTube platform by the authors themselves. For an increased protection of user identities, in the released corpus only the YouTube usernames of the authors are mentioned, which are not unique identifiers. The YouTube IDs of the corresponding channels, which are instead unique identifiers on the platform and would allow to trace back the identity of the authors, are not released. The corpus was created for academic research purposes, and is not intended for commercial deployment or applications.

3.1   Source and Theoretical Model

YouTube is the source of data for our corpus. The decision is grounded on the fact that compared to the more commonly collected tweets, YouTube comments can be longer, so that users are freer to express themselves without limitations. Additionally, there is a substantial amount of available data on the YouTube platform, which is easy to access thanks to the free YouTube APIs.

Our theoretical trait model of choice is MBTI. Although it has been extensively criticized for a number of limitations (McCrae and Costa, 1989; Boyle, 1995 03; Pittenger, 2005), and the Big Five model seems to be more widely accepted in psychology, our choice has been driven by two main reasons. The first benefit of this decision is that MBTI is easy to use in association with a Distant Supervision approach (just checking if a message contains one of the 16 personality types; see Section 3.2). Another benefit is related to the existence of TwiSTY. Since both TwiSTY and Personal-ITY implement the MBTI model, analyses and experiments over personality detection can be carried out also in a cross-domain setting.

3.2   Corpus Creation and Description

The fact that users often self-disclose information about themselves on social media makes it possible to adopt *Distant Supervision* (DS) for the acquisition of training data. DS is a semi-supervised method that has been abundantly and successfully used in affective computing and profiling to assign silver labels to data on the basis of indicative proxies (Go et al., 2009; Pool and Nissim, 2016; Emmery et al., 2017).

We observed that some YouTube Italian users were used to leave comments to videos on the MBTI theory, in which they were stating their own personality type (e.g. *Sono ENTJ...chi altro?* [en: "I'm ENTJ...anyone else?"]; *INTP, primo test che effettivamente ha ragione* [en: "INTP, the first test that is actually right"]). We exploited such comments to create Personal-ITY.

The methodology, explained in detail in (Bassignana et al., 2020), consisted in creating automatically a list of YouTube users annotated with MBTI personality labels starting from the comments cited above. In the second macro-step, we adopted a Distant Supervision approach in order to retrieve as much as possible texts written by the authors whose personality was known. The result of this procedure led to a final corpus with a conspicuous number of users and comments, where only authors with at least five comments, each at least five token long, are included.

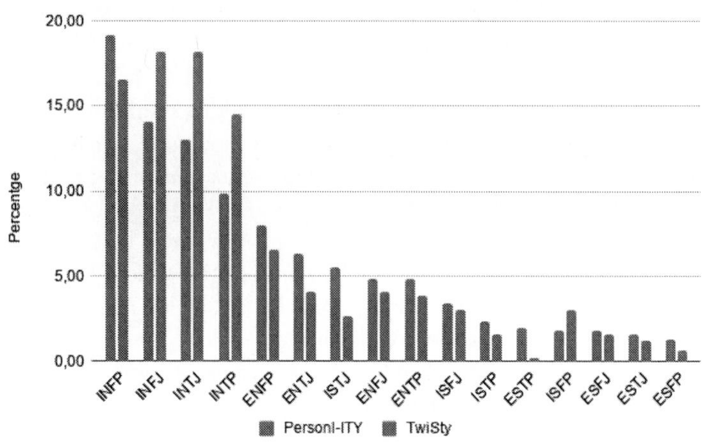

Figure 1: Distribution of the 16 labels in the YouTube corpus and in the Italian part of TwiSTY.

Personal-ITY contains 1048 users, each annotated with an MBTI label. The average number of comments per user is 92 and each message is on average 115 tokens. Table 2 shows explicitly the comparison between our new corpus and TwiSTY.

Corpus	# Users	Avg. comments/user	Avg. tokens/comment	Avg. tokens/user
Personal-ITY	1048	92	115	10,585
TwiSTY	490	1,903	11	21,343

Table 2: Statistical comparison between Personal-ITY and TwiSTY.

The amount of the 16 personality types in the corpus is not uniform. Figure 1 shows such distribution and also compares it with the one in TwiSTY. It can be observed that the two corpora present quite similar percentages of personality types. Some little differences (e.g., *INFJ*, *INTJ*, *INTP*) can be explained considering the different data sources: Personal-ITY is collected from YouTube, while TwiSTY is collected from Twitter. The general unbalanced distribution can be due to personality types not being uniformly distributed in the population, and to the fact that different personality types can make different choices about their online presence. Goby (2006) for example, observed that there is a significant correlation between online–offline choices and the MBTI dimension of EXTRAVERT-INTROVERT: extroverts are more likely to opt for offline modes of communication, while online communication is presumably easier for introverts. Figure 1 confirms this theory as the four most frequent types are introverts in both datasets. The conclusion is that, despite the different biases, collecting linguistic data in this way has the advantages that it reflects actual language use and allows large-scale analysis (Plank and Hovy, 2015).

4   Experiments

We ran a series of initial experiments on Personal-ITY, which we use to peek into the relationship between labels and theory, and which can also serve as a baseline for future work on this dataset.

The choices related to the experimental framework have been driven by the interest on investigating signals and linguistic cues for personality traits, analyzed through the lens of psychological studies on personality. This perspective has therefore led us not use deep learning techniques that would have made this analysis task more complex. Rather, we opt for state-of-the-art approaches commonly used in author profiling, developing interpretable models that can aid the analysis process. These will make it possible to perform a linguistic and psychological analysis, though perhaps at the expense of performance.

Specifically, we used the `sklearn` (Pedregosa et al., 2011) implementation of a linear SVM

(LinearSVM), with standard parameters, and tested three types of features: lexical-, stylistic-, and embeddings-based. We used four placeholders for hashtags, urls, usernames and emojis.

At the lexical level, we experimented with word (1-2) and character (3-4) n-grams, both as raw counts as well as tf-idf weighted. Character n-grams were tested also with a word-boundary option. Considering stylistic features, we investigated the use of emojis, hashtags, pronouns, punctuation and capitalisation. Lastly, we also experimented with embeddings-based representations, using more generic (Pennington et al., 2014) and YouTube-specific (Nieuwenhuis and Nissim, 2019) pre-trained models. We created one representation per user by averaging the vectors for all words written by that user.

We used 10-fold cross-validation, and assessed the models using macro f-score. We deem this way of averaging over f-scores per class appropriate, since the dataset is quite unbalanced, but we want good performance for each class. For comparison, we calculated a majority baseline (MAJ).

Table 3 shows the results of our experiments with the different feature types described above. Regarding n-grams and embeddings representations, we report results for the best configurations, namely character n-grams for the lexical features, and GloVe embeddings. Overall, lexical features perform best. Combining different feature types did not lead to any improvement. Classification was performed both with four separate binary classifiers (one per dimension), as well as with one single classifier predicting a total of four classes, i.e, the whole MBTI labels at once. Interestingly, in the latter case, we observe that the results are quite high considering the increased difficulty of the task.

Table 4 reports the scores of our models on TwiSTy. Because the original TwiSTy paper uses micro f-score, for the sake of comparison, in Table 4a we include the results of our experiments using micro-f for the MAJ baseline and our lexical n-gram model. For all traits, our models achieve better results (micro-f) than those reported in the original TwiSTy paper (Verhoeven et al., 2016). In Table 4b, instead, there are the macro-f of the experiments we performed on TwiSTy. As for Personal-ITY, best results were achieved using lexical features (tf-idf word n-grams); results of models with stylistic features and embeddings were just above the baseline.

Trait	Binary classification				Full label at once
	MAJ	n-grams	Sty	Emb	n-grams
EI	40.55	51.85	40.46	40.55	51.65
NS	44.34	51.92	44.34	44.34	49.04
FT	35.01	50.67	36.27	35.01	50.86
PJ	29.49	50.53	51.04	47.06	51.03
Avg	37.35	**51.24**	43.03	41.74	50.65

Table 3: Results of the experiments on Personal-ITY. Predictions of the full MBTI label at once were performed using the model performing best in the binary classification.

	(Verhoeven et al., 2016)			Our experiments	
Trait	WRB	MAJ	Lex	MAJ	n-grams
EI	65.54	77.88	77.78	77.75	**79.18**
NS	75.60	85.78	79.21	85.92	**85.92**
FT	50.31	53.95	52.13	53.67	**55.31**
PJ	50.19	53.05	47.01	53.06	**54.08**
Avg	60.41	67.67	64.06	67.6	**68.62**

(a) Comparison between our experiments on TwiSTy and the ones in (Verhoeven et al., 2016). Scores reported are micro f-scores. WRB = weighted random baseline. MAJ = majority baseline.

Trait	MAJ	n-grams	Sty	Emb
EI	43.69	55.23	43.69	43.69
NS	46.15	46.15	46.15	46.15
FT	34.79	52.98	35.34	34.70
PJ	34.56	53.01	35.20	34.90
Avg	39.80	**51.84**	40.09	39.86

(b) Results of our experiments on TwiSTy by using macro f-scores.

Table 4: Results of our experiments on TwiSTy.

To test compatibility of resources and to assess model portability, we also ran cross-domain experiments on Personal-ITY and TwiSTY. We divided both corpora in fixed training and test sets with a proportion of 80/20 so that the test set stays the same for in-domain and cross-domain settings. Indeed, we run the in-domain models again using this split. The models use lexical features as they are the one performing better overall the others. Results are shown in Table 5. We ran the experiments both using a binary classification of each trait separately and with the prediction of the full MBTI label at once. This latter leads to results even better on the considered sets. Cross-domain scores are obtained with the best in-domain model[2,3]. They drop substantially compared to in-domain, but are always above the baseline.

We specify that in every experiments done (Tables 3–4–5) we chose to look for the best model able to predict the whole MBTI personality and so we report the highest scores based on averages of the four traits. Considering the four dimensions individually better results can be obtained by using specific models. Table 6 shows an overview of the best models considering each trait independently for each source of data we tested. Results are quite scattered: there is no a single best model for personality predictions, as feature contribution depends on the dimension considered, and on the dataset. This observation confirms the inherent difficulty of the Personality Detection task from written texts.

Train	Binary classification						Full MBTI label at once					
	Personal-ITY		TwiSTY				Personal-ITY		TwiSTY			
	IN	CROSS		IN	CROSS		IN	CROSS		IN	CROSS	
Test	Pers	MAJ	TwI	TwI	MAJ	Pers	Pers	MAJ	TwI	TwI	MAJ	Pers
EI	58.94	44.94	49.33	55.66	44.59	44.59	54.67	44.94	44.94	59.77	44.59	44.59
NS	52.88	47.87	47.31	47.87	45.31	45.31	48.65	47.87	47.59	47.87	45.31	45.31
FT	49.20	37.58	47.09	65.26	39.13	51.04	54.18	37.58	46.38	61.98	26.32	46.71
PJ	54.43	32.41	32.50	56.87	36.56	38.54	58.07	32.41	38.08	50.27	36.56	46.80
Avg	53.86	40.70	44.06	56.42	41.40	44.87	53.89	40.70	**44.25**	54.97	38.20	**45.85**

Table 5: Results of the cross-domain experiments. MAJ = baseline on the cross-domain testset.

| Source | Trait | Tf-idf | | | Count | | |
		word	char	char_wb	word	char	char_wb
Personal-ITY	EI						X
	NS						X
	FT			X			
	PJ		X				
TwiSTY	EI	X					
	NS					X	
	FT			X			
	PJ	X					
Cross-domain: Tr: Personal-ITY Te: TwiSTY	EI				X		
	NS			X			
	FT						X
	PJ						X
Cross-domain: Tr: TwiSTY Te: Personal-ITY	EI					X	
	NS					X	
	FT	X					
	PJ						X

Table 6: Best model for each trait considering each source individually.

The in-domain experiments show that performance over the two datasets is very similar overall, though

---

[2]Binary classification: Train on Personal-ITY: character n-grams. Train on TwiSTY: tf-idf character n-grams.
[3]Full MBTI label at once: Train on Personal-ITY: character n-grams. Train on TwiSTY: tf-idf word n-grams.

with some differences regarding the best and worst predicted traits. However, we observe that cross-domain performance drops by approximately 10 points, independently of the direction of training and testing taken. This underlines differences in the dataset which might not make them fully compatible. For our in-depth linguistic analysis, we choose to concentrate on Personal-ITY, mainly due to the availability of longer author's comments, which can give rise to more interesting insights when studying word-based feature contribution in connection with the source MBTI personality theory.

5 Feature Analysis and Linguistic Cues for Personality Traits

In this section we discuss possible correlations between linguistic cues derived from the experiments described in Section 4 on the Personal-ITY corpus and psychological traits descriptions deriving from the field of Psychology. Table 7 shows the most important features on which our classifier bases its decisions (i.e., the most relevant ones based on the weight they have on the model prediction). We report word n-gram features as they are the most interpretable for a psychological analysis.

	Extravert	Introvert	Sensing	Intuition	Thinking	Feeling	Judging	Perceiving
Count word (1,2)	punti	sbagliato	adoro	fuori	**ma io**	**io sono**	**alle**	**bene**
	poi	**che era**	**gli**	**ehm**	nel	giorno	**un video**	12
	ora	fa	**del**	sbagliato	**vero**	beh	**nella**	**emoji ho**
	ne	via	oddio	**vorrei**	anni	marco	ancora	che ti
	ancora	**anzi**	credo	morto	**vedo**	nero	**tuoi**	non ci
	emoji non	hashtag se	qualcuno	che tu	17	sotto	**minecraft**	ho fatto
	volevo	**lui**	solo	alcune	tanto	più	so se	**beh**
	midna	sia	io mi	serie	con le	avevo	**te**	**nether**
	dal	**era**	idea	tutto il	chi	**dentro**	**metti**	tanto
	fosse	**penso**	va	secondo	**capire**	**trovo**	**neanche**	test
Tf-idf word (1,2)	in	nn	matteo	die	**perchè**	più	**user**	perchè
	xd	eren	ahah	die die	emoji	emoji emoji	nn	**emoji**
	che	bella playerinside	**del**	raiden	**vedo**	marco	**minecraft**	test
	ancora	genio genio	adoro	cane	lullaby	nn	**da**	**anche**
	ci	playerinside xd	**di**	cuticole	dei	avevo	**tuoi**	genio genio
	davvero	**marco**	erenblaze	anche	xd	test	hashtag	non
	molto	die	libro	tano	un	genio genio	**alle**	u3000
	di	tifo	marco	**ehm**	**questa**	raiden	di eren	**bene**
	perchè	bella	**in**	copia	eren	in	leo	u3000 u3000
	dei	pixelmon	persone	00 00	grazie	u3000	puoi	un

Table 7: Most predictive word n-grams on Personal-ITY.

Below we are going to analyze each MBTI trait independently by interpreting observed features with existing theoretical definitions of the personality types, which we take from (Geyer, 2014).

- EXTRAVERT vs. INTROVERT trait:
    - EXTRAVERT: extraverts tend to use abstract words, to be vague and to use adjectives. They talk a lot (in respect to their opposite) about family, friends, groups and social activities.
    - INTROVERT: introverts, on the other side, tend to use concrete words, to be more precise and so to use nouns, pronouns, articles, numbers and distinctions (*but, except...*).

Referring to Table 7, we find *emoji* in the extraversion pole (recall that we normalized all the emojis in the corpus[4]), while it is not present in the opposite pole. Looking at the definition, we linked this to a more extroverted behavior, people talking about friends, groups and social activities. Similar to that label there is, in the same column, *xd*, that we intended as an emoticon. Moreover, closely related to the definition (being abstract and vague) there is the word *fosse* (subjunctive form of the verb 'to be'). In the introversion column, instead, there are more concrete and precise words as *che era* ('which was'), *era* ('it was') and *penso* ('I think'). With the same intention to be concrete and precise, those people use (proper) nouns and pronouns as *lui* ('he') and *marco*. Lastly, coherently with the introvert definition, we find *anzi* ('rather', 'instead'), word belonging to the distinction set.

---

[4] https://pypi.org/project/emojis/

- SENSING vs. INTUITION trait:

    - SENSING: these people are realistic, they usually talk about practical activities and about what is already happened. They describe facts specifying a lot of details, tangible information and rely a lot on senses.
    - INTUITION: people with this personality follow intuition, fantasy, imagination and ideas. They usually talk about what is going to happen, future possibilities and relate their discourses to abstract and general principles.

In the sensing list of words we highlighted *gli* ('the'), *del* ('of the'), *di* ('of') and *in* ('in') as those tokens are used to specify details. In the opposite column, in line with the definition, we just found the words *ehm* and *vorrei* ('I would like to').

- THINKING vs. FEELING trait:

    - THINKING: these people follow logic, objectivity, rationality, causality and consistency.
    - FEELING: their opposite, instead, are more inclined to follow the heart and principles; they look for cooperation, harmony and are more sensitive.

In line with the definition of thinking we highlighted the *n*-grams *ma io* ('but I'), *vero* ('true'), *vedo* ('I see'), *capire* ('to understand'), *perchè* ('because') and *questa* ('this'). For their opposite we found *io sono* ('I am'), *dentro* ('inside') and *trovo* ('I think', 'I find').

- JUDGING vs. PERCEIVING trait:

    - JUDGING: this trait indicates determined people, who are used to plan everything and that are comfortable with rules and guide lines.
    - PERCEIVING: the opposite are people who like improvisation and tend to keep open options. They are more relaxed and look for liberty.

In the judging column there are words such as *alle* ('at'), *nella* ('in'), *tuoi* ('yours'), *te* ('you'), *metti* ('put'), *neanche* ('neither'), *da* ('from', 'by') and *user* (which is a normalized label deriving from pre-processing; it replaces references to specific users). These can all be used to make precise plans, and fit with the description of determined people, comfortable with rules and guidelines. The more interesting word *n*-grams in this set, is *minecraft*, which is the name of a video game where planning skills are fundamental. In the opposite pole, perceiving, some distinctive words are: *bene* ('good'), *beh*, the label *emoji* and *anche* ('also').

A final consideration about the analysis above is that the correlations we found are sometime weak and not so explicit, especially for the S-N trait and we observed that this is coherent with the not so high results obtained from experiments in Section 4: it is likely that the absence of strong evidences linking linguistic cues with psychological ones, makes the decision of the classifier hard. Notice that a similar observation concerning the difficulty to predict the S-N trait has been reported in (Plank and Hovy, 2015) on an English corpus, suggesting that such trait could in general be more related to perception, with a weak linguistic signal. A second observation is that Table 7 contains many unexpected tokens which apparently have no explanation. Some examples are: *midna* for extravert, *eren*, *die playerinside* and *pixelmon* for introvert, *erenblaze* for sensing, *die* again also for intuition, *eren*, *17* and *lullaby* for thinking, *raiden* for feeling, *eren* again for judging and *u3000* for perceiving. The explanation we give to the presence of such 'specific' tokens is to be found in the source and in the way we collected the corpus. Channels on YouTube gather a community of users with similar interests and common saying. It is therefore likely that users commenting videos from a given channel develop some sort of shared, own slang. In this perspective, a further analysis of the dataset aimed at detecting topics and word distribution would be useful to identify the presence of a narrow set of specific-domain texts.

For a second qualitative analysis we used *Wordify*[5], a tool developed by Bocconi University whose intent is to identify words that discriminate categories in textual data. Table 8 reports the results of such

---

[5]`https://wordify.unibocconi.it/index`

tool on Personal-ITY, and we can observe various correspondences with Table 7 (terms appearing in both Tables) such as, regarding the first trait, *xd* and *davvero* for EXTRAVERT and *eren*, *playerinside xd* and *nn* for INTROVERT. This 'double check' makes bold words in Table 8 reliable features in MBTI personality prediction, even if for most of them we didn't find a direct psychological explanation coherent with the trait definitions.

Trait	Term	Score	Label	Trait	Term	Score	Label
First trait	sì	0,384	E	Second trait	emoji	0,312	N
	xd	0,352	E				
	davvero	0,328	E				
	eren	0,474	I				
	emoji	0,466	I				
	bello **playerinside**	0,400	I				
	playerinside xd	0,324	I				
	nn	0,312	I				
Third trait	**test**	0,414	F	Fourth trait	**hashtag**	0,344	J
	qi	0,364	F		**nn**	0,336	J
	commento	0,338	F		**eren**	0,306	J
	ahah	0,420	T		**test**	0,414	P
	perché	0,336	T		ahah	0,33	P
	ahahah	0,306	T		xd	0,330	P
					sì	0,318	P

Table 8: Results of the *Wordify* tool on Personal-ITY.

6 Conclusions

We presented Personali-ITY, a novel YouTube-based Corpus for Personality Prediction in Italian. An exploratory empirical investigation on our new corpus confirms that identifying MBTI personality trait from social media texts is challenging. Lexical features perform best, but they tend to be strictly related to the context in which the model is trained and so to overfit. Concerning our experiments on TWISTY, our model outperforms the original TWISTY results (Verhoeven et al., 2016) for Italian and provides a new baseline on this corpus. Moreover we performed cross-domain experiments between YouTube and Twitter data, achieving scores above the baseline. Performance drops from the in- to the cross-genre setting show limits in portability, and leave a lot of space for improvements.

In general, better results could, probably, be obtained using more complex models by using neural networks (e.g. LSTM) (Mehta et al., 2019). The choice to use a simpler SVM model was driven by its greater understandability and transparency. These qualities allowed the features analysis of Section 5.

The inherent difficulty of the task itself is confirmed and deserves further investigations, as assigning a definite personality is an extremely subjective and complex task even for humans. The distant supervision approach remains promising, also applied to YouTube data. Indeed, assigning an 'absolute' personality to an individual is difficult. Even if, to some extent, distant supervision is inaccurate and can lead to the creation of corpus containing bias and noise, since there is no control on user statements, we cannot avoid considering that according to the literature also professional psychological tests can lead to inaccurate results. Moreover, DS, despite its inaccuracy, allows the availability of a large amount of data, necessary for addressing the task by using machine learning approaches.

Acknowledgments

The work of Elisa Bassignana was partially carried out at the University of Groningen within the framework of the Erasmus+ program 2019/20.

References

Nazar Akrami, Johan Fernquist, Tim Isbister, Lisa Kaati, and Björn Pelzer. 2019. Automatic extraction of personality from text: Challenges and opportunities. In *2019 IEEE International Conference on Big Data (Big Data)*, pages 3156–3164. IEEE.

Shlomo Argamon, Moshe Koppel, James W. Pennebaker, and Jonathan Schler. 2009. Automatically profiling the author of an anonymous text. *Commun. ACM*, 52(2):119–123, February.

Elisa Bassignana, Malvina Nissim, and Viviana Patti. 2020. Personal-ity: A novel youtube-based corpus for personality prediction in italian. In Felice Dell'Orletta, Johanna Monti, and Fabio Tamburini, editors, *Proceedings of the Seventh Italian Conference on Computational Linguistics (CLiC-it 2020), Bologna, Italy, March 1-3, 2021*, CEUR Workshop Proceedings. CEUR-WS.org.

Joan-Isaac Biel and Daniel Gatica-Perez. 2013. The youtube lens: Crowdsourced personality impressions and audiovisual analysis of vlogs. *Multimedia, IEEE Transactions on*, 15(1):41–55.

Gregory J Boyle. 1995-03. Myers briggs type indicator (mbti): some psychometric limitations. *Australian Psychologist*, 30(1):71–74.

Fabio Celli and Bruno Lepri. 2018. Is big five better than mbti? a personality computing challenge using twitter data. In *CLiC-it*.

Fabio Celli, Fabio Pianesi, David Stillwell, and Michal Kosinski. 2013. Workshop on computational personality recognition: Shared task. In *Seventh International AAAI Conference on Weblogs and Social Media*.

Chris Emmery, Grzegorz Chrupała, and Walter Daelemans. 2017. Simple queries as distant labels for predicting gender on Twitter. In *Proceedings of the 3rd Workshop on Noisy User-generated Text*, pages 50–55, Copenhagen, Denmark, September. Association for Computational Linguistics.

Adrian Furnham, Joanna Moutafi, and John Crump. 2003. The relationship between the revised neo personality inventory and the myers briggs type indicator. *Social Behavior and Personality - SOC BEHAV PERSONAL*, 31:577–584, 01.

Peter Geyer. 2014. C.G.Jung's psychological types, the MBTI, and ideas of social adjustment. In *Proceedings of AusAPT Meeting Adelaide*, 03.

Alec Go, Richa Bhayani, and Lei Huang. 2009. Twitter sentiment classification using distant supervision. *CS224N project report, Stanford*, 1(12):2009.

Valerie Goby. 2006. Personality and Online/Offline Choices: MBTI Profiles and Favored Communication Modes in a Singapore Study. *Cyberpsychology & behavior : the impact of the Internet, multimedia and virtual reality on behavior and society*, 9:5–13, 03.

Oliver P. John and Sanjay Srivastava. 1999. The big five trait taxonomy: History, measurement, and theoretical perspectives. In L. A. Pervin and O. P. John, editors, *Handbook of personality: Theory and research*, page 102–138. Guilford Press.

Pratik Joshi, Sebastin Santy, Amar Budhiraja, Kalika Bali, and Monojit Choudhury. 2020. The state and fate of linguistic diversity and inclusion in the NLP world. In *Proceedings of the 58th Annual Meeting of the Association for Computational Linguistics*, pages 6282–6293, Online, July. Association for Computational Linguistics.

Tatiana Litvinova, P. Seredin, Olga Litvinova, and Olga Zagorovskaya. 2016. Profiling a set of personality traits of text author: What our words reveal about us. *Research in Language*, 14, 12.

Yukun Ma, Khanh Linh Nguyen, Frank Z. Xing, and Erik Cambria. 2020. A survey on empathetic dialogue systems. *Information Fusion*, 64:50 – 70.

François Mairesse, Marilyn A. Walker, Matthias R. Mehl, and Roger K. Moore. 2007. Using linguistic cues for the automatic recognition of personality in conversation and text. *Journal of Artificial Intelligence Research*, 30:457–500, sep.

Navonil Majumder, Soujanya Poria, Alexander Gelbukh, and Erik Cambria. 2017. Deep learning-based document modeling for personality detection from text. *IEEE Intelligent Systems*, 32:74–79, 03.

Robert McCrae and Paul Costa. 1989. Reinterpreting the myers-briggs type indicator from the perspective of the five-factor model of personality. *Journal of personality*, 57:17–40, 03.

Yash Mehta, Navonil Majumder, Alexander Gelbukh, and Erik Cambria. 2019. Recent trends in deep learning based personality detection. *Artificial Intelligence Review*, pages 1–27.

I.B. Myers and P.B. Myers. 1995. *Gifts Differing: Understanding Personality Type*. Mobius.

Moniek Nieuwenhuis and Malvina Nissim. 2019. The Contribution of Embeddings to Sentiment Analysis on YouTube. In *Proceedings of the Sixth Italian Conference on Computational Linguistics, Bari, Italy, November 13-15, 2019*, volume 2481 of *CEUR Workshop Proceedings*. CEUR-WS.org.

Francisco M. Rangel Pardo, Fabio Celli, Paolo Rosso, Martin Potthast, Benno Stein, and Walter Daelemans. 2015. Overview of the 3rd Author Profiling Task at PAN 2015. In *Working Notes of CLEF 2015 - Conference and Labs of the Evaluation forum, Toulouse, France, September 8-11, 2015*, volume 1391 of *CEUR Workshop Proceedings*. CEUR-WS.org.

Laura Parks and Russell P Guay. 2009. Personality, values, and motivation. *Personality and individual differences*, 47(7):675–684.

F. Pedregosa, G. Varoquaux, A. Gramfort, V. Michel, B. Thirion, O. Grisel, M. Blondel, P. Prettenhofer, R. Weiss, V. Dubourg, J. Vanderplas, A. Passos, D. Cournapeau, M. Brucher, M. Perrot, and E. Duchesnay. 2011. Scikit-learn: Machine learning in Python. *Journal of Machine Learning Research*, 12:2825–2830.

James Pennebaker and Laura King. 2000. Linguistic styles: Language use as an individual difference. *Journal of personality and social psychology*, 77:1296–312, 01.

Jeffrey Pennington, Richard Socher, and Christopher D. Manning. 2014. Glove: Global vectors for word representation. In *Empirical Methods in Natural Language Processing (EMNLP)*, pages 1532–1543.

David Pittenger. 2005. Cautionary comments regarding the myers-briggs type indicator. *Consulting Psychology Journal: Practice and Research*, 57:210–221, 06.

Barbara Plank and Dirk Hovy. 2015. Personality traits on Twitter—or—How to get 1,500 personality tests in a week. In *Proceedings of the 6th Workshop on Computational Approaches to Subjectivity, Sentiment and Social Media Analysis*, pages 92–98, Lisboa, Portugal, September. Association for Computational Linguistics.

Chris Pool and Malvina Nissim. 2016. Distant supervision for emotion detection using Facebook reactions. In *Proceedings of the Workshop on Computational Modeling of People's Opinions, Personality, and Emotions in Social Media (PEOPLES)*, pages 30–39, Osaka, Japan, December. The COLING 2016 Organizing Committee.

Qiao Qian, Minlie Huang, Haizhou Zhao, Jingfang Xu, and Xiaoyan Zhu. 2018. Assigning personality/profile to a chatting machine for coherent conversation generation. In *Proceedings of the Twenty-Seventh International Joint Conference on Artificial Intelligence, IJCAI-18*, pages 4279–4285. International Joint Conferences on Artificial Intelligence Organization, 7.

H. Andrew Schwartz, Johannes C. Eichstaedt, Margaret L. Kern, Lukasz Dziurzynski, Stephanie M. Ramones, Megha Agrawal, Achal Shah, Michal Kosinski, David Stillwell, Martin E.P. Seligman, et al. 2013. Personality, gender, and age in the language of social media: The open-vocabulary approach. *PloS one*, 8(9):e73791.

Mark Snyder. 1983. The influence of individuals on situations: Implications for understanding the links between personality and social behavior. *Journal of personality*, 51(3):497–516.

Jacopo Staiano, Bruno Lepri, Nadav Aharony, Fabio Pianesi, Nicu Sebe, and Alex Pentland. 2012. Friends don't lie - inferring personality traits from social network structure. In *UbiComp'12 - Proceedings of the 2012 ACM Conference on Ubiquitous Computing*, pages 321–330, 09.

Ben Verhoeven, Walter Daelemans, and Barbara Plank. 2016. TwiSty: A multilingual Twitter stylometry corpus for gender and personality profiling. In *Proceedings of the Tenth International Conference on Language Resources and Evaluation (LREC'16)*, pages 1632–1637, Portorož, Slovenia, May. European Language Resources Association (ELRA).

Alessandro Vinciarelli and Gelareh Mohammadi. 2014. A survey of personality computing. *IEEE Transactions on Affective Computing*, 5(3):273–291.

Irving B. Weiner and Roger L. Greene, 2017. *Ethical Considerations In Personality Assessment*, chapter 4, pages 59–74. Wiley.

Susan Whelan and Gary Davies. 2006. Profiling consumers of own brands and national brands using human personality. *Journal of Retailing and Consumer Services*, 13(6):393–402.

Wu Youyou, Michal Kosinski, and David Stillwell. 2015. Computer-based personality judgments are more accurate than those made by humans. *Proceedings of the National Academy of Sciences*, 112(4):1036–1040.

Red Is Open-Minded, Blue Is Conscientious: Predicting User Traits From Instagram Image Data

Lisa Branz
Technische Hochschule
Georg Simon Ohm
Nuremberg
`lisa.branz`
`@yahoo.de`

Patricia Brockmann
Technische Hochschule
Georg Simon Ohm
Nuremberg
`patricia.brockmann`
`@th-nuernberg.de`

Annika Hinze
University of Waikato

Hamilton
`annika.hinze`
`@waikato.ac.nz`

Abstract

Various studies have addressed the connection between a user's traits and their social media content. This paper explores the relationship between gender, age and Big Five personality traits of 179 university students from Germany and their Instagram images. With regards to both image features and image content, significant differences between genders as well as preferences related to age and personality traits emerged. Gender, age and personality traits are predicted using machine learning classification and regression methods. This work is the first of its kind to focus on data from European Instagram users, as well as to predict age from Instagram image features and content on a fine-grained level.

1 Introduction

The rise of machine learning methods has opened up novel possibilities to extract patterns from social media data that allow researchers to identify and predict user traits based on data features. This work presents an approach towards finding connections between a user's traits and their social media image data as well as predicting a user's traits from their data. Focusing on Instagram data of German university students, we analyze the connection of image features and image content with a user's gender, age and personality traits. While some studies with similar approaches will be used for comparison, some novel insights regarding the connection of image data and user traits as well as their prediction will be presented.

2 Related Work

A meta-analysis published by (Azucar et al., 2018) gives an overview of 28 studies exploring the connection between digital footprints and users' Big Five personality traits. The authors conclude that personality traits can be inferred with high accuracy from information shared by users on social media platforms. However, only four out of 28 studies included take image content into account and only one of the studies focuses on Instagram. Ferwerda et al. provided deeper insights into the area by exploring the correlation between Big Five personality traits and image features (Ferwerda et al., 2015) as well as image content (Ferwerda and Tkalcic, 2018b) and their suitability for predicting a user's personality (Ferwerda and Tkalcic, 2018a). Kim et al. explored the connection between Instagram image color characteristics (Kim and Kim, 2019) as well as image features, image content and emotional expressions in images (Kim and Kim, 2018) with user traits, such as personality or gender. (You et al., 2014) aimed at predicting a user's gender from posting behavior and image content on Pinterest and identified a number of image content categories suitable for classifying a user's gender. (Song et al., 2018) explored correlations between an Instagram user's image content with their gender and age group, and successfully predicted these user traits from image content. However, only two large age groups were distinguished and age group as well as gender were inferred from a user's profile information and could, therefore, not be verified. (Han et al., 2016) successfully predicted a user's age group from user activities on Instagram. Like (Song et al., 2018), the researchers predicted age only on a coarse-grained level and inferred age information from

Proceedings of the Third Workshop on Computational Modeling of PEople's Opinions, PersonaLity, and Emotions in Social media, pages 23–28
Barcelona, Spain (Online), December 13, 2020.

a user's Instagram account. At this point there is, to our knowledge, no study predicting an Instagram user's age on a fine-grained level. This requires collecting a user's age directly through a survey in order to obtain the exact age in years. Moreover, all studies mentioned above were conducted using data from the US, South Korea or randomly selected locations. Hitherto there is, to our knowledge, no study specifically focusing on data from European Instagram users.

3 Method

Participants were students of Technische Hochschule Nuremberg, Germany taking an online survey. The user traits assessed included a participant's age, gender and Big Five personality traits openness (O), conscientiousness (C), extraversion (E), agreeableness (A) and neuroticism (N). Personality traits were assessed using the German version of the Big Five Inventory 2 (BFI-2) (Danner et al., 2016). The data sample consisted of 16,458 images and survey data of 182 participants (100 female, 79 male, 3 non-binary (excluded)) between the ages of 18 and 36 years with a mean age of 23 years ($SD = 3.29$). Instagram-scraper for Python (rarcega, 2017) was used to download all image content from the participants' Instagram profiles. Saturation-related, hue-related and value-related features were extracted from every image, and average values for each user were calculated. Following the approach in (Ferwerda et al., 2015) and (Kim and Kim, 2018), the Pleasure-Arousal-Dominance model of Valdez and Merhabian (Valdez and Mehrabian, 1994) was adopted. The author found specific combinations of brightness and saturation to represent different emotional states, which are calculated as follows: **Pleasure** = .69 Brightness + .22 Saturation, **Arousal** = -.31 Brightness + .60 Saturation, **Dominance** = -.76 Brightness + .32 Saturation.

Image features used for analysis are displayed in Table 1. Using Google Vision API, every image was annotated with multiple labels describing the depicted objects. This yielded a list of 4,537 unique labels, which were classified into 29 categories (Figure 1). The sum of category occurrences for each user across all images was calculated and normalized in order to account for varying numbers of images among participants. An independent sample t-test was performed in order to compare mean values between gender groups for each image feature and image content score. For the user traits age, openness, conscientiousness, extraversion, agreeableness and neuroticism, statistical correlations were calculated with all of the image feature scores and content scores. To ensure comparability with previous research (((Ferwerda et al., 2015), (Ferwerda and Tkalcic, 2018b), (Kim and Kim, 2018), (Song et al., 2018)), the Random Forest approach was chosen for both regression and classification in the prediction step. A 10-fold cross-validation was employed. F1 score, AUC (Area Under The Curve) ROC (Receiver Operating Characteristics) as well as root-mean-square-error (RMSE) were calculated as performance measures for classifier and regressors, respectively.

4 Results

4.1 Statistical Correlations Between User Traits and Social Media Data

Significant gender differences were revealed with regards to image features as well as image content which are displayed in Table 3. Table 2 displays statistical correlations between image features and age as well as personality traits. Table 4 displays statistical correlations between content categories and age as well as personality traits.

Saturation-related features	A. Average saturation B. Saturation variance
Hue-related features	C. % Red pixels D. % Orange pixels E. % Yellow pixels F. % Green pixels G. % Blue pixels H. % Purple pixels I. % Warm pixels J. % Cold pixels
Value-related features	K. Normalized brightness L. Contrast
PAD	M. Pleasure N. Arousal O. Dominance

Table 1: Image features extracted from all images

	O	C	E	A	N	Age		O	C	E	A	N	Age
A	**-0.17**	0.00	-0.08	-0.10	-0.04	0.08	I	**0.25**	**-0.17**	0.01	0.08	0.03	0.11
B	0.10	**-0.15**	0.04	-0.13	-0.05	0.00	J	**-0.25**	**0.17**	-0.01	-0.08	-0.03	-0.11
C	**0.24**	**-0.20**	0.05	-0.09	0.03	-0.07	L	**-0.21**	0.05	-0.02	0.06	-0.07	-0.14
D	-0.03	0.00	-0.03	0.09	0.10	**0.15**	N	**-0.19**	-0.05	-0.05	-0.07	-0.09	0.02
F	-0.07	0.03	**-0.15**	0.04	0.01	-0.07	O	**-0.18**	-0.09	0.00	-0.02	-0.13	-0.05
G	**-0.25**	**0.20**	0.05	-0.07	-0.03	**-0.20**							

Table 2: Spearman's correlation between image features and user traits. Only features with significant correlations are shown. Significant correlations ($p \leq .05$) are shown in boldface.

1. Food and drinks	9. Art	15. Dance and performance
2. Animals	10. Clothing and accessories	16. Fabric and material
3. Botanical	11. Home and interior	17. People
4. Body parts	12. Fantasy and fiction	18. Weapons
5. Architecture	13. Sports	19. Vehicles and transport
6. Beauty and care	14. Music	20. Tools and machine
7. Landscape and nature		21. Electronics
8. Colors		22. Events, holidays and gatherings
		23. Human emotions and behavior
24. Leisure and play	27. Services	
25. Business and education	28. Jewelry	
26. Crafts	29. Humans	

Figure 1: Image content catgeories identified from the data sample

Image Feature	Female	Male	Image Feature	Female	Male
% Orange pixels**	**0.317**	0.267	Beauty and care***	**0.018**	0.004
Brightness*	**0.633**	0.589	Landscape and nature**	0.092	**0.120**
Pleasure*	**0.502**	0.474	Clothing and accessories*	**0.030**	0.021
Dominance*	-0.385	**-0.348**	Jewelry*	**1.510**	0.203
Body parts***	**0.061**	0.0265	Sports**	0.015	**0.026**
Architecture**	0.035	**0.051**	Humans***	**0.073**	0.040

$(p \leq .05), **(p \leq .01), ***(p \leq .001)$

Table 3: Significant gender differences in regards to image features and content categories

	O	C	E	A	N	Age		O	C	E	A	N	Age
1	0.08	0.06	0.01	-0.04	-0.01	**0.32**	18	0.12	0.07	0.00	0.13	**-0.16**	0.00
2	0.10	-0.05	-0.12	0.09	0.02	**0.16**	21	**0.23**	-0.14	0.01	0.00	-0.01	**0.15**
6	-0.01	0.06	0.02	0.14	**0.16**	**-0.16**	22	**-0.23**	0.01	0.07	-0.09	0.05	**-0.21**
8	**0.16**	0.00	-0.05	0.07	0.04	-0.06	23	-0.12	0.01	**0.22**	0.03	-0.03	**-0.18**
9	**0.28**	**-0.19**	0.00	0.10	-0.06	-0.14	24	**-0.26**	0.08	0.10	-0.02	0.03	**-0.22**
12	**0.26**	**-0.18**	-0.05	-0.05	0.07	0.04	25	**0.21**	-0.05	0.03	-0.01	0.03	0.14
13	**-0.18**	0.07	0.14	**-0.15**	-0.02	-0.04	26	0.10	-0.02	-0.10	0.06	-0.07	**0.15**
16	**0.15**	0.01	-0.04	0.06	-0.03	0.04	27	0.06	0.08	0.05	**-0.22**	-0.04	0.07
17	**-0.15**	0.03	0.10	0.02	-0.01	**-0.17**							

Table 4: Spearman's correlation between content categories and user traits. Only categories with significant correlations are shown. Significant correlations ($p \leq .05$) are shown in boldface.

4.2 Prediction of User Traits

The prediction of gender using all image features and content categories yielded an F1 score of 0.79 as well as an AUC ROC of 0.78. Performance measures for gender are not compared to previous research as gender was, unlike in previous studies, not inferred from Instagram data. The respective RMSE as well as the interval it refers to for age, openness, conscientiousness, extraversion, agreeableness and neuroticism are displayed in Table 5.

User trait	RMSE [Interval]	User trait	RMSE [Interval]
Openness	**0.62** [1,5] (0.62)	Agreeableness	**0.55** [1,5] (0.56)
Conscientiousness	0.67 [1,5] (0.58)	Neuroticism	0.79 [1,5] (0.67)
Extraversion	0.72 [1,5] (0.61)	Age	**2.88** [18,36] (-)

Table 5: RMSE and reference interval for prediction of user traits with results of (Kim and Kim, 2018) in parantheses. Novel results and results equal to or outperforming results from previous comparable research are shown in boldface.

5 Discussion

In regards to the user trait gender, results align well with (Song et al., 2018) and (Kim and Kim, 2018). Women posting more warm-toned, pleasurable images and displaying a preference for fashion and beauty-related topics as well as social scenes as opposed to men whose images exude more dominance and who tend to display a preference for architecture, sports and outdoor scenes are also in line with common expectations and, therefore, emphasize the validity of results. In regards to age, the preference for social scenes in younger users could be rooted in their stronger desire for social validation and feedback (Somerville, 2013) (Chua and Chang, 2016) in order to build social identity and develop relations (Dhir et al., 2016) (Brown, 1999). In regards to personality traits, only some findings of (Kim and Kim, 2018) and (Ferwerda et al., 2015) (Ferwerda and Tkalcic, 2018b) could be reproduced while in some cases findings even contradict each other (e.g. a preference for red in conscientious users (Kim and Kim, 2018) vs. blue in conscientious users (this study as well as (Labrecque and Milne, 2012), (Navarro et al., 2018))) even though a very similar approach was adopted. Reasons for the discrepancies might include the composition of the user sample in regards to location or socio-economic status as well as current posting and editing trends on social media. However, more research in the area based on larger and more diverse data samples is required to obtain a clearer picture. Preferences that emerged in this work as well as other studies include a preference for art-related topics vs. social scenes in open-minded users (Ferwerda and Tkalcic, 2018b) (Marshall et al., 2015) as well as a preference for warmer colors and social scenes in extraverts and cooler colors in introverts (Kim and Kim, 2018) (Robinson, 1975). These findings are in line with attributes ascribed to these personality traits (Wirtz et al., 2014). The trait agreeableness generally shows a statistical correlation with a user's gender (Vecchione et al., 2012) (Weisberg et al., 2011), with women also scoring significantly higher in our sample. In the light of this connection, both the aversion against sports-related images found in this study as well as the preference for fashion found by (Ferwerda and Tkalcic, 2018b) are in line with expectations. The same holds true for the trait neuroticism, explaining the preference for beauty products and aversion against weapons in images in highly neurotic users. Regarding the prediction of gender, this study outperformed (Kim and Kim, 2018) by a large margin. While (Song et al., 2018) did achieve better results, it has to be noted that their study predicted gender as inferred from image content, not a user's verified gender. Regarding the prediction of personality traits, the prediction in this study outperformed (Ferwerda and Tkalcic, 2018a) in regards to all five personality traits. While (Kim and Kim, 2018) achieved better results predicting conscientiousness, extraversion and neuroticism, this study achieved the same or better results for openness and agreeableness.

6 Strengths and Limitations

While other researchers (e.g. (Song et al., 2018)) inferred a user's gender and age group from their profile information, we tested our results against survey data. Our approach holds two main benefits. Firstly, in order to make age groups clearly distinguishable, (Song et al., 2018) only included teenagers (age < 20 years) and adults (age > 30 years). This approach forced the researchers to exclude all users estimated to be in their twenties, which represents a very large group among Instagram users in general as well as in the data sample for our study. Secondly, it is crucial to mention that predicting a user's age from their Instagram profile might not be reliable. Errors can easily be introduced into the ground truth by users not disclosing their real age, by lack of precision in face recognition tools as well as image editing and the common use of filters. Moreover, in our study we are looking at a user's age on a fine-grained level. This way we are accounting for the fact that particularly among teenagers and young adults, an age difference of a few years can have a large impact on preferences, habits and aversions which cannot be captured as precisely when working with age groups. Another strength of this study is that it is, to our knowledge, the first study of its kind to focus on data from European users, opening up more possibilities for comparison of results across cultures and geographic locations. Limitations include the limited age range of participants as well as the data sample mostly consisting of university students. Future studies should also focus on other age groups and socio-economic groups as well as collect sufficient data from participants of non-binary gender identity. Another limitation is the assignment of each image content label to only one category to avoid statistic interaction between categories. While this makes sense from a statistical point of view, many labels could be assigned to more than one category, which might yield more accurate results in regards to the occurrence of a specific category.

7   Outlook

Possible areas of application could be the non-invasive acquisition of personality data for statistics or research when conducting a survey is not feasible as well as the generation of targeted content in areas such as advertising or usability. However, ethical concerns will have to be addressed when inferring user traits from image data, particularly in areas such as health or employment. The question whether users can consent to the extraction of information from their publicly visible image data with machine learning methods largely incomprehensible to humans will have to be discussed. While some overlap between results of studies in the area is emerging, more research on larger and more diverse data samples is still required to obtain robust results on the connection between user traits and social media image data. Based on the results of this work and related studies, image features and content categories that hold the most and least predictive value in regards to user traits should be identified and used to improved the proposed approach. As data for this study was collected shortly before the onset of the COVID-19 pandemic, future research should explore its impact on how user traits manifest in social media content.

References

Danny Azucar, Davide Marengo, and Michele Settanni. 2018. Predicting the big 5 personality traits from digital footprints on social media: A meta-analysis. *Personality and individual differences*, 124:150–159.

B Bradford Brown. 1999. " you're going out with who?": Peer group influences on adolescent romantic relationships.

Trudy Hui Hui Chua and Leanne Chang. 2016. Follow me and like my beautiful selfies: Singapore teenage girls' engagement in self-presentation and peer comparison on social media. *Computers in Human Behavior*, 55:190–197.

Daniel Danner, Beatrice Rammstedt, Matthias Bluemke, Lisa Treiber, Sabrina Berres, Christopher Soto, and Oliver John. 2016. Die deutsche version des big five inventory 2 (bfi-2). In *Zusammenstellung Sozialwissenschaftlicher Items und Skalen*.

Amandeep Dhir, Ståle Pallesen, Torbjørn Torsheim, and Cecilie Schou Andreassen. 2016. Do age and gender differences exist in selfie-related behaviours? *Computers in Human Behavior*, 63:549–555.

Bruce Ferwerda and Marko Tkalcic. 2018a. Predicting users' personality from instagram pictures: Using visual and/or content features? In *Proceedings of the 26th Conference on User Modeling, Adaptation and Personalization*, pages 157–161.

Bruce Ferwerda and Marko Tkalcic. 2018b. You are what you post: What the content of instagram pictures tells about users' personality. In *The 23rd International on Intelligent User Interfaces, March 7-11, Tokyo, Japan*.

Bruce Ferwerda, Markus Schedl, and Marko Tkalcic. 2015. Predicting personality traits with instagram pictures. In *Proceedings of the 3rd Workshop on Emotions and Personality in Personalized Systems 2015*, pages 7–10. ACM.

Kyungsik Han, Sanghack Lee, Jin Yea Jang, Yong Jung, and Dongwon Lee. 2016. Teens are from mars, adults are from venus: analyzing and predicting age groups with behavioral characteristics in instagram. In *Proceedings of the 8th ACM Conference on Web Science*, pages 35–44.

Yunhwan Kim and Jang Hyun Kim. 2018. Using computer vision techniques on instagram to link users' personalities and genders to the features of their photos: An exploratory study. *Information Processing & Management*, 54(6):1101–1114.

Jang Hyun Kim and Yunhwan Kim. 2019. Instagram user characteristics and the color of their photos: Colorfulness, color diversity, and color harmony. *Information Processing & Management*, 56(4):1494–1505.

Lauren I Labrecque and George R Milne. 2012. Exciting red and competent blue: the importance of color in marketing. *Journal of the Academy of Marketing Science*, 40(5):711–727.

Tara C Marshall, Katharina Lefringhausen, and Nelli Ferenczi. 2015. The big five, self-esteem, and narcissism as predictors of the topics people write about in facebook status updates. *Personality and Individual Differences*, 85:35–40.

Remedios T Navarro, Edelyn A Cadorna, Lourdes P Llanes, and Michael Esta. 2018. Color preferences and personality traits of cas faculty: Gender differences. *UNP Research Journal*, 22:110–127.

rarcega. 2017. instagram-scraper.

Carl Robinson. 1975. Color preference as a function of introversion and extraversion. *Perceptual and Motor Skills*.

Leah H Somerville. 2013. The teenage brain: Sensitivity to social evaluation. *Current directions in psychological science*, 22(2):121–127.

Junho Song, Kyungsik Han, Dongwon Lee, and Sang-Wook Kim. 2018. "is a picture really worth a thousand words?": A case study on classifying user attributes on instagram. *PloS one*, 13(10):e0204938.

Patricia Valdez and Albert Mehrabian. 1994. Effects of color on emotions. *Journal of experimental psychology: General*, 123(4):394.

Michele Vecchione, Guido Alessandri, Claudio Barbaranelli, and Gianvittorio Caprara. 2012. Gender differences in the big five personality development: A longitudinal investigation from late adolescence to emerging adulthood. *Personality and Individual Differences*, 53(6):740–746.

Yanna J Weisberg, Colin G DeYoung, and Jacob B Hirsh. 2011. Gender differences in personality across the ten aspects of the big five. *Frontiers in psychology*, 2:178.

Markus Antonius Wirtz, Janina Strohmer, and Verlag Hans Huber. 2014. Dorsch-lexikon der psychologie.

Quanzeng You, Sumit Bhatia, Tong Sun, and Jiebo Luo. 2014. The eyes of the beholder: Gender prediction using images posted in online social networks. In *2014 IEEE International Conference on Data Mining Workshop*, pages 1026–1030. IEEE.

Persuasiveness of News Editorials depending on Ideology and Personality

Roxanne El Baff [1,2] **Khalid Al-Khatib** [2] **Benno Stein** [2] **Henning Wachsmuth** [3]
[1] German Aerospace Center (DLR), Germany, `roxanne.elbaff@dlr.de`
[2] Bauhaus-Universität Weimar, Weimar, Germany, `<first>.<last>@uni-weimar.de`
[3] Paderborn University, Paderborn, Germany, `henningw@upb.de`

Abstract

News editorials aim to shape the opinions of their readership and the general public on timely controversial issues. The impact of an editorial on the reader's opinion does not only depend on its content and style, but also on the reader's profile. Previous work has studied the effect of editorial style depending on general political ideologies (liberals vs. conservatives). In our work, we dig deeper into the persuasiveness of both content and style, exploring the role of the intensity of an ideology (lean vs. extreme) and the reader's personality traits (agreeableness, conscientiousness, extraversion, neuroticism, and openness). Concretely, we train content- and style-based models on New York Times editorials for different ideology- and personality-specific groups. Our results suggest that particularly readers with extreme ideology and non "role model" personalities are impacted by style. We further analyze the importance of various text features with respect to the editorials' impact, the readers' profile, and the editorials' geographical scope.

1 Introduction

News editorials are considered the backbone of a community in which they tackle timely controversial issues, aiming to sway readers towards certain opinions. Nowadays, editorials do not only focus on issues affecting their close entourage (e.g., within a state or a country), but rather tackle issues relevant across continents to shape the views of those living there and worldwide. For example, *The New York Times* and *Der Spiegel*[1] lately invested resources to write news editorials about the August 4th Beirut blast. As such, news editorials represent an important source for research on computational social science.

To be persuasive, a news editorial should comply with the communication-persuasion paradigm defined by O'Keefe (2015) consisting of five factors: source, message, target, impact, and channel: (1) The *source* represents an editorial's author who tries to persuade the readers. Usually, authors reflect the ideology of their newspaper. For example, The New York Times is considered a liberal news portal and its editorials reflect this ideology. (2) The *message* represents an editorial's content and the linguistic choices it made, e.g., in terms of style. (3) The *target* represents the readers, their prior beliefs (e.g., their political ideology or its intensity) and their characteristics (e.g., personality traits or gender). (4) The *impact* represents the actual effect of an editorial on a reader. Halmari and Virtanen (2005) states that persuasive text aims at changing or affecting the behavior of others or at strengthening the existing beliefs of those who already agree. And (5) the *channel* represents the mean used to read the editorial, e.g., an online news portal. We leave an analysis of the impact of the medium used on the editorial's effectiveness to future research.

Previous research tackled how people are affected by arguments depending on their personality traits, interests, and beliefs. However, most studies conducted their analysis on dialogical text from debate portals and similar (Lukin et al., 2017; Durmus and Cardie, 2018; Al Khatib et al., 2020). For news editorials, we recently revealed that liberal readers, unlike conservatives, are affected by the linguistic style (El Baff et al., 2020). Still, it remains unexplored to what extent also the intensity of a political ideology plays a role, let alone a reader's personality traits. In our work here, we fill this gap, and we consider both the content and the style of an editorial.

---

[1] A German newspaper: `https://www.spiegel.de/international/`

Proceedings of the Third Workshop on Computational Modeling of PEople's Opinions, PersonaLity, and Emotions in Social media, pages 29–40
Barcelona, Spain (Online), December 13, 2020.

In particular, this paper analyzes the persuasive effect (the impact) of linguistic content and style choices of news editorials (the message) on readers (the target) with two profile varieties, the intensity of their political ideology and their personality traits. We distinguish *lean* and *extreme* intensity of ideology, and we resort to the "Big Five" personality traits (Goldberg, 1990): *agreeableness, conscientiousness, extraversion, neuroticism,* and *openness.*

For our analysis, we employ a corpus with 1000 New York Times news editorials (El Baff et al., 2018). Each editorial is annotated for a notion of impact that defines the editorial to either *challenge* its readers' stance, by making them rethink their current opinion towards a topic, to *reinforce* their stance, by helping them argue better about a certain issue, or neither. The annotations were added by 24 readers with different political ideologies (liberals and conservatives). For each reader, also the ideology intensity and the Big Five personality traits are reported, but this information has not been used so far to our knowledge.

For each intensity and personality group in the corpus, we train one model to predict the persuasive effectiveness of an editorial, using various content and style features. Our results show that people with extreme ideology are somewhat impacted by style, and the same holds for readers whose personality is relatively high in neuroticism and low in extraversion. We further investigate the role of editorials' geographical scope; whether it tackles a *global*, *national*, or *state* topics.

2 Related Work

News editorials reflect argumentation related to political issues and, therefore, comprise hidden rhetorical means (van Dijk, 1995), which makes them a challenging genre to study. Some works dealt with news editorials for information retrieval purposes (Yu and Hatzivassiloglou, 2003; Bal, 2009) or for analyzing arguments (Bal and Dizier, 2010; Kiesel et al., 2015; Scheffler and Stede, 2016). Al Khatib et al. (2016) represent editorial argumentation explicitly by annotating 300 news editorials with argumentative discourse units on the sub-sentence level. We employ their model to extract features from news editorials for predicting the persuasive effectiveness of news editorials, as detailed in Section 4.

Aristotle (2007) argued that a persuasive effect is best achieved by providing showing a good character (ethos), evoking the right emotions (pathos), and providing logically reasoned arguments (logos) in a well-arranged and well-phrased way. This view was modeled by Wachsmuth et al. (2018) for argumentation synthesis. Instead, we here follow the communication-persuasion paradigm of O'Keefe (2015), stating that an argumentative text, and hence a news editorial, should comply with five factors to be persuasive, as already indicated in Section 1. Each of them is tackled in some way in related work:

(1) *Source* refers to the prior beliefs and behaviors of the writer. Each news portal reflects its beliefs (van Dijk, 1995). (2) *Message* deals with the linguistic choices in the content. In this regard, Hidey et al. (2017) study the semantic types of argument components in an online forum, and El Baff et al. (2020) analyze the persuasive effect of linguistic style on readers. Also, Hidey and McKeown (2018) and Durmus et al. (2020), respectively, exploit the role of argument sequencing in detecting persuasive influence, and the role of pragmatics and discourse context in determining argument impact. (3) *Target* includes the prior beliefs of readers. Lukin et al. (2017) find that emotional and rational arguments are effective depending on the Big Five personality traits (John et al., 1991). Also, Durmus and Cardie (2018) provide a debate portal dataset with a controlled task setting that takes into consideration the reader's religious and political ideology, and Al Khatib et al. (2020) exploit the personal characteristics of debaters to improve persuasiveness prediction. (4) *Impact* reflects the effect of a text, which has been assessed for essays (Persing and Ng, 2015; Wachsmuth et al., 2016) and debate portal arguments (Habernal and Gurevych, 2016; Persing and Ng, 2017). (5) *Channel*, finally, means the communication medium. Joiner and Jones (2003) study the effect of the medium on argumentation. They found that the quality of argumentation in face-to-face discussions is higher than in online discussions.

In previous work, we annotated news editorials at the document level, covering an editorial's persuasive effectiveness by reflecting to what extent a writer persuades a reader (El Baff et al., 2018); the effectiveness concept is based on the argumentation quality taxonomy defined by Wachsmuth et al. (2017). In our annotation setup, we considered the beliefs of readers by profiling annotators based on political ideology (liberals or conservatives). We also provides additional information about the annotators' ideology

(a) Intensity	Lean		Extreme	
Effect	Train	Test	Train	Test
Challenging	100	21	156	43
Ineffective	274	70	133	30
Reinforcing	409	105	494	123
Overall	783	196	783	196

(b) Personality	Role Models		Other	
Effect	Train	Test	Train	Test
Challenging	74	15	106	26
Ineffective	121	31	412	108
Reinforcing	588	150	265	62
Overall	783	196	783	196

Table 1: Distribution of the majority persuasive effect of the news editorials in the given training and test set for (a) ideology intensity, i.e., *lean* or *extreme*, and (b) the personality group, i.e., *role model* or *other*.

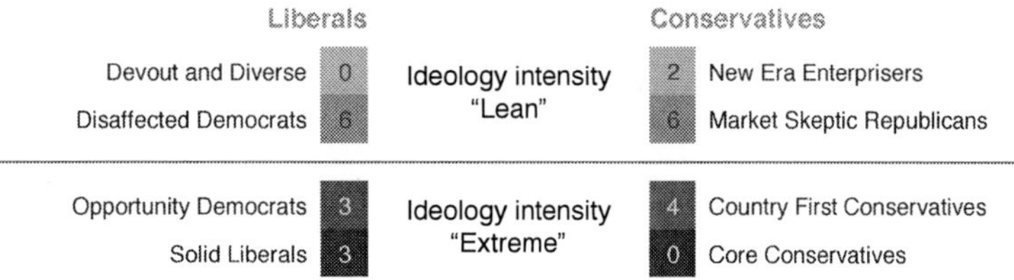

Figure 1: The distribution of the 24 selected annotators over the eight considered political ideologies, which we grouped by ideology intensity into *lean* and *extreme*.

intensity and personality traits. Later, we analyzed linguistic choices in news editorials with respect to the readers' ideology and reported effect (El Baff et al., 2020). However, we did not conduct our analysis on how content and style affect readers with different ideology intensity or with different personality traits. In the paper at hand, we fill this gap by using a similar methodology to detect the effect of style and content on readers with different ideology intensity and personality traits.

Conceptually, the studies of Lukin et al. (2017), Durmus and Cardie (2018), and Al Khatib et al. (2020) are closest to ours, but they tackle single arguments and dialogical argumentation respectively. To our knowledge, there is no computational analysis of linguistic choices related to ideology intensity and personality of readers and writers so far.

3 Data

The analysis is conducted using the Webis-Editorial-Quality-18 corpus (El Baff et al., 2018). 1000 New York Times editorials were annotated regarding their persuasive effects by three liberals and three conservatives each. The persuasive effect of each editorial was determined based on whether the editorial *challenged* their stance by making them rethink it, *reinforced* their stance by helping them argue better, or was *ineffective*. We previously utilized a corpus to investigate the role of editorial's style on readers with different political ideologies (El Baff et al., 2020). In order to ease the comparison to El Baff et al. (2020), we use the same dataset (with similar training/test split) in all our experiments. In particular, we chronologically split the dataset into 80% for training and 20% for testing (Table 1), based on editorials issue date, to imitate real-life prediction.[2] The majority effect votes vary depending on the annotators' profile (e.g., ideology intensity such as *lean*, personality trait such as *low agreeableness*).[3]

The corpus, in addition to the effect labels, includes information about the annotator's ideology and personality traits. In the following, we describe how we leverage this information here.

3.1 Ideology Intensity

The annotators of the Webis-Editorial-Quality-18 corpus took the PEW political typology quiz in order to determine their political ideology.[4] The ideology classes in this test ranges from *Solid Liberals* to *Core Conservatives*, as shown in Figure 1.

---

[2] In our previous work (El Baff et al., 2020), we found 21 duplicate editorials with the same content but different IDs — for these, they use the majority vote across all duplicates).

[3] In case of a tie between *effective* (challenging or reinforcing) and ineffective, we consider the majority effect as *effective*.

[4] PEW research quiz: https://www.pewresearch.org/politics/quiz/political-typology/

Trait	Effect	Low		Average		High	
		Train	Test	Train	Test	Train	Test
Agree-ableness	Challenging	123	30	n/a	n/a	86	17
	Ineffective	291	76	n/a	n/a	162	43
	Reinforcing	369	90	n/a	n/a	535	136
Conscien-tiousness	Challenging	157	48	77	12	64	9
	Ineffective	115	18	263	78	118	24
	Reinforcing	511	130	443	106	408	114
Extra-version	Challenging	106	22	83	18	171	53
	Ineffective	281	80	126	21	119	25
	Reinforcing	396	94	574	157	493	118

Trait	Effect	Low		Average		High	
		Train	Test	Train	Test	Train	Test
Neuro-ticism	Challenging	181	39	80	23	95	15
	Ineffective	104	36	114	28	311	70
	Reinforcing	498	121	396	96	377	111
Open-ness	Challenging	133	29	125	31	148	35
	Ineffective	316	93	220	42	106	28
	Reinforcing	334	74	438	123	529	133

Table 2: Distribution of the majority persuasive effect of the news editorials in the given training and test sets for the three values of the Big Five personality traits: *low*, *average*, and *high*. For agreeableness, *average* was combined with *low* due to the low number of annotators (two only) with *average* values.

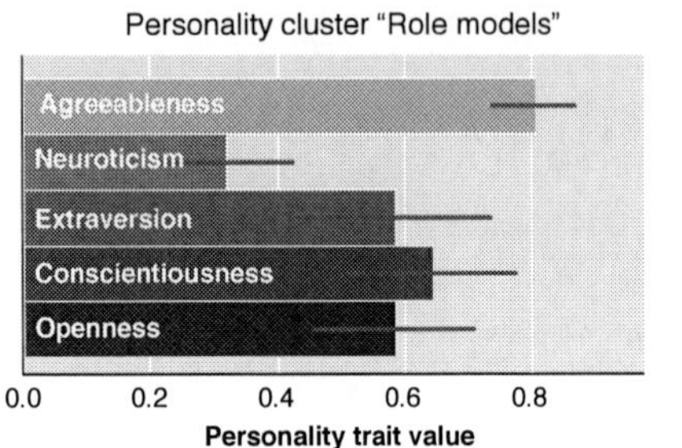

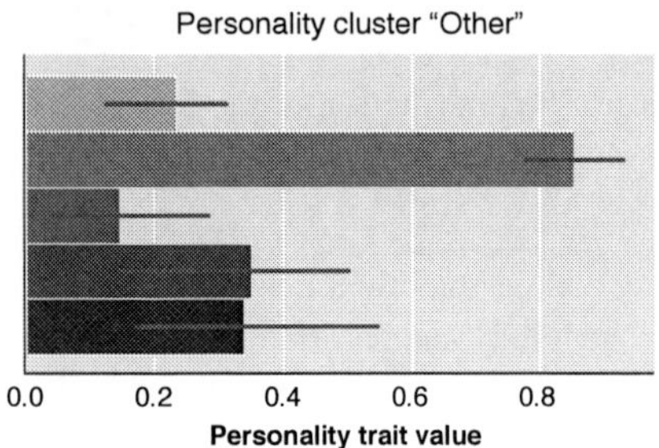

Figure 2: The two personality clusters, *role models* and *other*, based on the Big Five personality traits: agreeableness, conscientiousness, extraversion, neuroticism, and openness.

To analyze the effect of editorials on readers with different ideologies, we abstracted the annotators' ideologies into *Liberals* and *Conservatives* before (El Baff et al., 2018; El Baff et al., 2020). In contrast, we here decide to focus on the ideology intensities. Hence, we group the annotators into *lean* ("Market Skeptic Republicans", "New Era Enterprisers" and "Disaffected Democrats") and *extreme* ("Country First Conservatives", "Opportunity Democrats", "Solid Liberals"), illustrated in Figure 1. Table 1(a) shows the distribution of the persuasive effect (aggregated by majority vote) of the news editorials in the training and test sets for extreme and lean intensities.

3.2 Personality

Personality Traits   Besides the ideology test, the annotators took the personality test based on the "Big Five" (Goldberg, 1990) traits. Each annotator was assigned a numerical score (between 0 and 100) for each of five traits: "Agreeableness", "Conscientiousness", "Extraversion", "Neuroticism", and "Openness". Using this information, we investigate the impact of personality traits as follows. We use the same training and test sets mentioned before for each personality trait value of *Low* (≤ 32), *Average* (≥ 33 and ≤ 67), and *High*.[5] Table 2 shows the training and test distribution for each trait value (e.g. Openness *low*) across all effects (challenging, ineffective, and reinforcing).

Personality Groups   We categorize the annotators into two personality clusters. To do that, we apply cosine k-means, with $k = 2$, on the annotators' five personality trait values, as shown in Figure 2. The first group contains annotators with relatively high agreeableness, conscientiousness, extraversion, and openness, whereas the second group contains annotators with high neuroticism. Due to the small size of the dataset, we use $k = 2$ only.

---

[5]The *Low*, *Average* and *High* ranges were defined already in previous work (El Baff et al., 2018). There is one exception: for conscientiousness, the average range is ≥ 33 and < 67.

Feature Base	Overview	Reference	Label
Linguistic inquiry and word count	Psychological meaningfulness in percentile	Pennebaker et al. (2015)	liwc
NRC emotional and sentiment lexicon	Count of emotions (e,g. *fear,* *etc.) and polarity words*	Mohammad and Turney (2013)	emotion
Webis Argumentative Discourse Units	Count of each evidence type (*anecdote* and *testimony*)	Al Khatib et al. (2017)	evidence
MPQA Arguing Lexicon	Count of 17 types of arguing (*assessments, doubt,* etc.)	Somasundaran et al. (2007)	arguing
MPQA Subjectivity Classifier	Count of subjective and objective sentences	Riloff and Wiebe (2003)	subjectivity
Lemma 1–3-grams	Tfldf of lemma for 1–3-grams	Miller (1998)	lemma

Table 3: Summary of the six feature types used. Each feature is quantified at both the level of the editorial. The labels (rightmost column) are used to refer to the respective feature.

Gerlach et al. (2018) developed an approach to identify personality types, which they applied to more than 1.5 million participants. They found robust evidence for at least four distinct personality types and one of them is labeled as the "role model", who is low in *neuroticism* and high in all the other traits. Figure 2 shows that the upper cluster fits the description of the "role model". For simplicity, we refer to the two personality groups by *role models* and *other* reflecting the most discriminating personality trait between the two groups. Table 1(b) shows the distribution of the persuasive effect (majority vote) of the news editorials in the training and test sets for the two personality groups.

4   Features

In this section, we describe the set of features that we select to explore the linguistic choices in editorials. These features encode semantic and pragmatic properties that may manifest the author's means of persuasion, implicitly or explicitly, and follow those in previous work (El Baff et al., 2020): psychological meaningfulness, eight basic emotions, editorial evidence types, argumentativeness, and subjectivity. As those features essentially target the modeling of text style, we also consider standard text features to model text content. In the following, we describe all features in detail (an overview is given in Table 3):

Linguistic Inquiry and Word Count (liwc)   LIWC (Pennebaker et al., 2015) is a lexicon-based text analysis that counts words in psychologically meaningful categories (Tausczik and Pennebaker, 2010). It captures the narrative tone, the emotional tone, and the confidence tone among several other categories.

NRC Emotional and Sentiment Lexicons (emotion)   The NRC lexicon, compiled with crowdsourcing by Mohammad and Turney (2013), contains a set of English words and their associations with (1) *sentiment,* i.e., negative and positive polarities, and (2) *emotions,* i.e., the eight basic emotions as defined by Plutchik (1980): *anger, anticipation, disgust, fear, joy, sadness, surprise* and *trust.* We use this lexicon to generate features, where each category is represented as the count of words in an editorial (e.g., *sad* words).

Webis Argumentative Discourse Units (evidence)   Al Khatib et al. (2017) developed a computational model to classify the evidence types in news editorials. The model was trained and evaluated using the corpus of Al Khatib et al. (2016), which contains 300 editorials from The Guardian, Al Jazeera, and Fox News. Each segment in the editorial is labeled with six types, including three evidence types: (1) *anecdote,* giving a personal experience of the author, (2) *statistics* citing a quantitative study, and (3) *testimony* quoting an expert's argument. The classifier sees all remaining types (common ground, assumption, and other) as (4) *other.* We apply the evidence classifier at the sentence-level of each editorial and count the occurrence of each type (e.g., number of *testimony* sentences in an editorial).

MPQA Arguing Lexicon (arguing)   The MPQA Arguing lexicon, built by Somasundaran et al. (2007), includes various arguing patterns of different types such as *causation, conditionals, structure,* and *contrast.* Using the lexicon, we generate different features represented as the count of each arguing type in a text (e.g., number of *assessments* patterns in an editorial).

Features	A. Intensity		B. Personality	
	Extreme	**Lean**	**Role Model**	**Other**
liwc	0.28	0.29	0.32	0.29
emotion	0.34	0.32	0.31	0.30
evidence	0.34	0.28	0.24	0.36
arguing	0.29	0.34	0.30	0.29
subjectivity	0.23	0.21	0.29	0.37
Top Style	***0.40**	0.35	0.37	0.37
Content (lemma-based)	0.33	0.37	0.33	0.34
Top Content+Style	*0.38	**0.42**	**0.36**	***0.39**
Random baseline	0.27	0.32	0.23	0.34

Table 4: The macro F_1-score of each feature type and the best combinations in classifying the persuasive effect on readers with different profiles: *extreme* and *lean* ideology intensity (left), as well as *role models* and *other* personality group (right). $*$ indicates significant gains over the *Random baseline* at $p < 0.05$.

MPQA Subjectivity (subjectivity)   The MPQA subjectivity classifier, provided in OpinionFinder 2.0 (Riloff and Wiebe, 2003; Wiebe and Riloff, 2005), labels a text as *subjective* or *objective*. We apply the classifier to the editorials, and count the number of *subjective* and *objective* sentences.

Content Features (lemma)   We use the Tf-Idf score for lemma (Miller, 1998) 1–3-grams as the base of our content features.

5   Analysis of the Persuasive Effect

In this section, we assess the impact of the style and content of news editorials on their persuasive effectiveness for readers with different ideology intensities (extreme or lean), personality traits, and personality groups (role models or others). Similar to El Baff et al. (2020), we perform the analysis by approaching the following task: *Given a news editorial and a reader's profile characteristic (ideology intensity, personality trait, or personality group), predict the effect of the editorial.* This task is tackled by developing a separate effect prediction model for each ideology intensity (extreme or lean), each personality trait (e.g., low agreeableness), and each personality group (role models or others).

The prediction models use SVM classifiers (with a linear kernel), in which each classifier is trained using its corresponding profile training set and evaluated on the test set (See Section 3). The classifiers employ the features described in Section 4, considering both the style and the content of the editorials. The SVM cost was tuned using grid search with 5-fold cross-validation on the training set. We set the class weight to "balance" because of the skewed distribution of the data, as shown in Tables 1 and 2. The prediction results are reported using the macro-F_1 scores for each style feature alone, for the best combination of style features (*top style*), for the best combination of style and content (*top content+style*), and the *random baseline*. We measure significance using a t-test (Wilcoxon's test if normal distribution is missing) to quantify the differences between each two feature-based models among random baseline', content, top style, and top style+content.

In the following presentation of the results, we see readers as impacted by style and/or content if at least one model based on the respective feature manages to outperform the random baseline significantly.

5.1   Ideology Intensity

As shown in Table 4.A, for *extreme* intensity ideologies, the only two models that significantly beat the random baseline are *top style* (liwc, emotion, arguing) with macro-$F_1 = 0.40$ and *top content+style* (lemma, arguing, evidence) with macro-$F_1 = 0.38$. The *content* model alone did not significantly outperform the baseline. For the *lean* ideology, we did not observe any model that yield significant improvements.

5.2   Personality

Traits   Table 5 shows the macro-F_1 scores for each personality trait value. In general, the best combination of style and content, *top content+style*, performed best. In detail, we observe the following:

Features	Agreeable.		Conscientiousness			Extraversion			Neuroticism			Openness		
	Low	High	Low	Avg	High	Low	Avg	High	Low	Avg	High	Low	Avg	High
liwc	0.35	0.31	0.39	0.35	0.33	0.35	0.27	0.33	0.35	0.28	0.30	0.26	0.30	0.28
emotion	0.30	0.31	0.29	0.34	0.34	0.35	0.26	0.30	0.28	0.23	0.35	0.29	0.35	0.27
evidence	0.37	0.27	0.25	0.28	0.29	0.31	0.21	0.29	0.28	0.27	0.28	0.32	0.31	0.28
arguing	0.29	0.28	0.28	0.28	0.29	0.31	0.26	0.28	0.26	0.18	0.23	0.32	0.22	0.25
subjectivity	0.29	0.28	0.27	0.26	0.30	0.24	0.16	0.23	0.27	0.35	0.25	0.19	0.24	0.31
Top Style	0.39	0.32	0.39	0.36	*0.42	0.40	*0.33	*0.35	0.38	0.35	0.35	0.34	0.37	0.35
Content (lemma-based)	0.34	0.32	*0.40	0.39	0.38	0.35	*0.38	*0.35	0.35	**0.42**	0.33	‡0.39	**0.40**	0.39
Top Content+Style	†**0.41**	**0.37**	***0.44**	‡***0.43**	***0.43**	**0.41**	***0.42**	**0.37**	**0.38**	0.41	**0.42**	‡**0.41**	**0.40**	†**0.43**
Random baseline	0.31	0.26	0.25	0.34	0.21	0.29	0.25	0.30	0.29	0.35	0.23	0.33	0.29	0.26

Table 5: The macro F_1-scores of each feature type and their best combinations in classifying the persuasive effect on readers with different profiles. * and † and ‡ indicate significant differences at $p < 0.05$ against the *Random baseline*, *content* and *style* respectively.

- *Agreeableness.* For the readers with *low* agreeableness, the top content+style model (liwc, evidence and lemma) model was significantly better than the content model. In contrast, for the readers with *high* agreeableness, no model significantly outperformed the baseline.

- *Conscientiousness.* Readers with *low* and *average* values seem to be impacted by content. However, readers with *high* conscientiousness are more impacted by style, i.e., both top style (liwc, emotion, arguing) and top content+style (lemma, liwc, emotion, arguing, subjectivity) models significantly outperformed the baseline.

- *Extraversion.* For the *average* and *highly* extraverted readers, style and content have a similar impact. For *average*, the content, top style (liwc, subjectivity, evidence), and top content+style ({lemma, liwc, subjectivity, evidence} and {lemma, liwc}) models significantly outperformed the baseline. The analog holds for *high* extraversion with content and top style (emotion, arguing) models.

- *Neuroticism.* Here we find that the top content+style model performed best for *low* and *high* neuroticism, while the content model performed better for *average* neuroticism, however, without observed significance.

- *Openness.* Readers with *low* openness are impacted by content (content and top content+style were significantly better than style). However, those with *high* openness are impacted by style since we observe that top content+style is significantly better than the content model.[6]

Groups As shown in Table 4.B, for *other* personalities, the only models that significantly outperformed the random baseline are the two top content+style models ({lemma, liwc, arguing, evidence} and {lemma, liwc, emotion, arguing, evidence}) with macro-$F_1 = 0.39$. Content alone did not significantly outperform the baseline. On the contrary, *role model* readers seem not to be impacted by style, i.e., we did not observe any significant differences between the style models and the baseline.

6 Analysis of the Impact of Geographical Scopes

Given the importance of the *topic* and its role in persuasive text (Al Khatib et al., 2017), we conduct an analysis study considering both the readers' profiles and the topic of the editorials. In particular, we cluster the topics of the editorials and group them into three geographical scopes: (1) *Global* discusses global issues, such as the Iraq war. (2) *National* discusses national issues such as election, and (3) *State* discusses state (e.g. New York) related issues such as New York governor.

We conduct our analysis on the training sets as in section 5, following two settings: (i) using the whole training sets, and (ii) using the editorials that belong to each geographical scope in the training sets

---

[6]For *high* openness, two sets of top content+style outperform the content model: {lemma, liwc, emotion, evidence} and {lemma, emotion, subjectivity, evidence}.

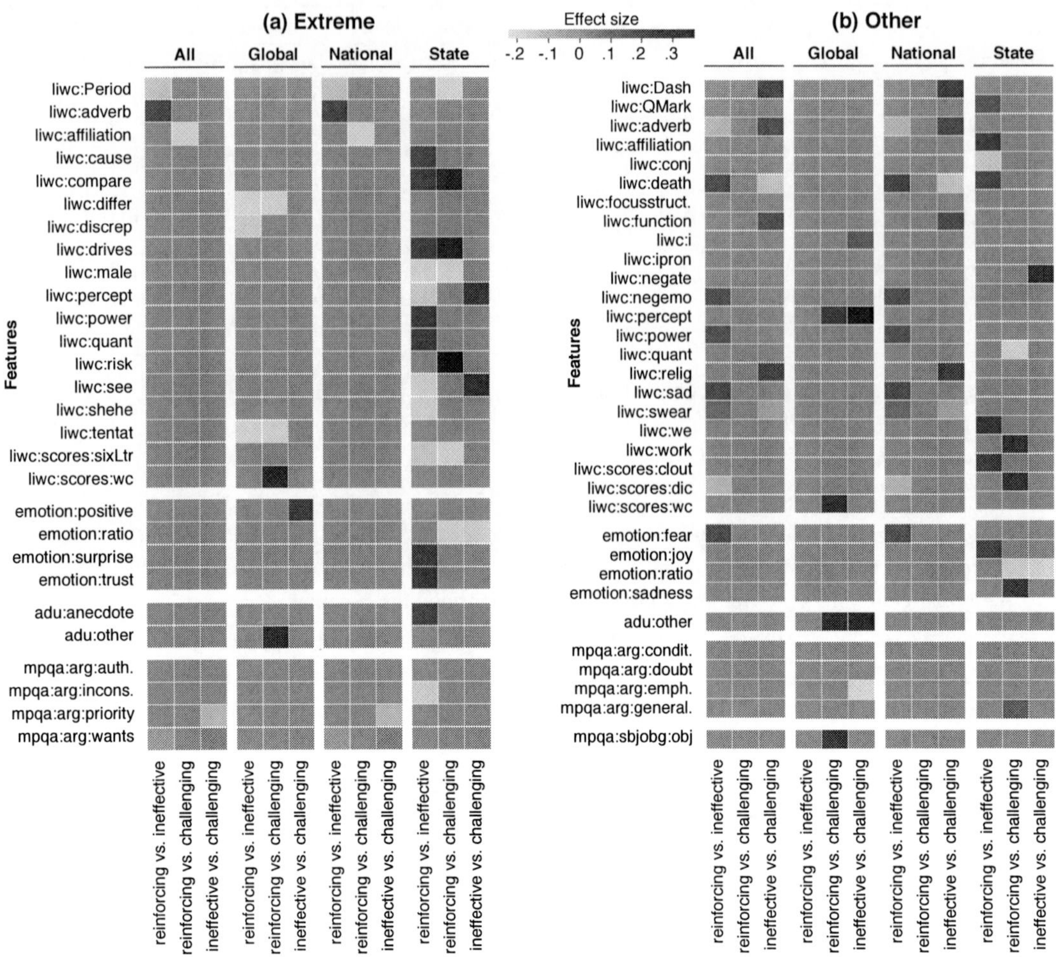

Figure 3: Heatmaps for each feature style for the two reader's profiles: extreme ideology ((a) Extreme) and and "Other" personality group ((b) Other). Each profile has four heatmaps, for each editorials' geographical scopes: *All*, *Global*, *National* and *State*. The y-axis represents the style features and the x-axis represents each effect-pair (*a vs. b*). Each effect size r value is indicated by a cube color: dark (light) color indicates that effect *a* (*b*) has significantly higher numbers of a style feature than effect *b* (*a*).

separately. For the reader profiles, we only consider the ones that were impacted by style (see Section 5), *extreme* ideology readers and non-*role models* ones.

Overall, our approach is divided into two steps: (1) Cluster the editorials into their three geographical scopes: *Global*, *National* and *State*. And (2) extract feature importance for each setting (i, ii), and profile (ideology intensity, *extreme* and personality group, *Other*).

6.1 Editorial Scope

For editorials topic clustering, we use Mallet latent Dirichlet allocation (Mallet-LDA) (Blei et al., 2003; McCallum, 2002). We employ it for several k (number of topics) and we calculate the coherence value for each k ranging from 2 to 30. The highest coherence value (0.52) is achieved with $k = 18$. The 18 topics cover issues related to the Bush administration, supreme court, tax, Iraqi war, Palestinian/Israeli conflict, immigration, nuclear weapon, energy, election, and more. We, then, hire an American annotator to map the 18 topics into meaningful groups. After inspecting each topic's keywords, he divides these topics into three geographical scopes. In total, we end up with 225 Global editorials, 475 for National editorials and 277 for State editorials.

New York City was put on notice a full decade ago that its black and Hispanic students were on the verge of being shut out of the elite public high schools that serve as a gateway to first-tier colleges and universities. The most damning analysis came from the community group ACORN. It called for sweeping curriculum changes at minority neighborhood middle schools, which typically lack the math, science and critical reading instruction necessary to prepare students for the entry test at the city's flagship high schools – Stuyvesant, Bronx Science and Brooklyn Tech.
The city should have seized on these findings as an opportunity to build a new middle school infrastructure in underserved neighborhoods. Instead, it opted for a poorly conceived and poorly run tutoring program that has now been exposed as a failure. [...]
The idea that students with decent preparation in the lower grades will automatically thrive is faulty. The city needs to attack the weaknesses of middle schools with the same urgency it has directed toward the elementary schools. New York needs a kind of Marshall Plan for its middle schools, especially in minority areas, with the specific aim of producing more high-performing minority students.
Getting there won't be easy. But the city needs to move with urgency and with all the resources at its disposal.

Figure 4: An excerpt of the news editorial with a *State* geographical scope, "Shutting Out Minorities". This editorial challenged the stance of annotators with extreme ideology.

The Supreme Court has been struggling to address the thorny question of when, if ever, punitive damages become so large that they violate the Constitution. The court made a good start when it laid down guidelines on when punitive damages are excessive. But eventually, it went too far. Today, it hears arguments in a case that offers a perfect opportunity to pull back to a more reasonable position.
The case involves Philip Morris's challenge to damages awarded to the widow of a smoker who died of lung cancer. An Oregon jury awarded Jesse Williams's widow, Mayola Williams, more than $821,000 in actual damages, and $79.5 million in punitive damages. Mrs. Williams said Philip Morris had engaged in 40 years of publicity to undercut concerns about cigarettes, even though it knew for most or all of that time that smoking was deadly. [...]
A final problem with the Supreme Court's rule of thumb on punitive damages is that it has been far less restrictive when it comes to punishing people. In 2003, the court held that California did not violate the ban on cruel and unusual punishment when it sentenced a man under its three-strikes law to 50 years for a theft of $153.53 worth of videotapes. That is a far more disproportionate punishment than Philip Morris got, for far less offensive conduct.

Figure 5: An excerpt of the news editorial with a *National* geographical scope, "Assessing the Damages". This editorial reinforced the stance of annotators with *Other* personality.

6.2 Style Impact within Geographical Scopes

Here, we study the impact of style (using style features) on readers with respect to reader's profile (*extreme* and *Other*) and geographical scope (e.g., national, all). To this end, we calculate, for each profile-scope, the significant differences between the persuasive effects (*challenging* vs. *reinforcing* vs. *ineffective*), for each of the style features (e.g. nrc:sad).

More precisely, for each feature (e.g., adu:anecdote), we measure significance using Anova (in case of homogeneity and normality) or Kruskal (otherwise). In the case of $p < 0.05$, we conduct post-hoc analysis (independent t-test in case of normality, Mann-Whitney otherwise) with Bonferroni correction for each effect-pair, and we calculated the effect-size r. Each heatmap, in Figure 3, shows the effect size [-0.23, +0.37] between each persuasive effect pair (e.g. challenging vs. ineffective) for all features with entailing significant differences within a pair.

For each profile-scope, we show, in Figure 3, only the style features if at least one effect-pair (e.g. *challenging* vs. *reinforcing*) has a significant difference for this style feature.

Extreme Ideology As shown in Figure 3.a, *All* and *National* editorials have similar pattern[7]. Whereas, *State* editorials differ from the other scopes. We observe that *reinforcing* editorials have significantly higher *adverbs* (liwc:adverbs) than *ineffective* editorials in both scopes (National/All). Also, within *State* editorials, the *emotional* (emotion:ratio) words are higher in *challenging* than *reinforcing/ineffective* (an excerpt is shown in Figure 4). Whereas, within the same scope, the same can be observed for *non-evidence* sentences (adu:other) for *reinforcing vs. challenging*. Within the *Global* scope, *ineffective* editorials have higher *positive words* (emotion:positive) than challenging ones.

[7]This can be due to the high number of National editorials in the dataset.

Other Personality   We observe from Figure 3.b that *fear* (emotion:fear) words are higher in *reinforcing* editorials than *ineffective* ones within *All and National* scopes (an excerpt is shown in Figure 5). However, for *State* editorials, in general, emotional words (emotion:ratio) are higher for *challenging* editorials. And, the *liwc:clout*, which refers to the relative social status, confidence, and leadership displaced in a text, is significantly higher for *reinforcing* editorials compared to *ineffective*.

Figure 3 shows the difference of style features across the different geographical scopes and within different editorial's effect, revealing the importance of the topic when studying persuasiveness.

7   Conclusion

In this paper, we analyzed how linguistic choices, in news editorials, affect readers with different ideology intensities, personality traits and groups, filling the gap for El Baff et al. (2020) analysis. Argumentative text, especially editorials tend to be very challenging to study due to the strategic maneuver used by the authors who are considered (usually) expert writers. Therefore, the performance of predicting effectiveness is limited. In our work, we used one news editorial portal (The New York Times) with an obvious ideology (Liberal). The picture will be more complete if this analysis is conducted on news editorials with different ideologies. However, the purpose of this paper was to shed light on which linguistic choices affect which profile and on the importance of topical information when studying persuasiveness. Our findings can be employed in augmented writing tools, to help editorials writer improve their *message*, based on their *target*'s profile, to have a higher *impact*.

References

Khalid Al Khatib, Henning Wachsmuth, Johannes Kiesel, Matthias Hagen, and Benno Stein. 2016. A News Editorial Corpus for Mining Argumentation Strategies. In *26th International Conference on Computational Linguistics (COLING 2016)*, pages 3433–3443. Association for Computational Linguistics, dec.

Khalid Al Khatib, Henning Wachsmuth, Matthias Hagen, and Benno Stein. 2017. Patterns of Argumentation Strategies across Topics. In *2017 Conference on Empirical Methods in Natural Language Processing (EMNLP 2017*, pages 1362–1368. Association for Computational Linguistics, sep.

Khalid Al Khatib, Michael Völske, Shahbaz Syed, Nikolay Kolyada, and Benno Stein. 2020. Exploiting Personal Characteristics of Debaters for Predicting Persuasiveness. In *58th Annual Meeting of the Association for Computational Linguistics (ACL 2020)*, pages 7067–7072. Association for Computational Linguistics, July.

Aristotle. 2007. *On Rhetoric: A Theory of Civic Discourse* (George A. Kennedy, Translator). Clarendon Aristotle series. Oxford University Press.

Bal Krishna Bal and Patrick Saint Dizier. 2010. Towards building annotated resources for analyzing opinions and argumentation in news editorials. In *Proceedings of the Seventh conference on International Language Resources and Evaluation (LREC'10)*. European Languages Resources Association (ELRA).

Bal Krishna Bal. 2009. Towards an analysis of opinions in news editorials: How positive was the year? (project abstract). In *Proceedings of the Eight International Conference on Computational Semantics*, pages 260–263. Association for Computational Linguistics.

David M Blei, Andrew Y Ng, and Michael I Jordan. 2003. Latent dirichlet allocation. *Journal of machine Learning research*, 3(Jan):993–1022.

Esin Durmus and Claire Cardie. 2018. Exploring the Role of Prior Beliefs for Argument Persuasion. In *Proceedings of the 2018 Conference of the North American Chapter of the Association for Computational Linguistics: Human Language Technologies, Volume 1 (Long Papers)*, volume 1, pages 1035–1045.

Esin Durmus, Faisal Ladhak, and Claire Cardie. 2020. The role of pragmatic and discourse context in determining argument impact. *arXiv preprint arXiv:2004.03034*.

Roxanne El Baff, Henning Wachsmuth, Khalid Al Khatib, and Benno Stein. 2018. Challenge or empower: Revisiting argumentation quality in a news editorial corpus. In *Proceedings of the 22nd Conference on Computational Natural Language Learning*, pages 454–464. Association for Computational Linguistics.

Roxanne El Baff, Henning Wachsmuth, Khalid Al Khatib, and Benno Stein. 2020. Analyzing the persuasive effect of style in news Editorial Argumentation. In *Proceedings of the 58th Annual Meeting of the Association for Computational Linguistics*, pages 3154–3160, Online, July. Association for Computational Linguistics.

Martin Gerlach, Beatrice Farb, William Revelle, and Luís A Nunes Amaral. 2018. A robust data-driven approach identifies four personality types across four large data sets. *Nature human behaviour*, 2(10):735–742.

Lewis R. Goldberg. 1990. An alternative "description of personality": The Big-Five factor structure. *Journal of Personality and Social Psychology*, 59(6):1216–1229.

Ivan Habernal and Iryna Gurevych. 2016. Which argument is more convincing? Analyzing and predicting convincingness of web arguments using bidirectional LSTM. In *Proceedings of the 54th Annual Meeting of the Association for Computational Linguistics (Volume 1: Long Papers)*, pages 1589–1599. Association for Computational Linguistics.

Helena Halmari and Tuija Virtanen. 2005. *Persuasion across genres: a linguistic approach*, volume 130. John Benjamins Publishing.

Christopher Hidey and Kathleen R McKeown. 2018. Persuasive influence detection: The role of argument sequencing. In *AAAI*, pages 5173–5180.

Christopher Hidey, Elena Musi, Alyssa Hwang, Smaranda Muresan, and Kathy McKeown. 2017. Analyzing the semantic types of claims and premises in an online persuasive forum. In *Proceedings of the 4th Workshop on Argument Mining*, pages 11–21.

Oliver P John, Eileen M Donahue, and Robert L Kentle. 1991. The big five inventory – versions 4a and 54.

Richard Joiner and Sarah Jones. 2003. The effects of communication medium on argumentation and the development of critical thinking. *International journal of educational research*, 39(8):861–871.

Johannes Kiesel, Khalid Al Khatib, Matthias Hagen, and Benno Stein. 2015. A Shared Task on Argumentation Mining in Newspaper Editorials. In *Proceedings of the 2nd Workshop on Argumentation Mining*, pages 35–38. Association for Computational Linguistics.

Stephanie Lukin, Pranav Anand, Marilyn Walker, and Steve Whittaker. 2017. Argument Strength is in the Eye of the Beholder: Audience Effects in Persuasion. In *Proceedings of the 15th Conference of the European Chapter of the Association for Computational Linguistics: Volume 1, Long Papers*, pages 742–753. Association for Computational Linguistics.

Andrew Kachites McCallum. 2002. Mallet: A machine learning for language toolkit. http://mallet.cs.umass.edu.

George Miller. 1998. *WordNet: An electronic lexical database*. MIT press.

Saif M Mohammad and Peter D Turney. 2013. Crowdsourcing a word–emotion association lexicon. *Computational Intelligence*, 29(3):436–465.

Daniel J. O'Keefe. 2015. *Persuasion: Theory and research*. Sage Publications.

James W Pennebaker, Ryan L Boyd, Kayla Jordan, and Kate Blackburn. 2015. The Development and Psychometric Properties of LIWC2015.

Isaac Persing and Vincent Ng. 2015. Modeling Argument Strength in Student Essays. In *Proceedings of the 53rd Annual Meeting of the Association for Computational Linguistics and the 7th International Joint Conference on Natural Language Processing (Volume 1: Long Papers)*, pages 543–552. Association for Computational Linguistics.

Isaac Persing and Vincent Ng. 2017. Lightly-supervised modeling of argument persuasiveness. In *Proceedings of the Eighth International Joint Conference on Natural Language Processing (Volume 1: Long Papers)*, pages 594–604, Taipei, Taiwan, November. Asian Federation of Natural Language Processing.

Robert Plutchik. 1980. A general psychoevolutionary theory of emotion. In *Theories of emotion*, pages 3–33. Elsevier.

Ellen Riloff and Janyce Wiebe. 2003. Learning extraction patterns for subjective expressions. In *Proceedings of the 2003 conference on Empirical methods in natural language processing*.

Tatjana Scheffler and Manfred Stede. 2016. Realizing Argumentative Coherence Relations in German: A Contrastive Study of Newspaper Editorials and Twitter Posts. *Patrick Saint-Dizier*, page 73.

Swapna Somasundaran, Josef Ruppenhofer, and Janyce Wiebe. 2007. Detecting arguing and sentiment in meetings. In *Proceedings of the SIGdial Workshop on Discourse and Dialogue*, volume 6.

Yla R Tausczik and James W Pennebaker. 2010. The psychological meaning of words: LIWC and computerized text analysis methods. *Journal of language and social psychology*, 29(1):24–54.

Teun A. van Dijk. 1995. Opinions and Ideologies in Editorials. In *Proceedings of the 4th International Symposium of Critical Discourse Analysis, Language, Social Life and Critical Thought*, Athens, June.

Henning Wachsmuth, Khalid Al Khatib, and Benno Stein. 2016. Using Argument Mining to Assess the Argumentation Quality of Essays. In *Proceedings of COLING 2016, the 26th International Conference on Computational Linguistics: Technical Papers*, pages 1680–1691. The COLING 2016 Organizing Committee.

Henning Wachsmuth, Nona Naderi, Yufang Hou, Yonatan Bilu, Vinodkumar Prabhakaran, Tim Alberdingk Thijm, Graeme Hirst, and Benno Stein. 2017. Computational argumentation quality assessment in natural language. In *Proceedings of the 15th Conference of the European Chapter of the Association for Computational Linguistics: Volume 1, Long Papers*, pages 176–187. Association for Computational Linguistics.

Henning Wachsmuth, Manfred Stede, Roxanne El Baff, Khalid Al Khatib, Maria Skeppstedt, and Benno Stein. 2018. Argumentation synthesis following rhetorical strategies. In *Proceedings of the 27th International Conference on Computational Linguistics*, pages 3753–3765. Association for Computational Linguistics.

Janyce Wiebe and Ellen Riloff. 2005. Creating subjective and objective sentence classifiers from unannotated texts. In *International conference on intelligent text processing and computational linguistics*, pages 486–497. Springer.

Hong Yu and Vasileios Hatzivassiloglou. 2003. Towards answering opinion questions: Separating facts from opinions and identifying the polarity of opinion sentences. In *Proceedings of the 2003 Conference on Empirical Methods in Natural Language Processing*, pages 129–136. Association for Computational Linguistics.

HopeEDI: A Multilingual Hope Speech Detection Dataset for Equality, Diversity, and Inclusion

Bharathi Raja Chakravarthi

Insight SFI Research Centre for Data Analytics

Data Science Institute

National University of Ireland Galway

bharathiraja.akr@gmail.com

Abstract

Over the past few years, systems have been developed to control online content and eliminate abusive, offensive or hate speech content. However, people in power sometimes misuse this form of censorship to obstruct the democratic right of freedom of speech. Therefore, it is imperative that research should take a positive reinforcement approach towards online content that is encouraging, positive and supportive contents. Until now, most studies have focused on solving this problem of negativity in the English language, though the problem is much more than just harmful content. Furthermore, it is multilingual as well. Thus, we have constructed a Hope Speech dataset for Equality, Diversity and Inclusion (HopeEDI) containing user-generated comments from the social media platform YouTube with 28,451, 20,198 and 10,705 comments in English, Tamil and Malayalam, respectively, manually labelled as containing hope speech or not. To our knowledge, this is the first research of its kind to annotate hope speech for equality, diversity and inclusion in a multilingual setting. We determined that the inter-annotator agreement of our dataset using Krippendorff's alpha. Further, we created several baselines to benchmark the resulting dataset and the results have been expressed using precision, recall and F1-score. The dataset is publicly available for the research community. We hope that this resource will spur further research on encouraging inclusive and responsive speech that reinforces positiveness.

1   Introduction

With the expansion of the Internet, there has been substantial growth all over the world in the number of marginalised people looking for support online (Gowen et al., 2012; Yates et al., 2017; Wang and Jurgens, 2018). Recently, due to the lockdowns enforced as a consequence of the COVID-19 pandemic, people have started to look at online forums as an emotional outlet when they go through a tough time. The importance of the online life of the marginalised population, such as women in the fields of Science, Technology, Engineering, and Management (STEM), people who belong to the Lesbian, Gay, Bisexual, Transgender, Intersex and Queer/Questioning (LGBTIQ) community, racial minorities or people with disabilities have been studied, and it has been proven that the online life of vulnerable individuals produces a significant impact on their self-definition (Chung, 2013; Altszyler et al., 2018; Tortoreto et al., 2019). Furthermore, according to Milne et al. (2016), Burnap et al. (2017) and Kitzie (2018), the social networking activities of a vulnerable individual play an essential role in shaping the personality of the individual and how they look at society.

Comments/posts on online social media have been analysed to find and stop the spread of negativity using methods such as hate speech detection (Schmidt and Wiegand, 2017), offensive language identification (Zampieri et al., 2019a) and abusive language detection (Lee et al., 2018). According to Davidson et al. (2019), technologies developed for the detection of abusive language do not consider the potential biases of the dataset that they are trained on. The systematic bias in the datasets causes abusive language detection to be biased and may discriminate against one group over another. This will have a

Proceedings of the Third Workshop on Computational Modeling of PEople's Opinions, PersonaLity, and Emotions in Social media, pages 41–53
Barcelona, Spain (Online), December 13, 2020.

negative impact on minorities. We should turn our work towards spreading positivity instead of curbing an individual's freedom of speech by removing negative comments.

Therefore, we turn our research focus towards hope speech. Hope is commonly associated with the promise, potential, support, reassurance, suggestions or inspiration provided to participants by their peers during periods of illness, stress, loneliness and depression (Snyder et al., 2002). Psychologists, sociologists and social workers in the Association of Hope have concluded that hope can also be a useful tool for saving people from suicide or harming themselves (Herrestad and Biong, 2010). The Hope Speech delivered by gay rights activist Harvey Milk on the steps of the San Francisco City Hall during a mass rally to celebrate California Gay Freedom Day on 25 June 1978 [1] inspired millions to demand rights for equality, diversity and inclusion (Milk, 1997). However, to the best of our knowledge, no prior work has explored hope speech for women in STEM, LGBTIQ individuals, racial minorities or people with disabilities in general.

Moreover, although people of various linguistic backgrounds are exposed to online social media language, English is still at the centre of ongoing trends in language technology research. Recently, some research studies have been conducted on high resourced languages, such as Arabic, German, Hindi and Italian. However, such studies usually use monolingual corpora and do not examine code-switched textual data. Code-switching is a phenomenon where the individual switches between two or more languages in a single utterance (Sciullo et al., 1986). We introduce a dataset for hope speech identification not only in English but also in under-resourced code-switched Tamil (ISO 639-3: tam) and Malayalam (ISO 639-3: mal) languages (Chakravarthi et al., 2019; Jose et al., 2020; Priyadharshini et al., 2020).

The key contributions of this paper can be summarised as follows:

- We propose to encourage hope speech rather than take away an individual's freedom of speech by detecting and removing a negative comment.

- We apply the schema to create a multilingual, hostility-diffusing hope speech dataset for equality, diversity and inclusion. This is a new large-scale dataset of English, Tamil (code-switched), and Malayalam (code-switched) YouTube comments with high-quality annotation of the target.

- We performed an experiment on Hope Speech dataset for Equality, Diversity and Inclusion (HopeEDI) using different state-of-the-art machine learning models to create benchmark systems.

2 Related Works

When it comes to crawling social media data, there are many works on YouTube mining (Marrese-Taylor et al., 2017; Muralidhar et al., 2018), mainly focused on exploiting user comments. Krishna et al. (2013) did an opinion mining and trend analysis on YouTube comments. The researchers made an analysis of the sentiments to identify their trends, seasonality, and forecasts, and it was found that user sentiments are well correlated with the influence of real-world events. Severyn et al. (2014) did a systematic study on opinion mining targeting YouTube comments. The authors developed a comment corpus containing 35K manually labelled data for modelling the opinion polarity of the comments based on tree kernel models. Chakravarthi et al. (2020a) and Chakravarthi et al. (2020b) collected comments from YouTube and created a manually annotated corpus for the sentiment analysis of under-resourced Tamil and Malayalam languages.

Methods to mitigate gender bias in natural language processing (NLP) have been extensively studied for the English language (Sun et al., 2019). Some studies have investigated gender bias beyond the English language using machine translation to French (Vanmassenhove et al., 2018) and other languages (Prates et al., 2020). Tatman (2017) studied the gender and dialect bias in automatically generated captions from YouTube. Technologies for abusive language (Waseem et al., 2017; Clarke and Grieve, 2017), hate speech (Schmidt and Wiegand, 2017; Ousidhoum et al., 2019) and offensive language detection (Nogueira dos Santos et al., 2018; Zampieri et al., 2019b; Sigurbergsson and Derczynski, 2020) are being developed and applied without considering the potential biases (Davidson et al., 2019; Wiegand

---

[1] http://www.terpconnect.umd.edu/~jklumpp/ARD/MilkSpeech.pdf

et al., 2019; Xia et al., 2020). However, current gender debiasing methods in NLP are not sufficient to debias other issues related to EDI in end-to-end systems of many language technology applications, which causes unrest and escalates the issues with EDI, as well as leading to more inequality on digital platforms (Robinson et al., 2020).

Counter-narratives (i.e. informed textual responses) is another strategy, which has received the attention of researchers recently (Chung et al., 2019; Tekiroğlu et al., 2020). A counter-narrative approach was proposed to weigh the right to freedom of speech and avoid over-blocking. Mathew et al. (2019) created and released a dataset for counterspeech using comments from YouTube. However, the core idea to directly intervene with textual responses escalates hostility even though it is advantageous to the writer to understand why their comment/post has been deleted or blocked and then favourably change the discourse and attitudes of their comments. So we turn our research to finding positive information such as hope and encouraging such activities.

Recently, a work by Palakodety et al. (2020a) and Palakodety et al. (2020b) analysed how to use hope speech from a social media text to diffuse tension between two nuclear power nations (India and Pakistan) and support minority Rohingyas refugees. However, the author's definition of hope is just defined to diffuse tensions and violence. It does not take other perspectives of hope and EDI. The authors did not give more information such as the inter-annotator agreement, diversity in annotators and the details of the dataset. The dataset is not publicly available for research. It was created in English, Hindi and other languages related known to the Rohingyas. Our work differs from the previous works in that we define hope speech for EDI, and we introduce a dataset for English, Tamil and Malayalam on EDI of it. To the best of our knowledge, this is the first work to create a dataset for EDI in Tamil and Malayalam, which are under-resourced languages.

3   Hope Speech

Hope is considered significant for the well-being, recuperation and restoration of human life by health professionals. Hope can be defined as an optimistic state of mind that depends on a desire for positive results regarding the occasions and conditions of one's life or the world at large, and it is also present- and future-oriented (Snyder et al., 2002). Hope can also come from inspirational talk about how people face difficult situations and survive them. Hope speech engenders optimism and resilience that positively influences many aspects of life, including work (Youssef and Luthans, 2007), college (Chang, 1998) and other aspects that make us vulnerable (Cover, 2013). We define hope speech for our problem as "YouTube comments/posts that offer support, reassurance, suggestions, inspiration and insight".

Hope speech reflects the belief that one can discover pathways to their desired objectives and become roused to utilise those pathways. Our work aims to change the prevalent way of thinking by moving away from a preoccupation with discrimination, loneliness or the worst things in life to building the confidence, support and good qualities based on comments by individuals. Thus, we have provided instructions to annotators that if a comment/post meets the following conditions, then it should be annotated as hope speech.

- The comment contains inspiration provided to participants by their peers and others, offers support, reassurance, suggestions and insight

- The comment promotes well-being and satisfaction (past), joy, sensual pleasures and happiness (present).

- The comment triggers constructive cognition about the future – optimism, hope and faith.

- The comment contains an expression of love, courage, interpersonal skill, aesthetic sensibility, perseverance, forgiveness, tolerance, future-mindedness, praise for talents and wisdom.

- The comment encourages compliance with COVID-19 health guidelines.

- The comment promotes the values of equality, diversity and inclusion.

- The comment brings out a survival story of gay, lesbian or transgender individuals, women in science, or a COVID-19 survivor.

- The comment talks about fairness in the industry. (e.g., [I do not think banning all apps is right, we should ban only the apps which are not safe])

- Comments explicitly talking about a hopeful future. (e.g., [We will survive these things])

- Comments that explicitly talk about and say no to division in any form.

- The comment expresses positive peace-seeking intent (e.g., [We want peace]).

Non-hope speech includes comments that do not bring positivity, such as the following:

- The comment uses racially, ethnically, sexual or nationally motivated slurs.

- The comment produces hate toward a minority.

- The comment is very prejudiced and attacks people without thinking about the consequences.

- The comments do not inspire hope in the reader's mind.

Non-hope speech is different from hate speech. Some examples are shown below.

- **"How is that the same thing???"** This is non-hope speech but it is not hate speech either.

- **"Society says don't assume but they assume to anyways"** This is non-hope speech but it is not hate speech either.

Hate speech or offensive language detection dataset is not available for code-mixed Tamil and code-mixed Malayalam (Banerjee et al., 2020), and it does not take into account LGBTIQ, women in STEM and other minorities. Thus, we cannot use existing hate speech or offensive language detection datasets to detect hope or non-hope for EDI of minorities.

4   Dataset Construction

We focused on collecting data from the social media comments on YouTube [2], which is the most widely used platform in the world to express an opinion about a particular video. We avoided taking comments from personal coming out stories of LGBTIQ people as it had references to personal details, we manually removed the videos for personal coming out stories. For English, we collected data on recent topics of EDI, including women in STEM, LGBTIQ issues, COVID-19, Black Lives Matters, United Kingdom (UK) versus China, United States of America (USA) versus China and Australia versus China from YouTube video comments. The data was collected from videos of people from English-speaking countries, such as Australia, Canada, the Republic of Ireland, United Kingdom, the United States of America and New Zealand.

For Tamil and Malayalam, we collected data from India on the recent topics regarding LGBTIQ issues, COVID-19, women in STEM, the Indo-China war and Dravidian affairs. India is a multilingual and a multi-racial country. Linguistically, India can be divided into three major language families, namely Dravidian, Indo-Aryan and Tibeto-Burman languages (Chakravarthi et al., 2019; Chakravarthi et al., 2020c; Hande et al., 2020; Chakravarthi, 2020). The recent dispute on the Indo-China border has triggered racism on the internet towards people with Mongoloid features even though they are Indians from the North-Eastern states. Similarly, the National Education Policy, which advocates for the introduction of Sanskrit or Hindi has escalated issues regarding the linguistic autonomy of Dravidian languages in the state of Tamil Nadu. We used the YouTube comment scraper [3] to collect comments. We collected data on the above topics from November 2019 to June 2020 . We believe that our dataset will diffuse hostility and inspire hope. Our dataset is produced as a multilingual resource to allow cross-lingual studies and approaches. In particular, it contains hope speech in English, Tamil and Malayalam.

---

[2] https://www.youtube.com/
[3] https://github.com/philbot9/youtube-comment-scraper

4.1 Code-Mixing

Code-mixing is a phenomenon where the speaker uses two or more languages in a single utterance. It is prominent in multilingual speakers' social media discourse. Traditionally code-mixing has been associated with inadequate or informal knowledge of the language. However, research has shown that it is frequent in user-generated social media contents. For a multilingual country like India, code-mixing is quite frequent (Barman et al., 2014; Bali et al., 2014; Gupta et al., 2018). As our data comes from YouTube, our Tamil and Malayalam dataset is code-mixed. We have come across all the three types of code-mixing, such as tag, inter-sentential and intra-sentential in our corpus. Our corpus also has code-mixing using Latin script and native script.

4.2 Ethical Concerns

Social media data is highly sensitive, and even more so when it is related to the minority population, such as the LGBTIQ community or women. We have taken full consideration to minimise the risk associated with individual identity in the data by removing personal information from dataset, such as names but not celebrity names. However, to study EDI, we needed to keep information relating to the following characteristics; racial, gender, sexual orientation, ethnic origin and philosophical beliefs. Annotators were only shown anonymised posts and agreed to make no attempts to contact the comment creator. The dataset will only be made available for research purpose to the researcher who agree to follow ethical guidelines.

Language		English	Tamil	Malayalam
Gender	Male	4	2	2
	Female	5	3	5
	Non-binary	2	1	0
Higher Education	Undergraduate	1	0	0
	Graduate	4	4	5
	Postgraduate	6	2	2
Nationality		Ireland, UK, USA, Australia	India, Sri Lanka	India
Total		11	6	7

Table 1: Annotators

4.3 Annotation Setup

After the data collection phase, we cleaned the data using *Langdetect*[4] to identify the language of the comments and removed comments that were not in the specified languages. However, there were unintended comments of other languages in the cleaned corpus of the Tamil and Malayalam comments due to code-mixing at different levels. Finally, we identified three classes, two of which are hope- and not-hope based on our definition from Section 3, while the last (Other languages) were introduced to account for comments that were not in the required language. These specific sets of classes were selected because they provided an adequate level of generalisation for characterising the comments of the EDI hope speech dataset.

4.4 Annotators

We created Google forms to collect annotations from annotators. Each form contained a maximum of 100 comments, and each page contained a maximum of 10 comments to maintain the quality of annotation. We collected information on the gender, educational background and the medium of schooling of the annotator to know the diversity of the annotator and avoid bias. The annotators were warned that comments might have offensive language and abusive text. The annotator was given the choice to stop annotating if they found the comments to be too disturbing or something that they could not handle.

---

[4]https://pypi.org/project/langdetect/

We educated annotators by providing them with YouTube videos on EDI [5] [6] [7] [8]. A minimum of three annotators annotated each form. As a warm-up procedure, after the first form containing 100 comments were annotated by annotators, the results were checked manually. This scheme was utilised to refine their understanding of the assignment and to improve the understanding of EDI. A few annotators dropped out after the initial stage of annotating their first form, and those annotations were discarded. The annotators were asked to watch the EDI videos again and reread the annotation guidelines. From Table 1, we can see the statistics of annotators. For English language comments, annotators were from Australia, the Republic of Ireland, the United Kingdom and the United States of America. For Tamil, we were able to get annotations from both people from the state of Tamil Nadu of India and from Sri Lanka. Most of the annotators were graduate or post-graduate students.

4.5 Inter-Annotator Agreement

To aggregate the hope speech annotations from multiple annotators, we opted for the majority, the comments that did not have a majority in the first round were collected, and a separate Google form was created to annotate them by new annotators. We calculated the inter-annotator agreement after the final round of annotation. We report inter-annotator agreement using the Krippendorff's alpha for assessing the clarity of the annotation. The Krippendorff's alpha is a statistical measure of agreement among annotators to answer how much the resulting data can be relied upon to represent real data (Krippendorff, 1970). Although **Krippendorff's alpha** (α) is computationally complex, it is more relevant to our case as more than two annotators annotated the comments, and the same annotators did not annotate all the sentences. It is not affected by missing data, takes into account varying the sample sizes, categories, the numbers of raters and can also be employed for any measurement levels, such as nominal, ordinal, interval and ratio. We used *nltk*[9] for calculating Krippendorff's alpha (α) (Krippendorff, 2011). Our annotations produced an agreement of 0.63, 0.76, and 0.85 using nominal metric for English, Tamil and Malayalam respectively.

Language pair	English	Tamil	Malayalam
Number of Words	522,717	191,242	122,917
Vocabulary Size	29,383	46,237	40,893
Number of Comments/Posts	28,451	20,198	10,705
Number of Sentences	46,974	22935	13,643
Average number of words per sentences	18	9	11
Average number of sentences per post	1	1	1

Table 2: Corpus statistic

Class	English	Tamil	Malayalam
Hope	2,484	7,899	2,052
Not Hope	25,940	9,816	7,765
Other lang	27	2,483	888
Total	28,451	20,198	10,705

Table 3: Classwise Data Distribution

---

[5] https://www.youtube.com/watch?v=C-uyB5I6WnQ&t=6s

[6] https://www.youtube.com/watch?v=UcuS5glhNto

[7] https://www.youtube.com/watch?v=hNeR4bBUj68

[8] https://www.youtube.com/watch?v=LqP6iU3g2eE

[9] https://www.nltk.org/

	English	Tamil	Malayalam
Training	22,762	16,160	8564
Development	2,843	2,018	1070
Test	2,846	2,020	1071
Total	28,451	20,198	10,705

Table 4: Train-Development-Test Data Distribution

4.6 Corpus Statistics

In total, our dataset contains 59,354 comments from YouTube videos, where 28,451 comments in English, 20,198 comments in Tamil, and 10,705 comments in Malayalam. Table 2 shows the distribution of our dataset. We used *nltk* tool to tokenise words and sentences in the comments to calculate corpus statistics. As shown, the vocabulary for Tamil and Malayalam is high due to the different types of code-mixing.

Table 3 presents the distribution of the annotated dataset by label. The dataset is skewed, with almost the majority of the comments being labelled as not hope (NOT). This is common for user-generated content on online platforms, and an automatic detection system needs to be able to handle imbalanced data in order to be truly useful. We have a considerable amount of "Other language" labels for Tamil and Malayalam; this is also due to high code-mixing phenomenon occurring in the comments of these languages. The fully annotated dataset was split into a train, development and test set. The training set contains 80%, the development set contains 10% and finally, the test set contains the remaining 10% of the data shown in Table 4.

4.7 Ambiguous Comments

We found some ambiguous comments during the process of annotation.

- **"Chanting Black Lives Matter is Racist"** This sentence from the English corpus was confusing. The annotators were as confused as we were about comments like these.

- **"God gave us a choice"** This sentence was interpreted by some as hope and others as not-hope.

- Sri Lankan **Tamilar** history **patti pesunga** – *Please speak about history of Tamil people in Sri Lanka.* Inter-sentential switch in Tamil corpus written using Latin script. The history of Tamil people in Sri Lanka is both hopeful and non-hopeful due to the recent civil war.

- **Bro helo app ku oru alternate appa solunga.** – *Bro tell me an alternate app for Helo app.* Intra-sentential and tag switch in Tamil corpus written using Latin script.

5 Benchmark Experiments

We reported our dataset using a wide range of standard classifiers on the unbalanced settings of the dataset. The experiment was applied on the token frequency-inverse document frequency (Tf-Idf) of tokens. We used sklearn [10]library to create baseline classifiers. For the multinomial Naive Bayes, we set alpha = 0.7. We used a grid search for the k-nearest neighbors (KNN), support vector machine (SVM), decision tree and logistic regression. More details about the parameters of the classifier will be published in the code.

Our models were trained on the training dataset; the development set was used to fine-tune the model, and it was evaluated by predicting the labels for the held-out test set, as shown in Table 4. To report the performance of the classification, we used a macro-averaged F-score, calculated using macro-averaged precision and recall. The motivation behind such a choice is due to the imbalanced class distribution,

---

[10]https://scikit-learn.org/stable/

Classifier	Hope Speech	Not-Hope Speech	Other language	Macro Avg	Weighted Avg
Support	250	2,593	3		
Precision					
SVM	0.00	0.91	0.00	0.30	0.83
MNB	0.14	0.91	0.00	0.35	0.84
KNN	0.63	0.92	0.00	0.52	0.90
DT	0.46	0.94	0.00	0.47	0.90
LR	0.33	0.96	0.00	0.43	0.90
Recall					
SVM	0.00	1.00	0.00	0.33	0.83
MNB	0.00	1.00	0.00	0.33	0.91
KNN	0.14	0.99	0.00	0.38	0.92
DT	0.39	0.96	0.00	0.45	0.90
LR	0.59	0.88	0.00	0.49	0.86
F-Score					
SVM	0.00	0.95	0.00	0.32	0.87
MNB	0.01	0.95	0.00	0.31	0.87
KNN	0.23	0.96	0.00	0.40	0.89
DT	0.42	0.95	0.00	0.46	0.90
LR	0.43	0.92	0.00	0.45	0.87

Table 5: Precision, Recall, and F-score for English

Classifier	Hope Speech	Not-Hope Speech	Other language	Macro Avg	Weighted Avg
Support	815	946	259		
Precision					
SVM	0.00	0.47	0.00	0.16	0.22
MNB	0.58	0.57	0.74	0.63	0.60
KNN	0.48	0.55	0.55	0.53	0.52
DT	0.52	0.57	0.52	0.53	0.54
LR	0.59	0.59	0.47	0.55	0.58
Recall					
SVM	0.00	1.00	0.00	0.33	0.47
MNB	0.42	0.81	0.25	0.49	0.58
KNN	0.35	0.72	0.38	0.48	0.53
DT	0.40	0.71	0.41	0.51	0.55
LR	0.37	0.73	0.64	0.58	0.57
F-Score					
SVM	0.00	0.64	0.00	0.21	0.30
MNB	0.49	0.67	0.37	0.51	0.56
KNN	0.41	0.62	0.45	0.49	0.51
DT	0.45	0.63	0.46	0.51	0.53
LR	0.46	0.65	0.55	0.55	0.56

Table 6: Precision, Recall, and F-score for Tamil

which makes well-known measures such as accuracy and the micro-average F-score not well representative of the performance. Since the performance of all classes is of interest, we also reported the precision, recall and the weighted F-score of the individual classes. Table 5, Table 6 and Table 7 reports the precision, recall and F-score results of the test set of HopeEDI using baselines classifiers, alongside support from test data.

As shown, all the models performed poorly due to a class imbalance problem. The SVM classifier achieved the lowest performance on the HopeEDI dataset with a macro-average F-Score of 0.32, 0.21 and 0.28 for English, Tamil and Malayalam respectively. The decision tree had a higher macro F-Score for English and Malayalam while Tamil performed well in the logistic regression. We used language identification to remove the non-intended language comments from our dataset. However, there were some comments that were annotated by annotators as "Other language". This caused another imbalance in our dataset. Most of the macro scores were less for English due to the "Other language" label; this could be avoided for English by merely removing those comments in the dataset. However, for Tamil and Malayalam, this label was necessary as the comments in these languages were code-mixed and written using a non-native script (Latin script). For the Tamil language, the data distribution was somewhat

Classifier	Hope Speech	Not-Hope Speech	Other language	Macro Avg	Weighted Avg
Support	194	776	101		
Precision					
SVM	0.00	0.72	0.00	0.24	0.52
MNB	0.78	0.76	0.91	0.81	0.78
KNN	0.39	0.77	0.79	0.65	0.71
DT	0.51	0.81	0.52	0.61	0.73
LR	0.46	0.79	0.45	0.57	0.70
Recall					
SVM	0.00	1.00	0.00	0.33	0.72
MNB	0.16	1.00	0.10	0.42	0.76
KNN	0.12	0.96	0.37	0.48	0.75
DT	0.27	0.92	0.40	0.53	0.76
LR	0.25	0.89	0.39	0.51	0.73
F-Score					
SVM	0.00	0.84	0.00	0.28	0.61
MNB	0.26	0.86	0.18	0.44	0.69
KNN	0.19	0.86	0.50	0.51	0.70
DT	0.36	0.86	0.45	0.56	0.73
LR	0.33	0.84	0.41	0.53	0.70

Table 7: Precision, Recall, and F-score for Malayalam

balanced between hope and non-hope classes.

In order to evaluate the effectiveness of our dataset, we conducted experiments using machine learning algorithms. We believe the HopeEDI dataset, with its novel method of data collection and annotation, shall revolutionise research in language technology in the future broaden the horizon for further research on positivity.

6 Conclusion

As online content increases massively, it is necessary to encourage positivity such as in the form of hope speech in online forums to induce compassion and acceptable social behaviour. In this paper, we presented the largest manually annotated dataset of hope speech detection in English, Tamil and Malayalam, consisting of 28,451, 20,198 and 10,705 comments, respectively. We believe that this dataset will facilitate future research on encouraging positivity. We aim to promote research in hope speech and to encourage positive content in online social media for equality, diversity and inclusion. In the future, we plan to extend the study by introducing a larger dataset with further fine-grained classification and content analysis.

7 Acknowledgments

The author Bharathi Raja Chakravarthi was supported in part by a research grant from Science Foundation Ireland (SFI) under Grant Number SFI/12/RC/2289_P2 (Insight_2), co-funded by the European Regional Development Fund as well as by the EU H2020 programme under grant agreement 825182 (Prêt-à-LLOD), and Irish Research Council grant IRCLA/2017/129 (CARDAMOM-Comparative Deep Models of Language for Minority and Historical Languages) for his postdoctoral period at National University of Ireland Galway.

References

Edgar Altszyler, Ariel J. Berenstein, David Milne, Rafael A. Calvo, and Diego Fernandez Slezak. 2018. Using contextual information for automatic triage of posts in a peer-support forum. In *Proceedings of the Fifth Workshop on Computational Linguistics and Clinical Psychology: From Keyboard to Clinic*, pages 57–68, New Orleans, LA, June. Association for Computational Linguistics.

Kalika Bali, Jatin Sharma, Monojit Choudhury, and Yogarshi Vyas. 2014. "I am borrowing ya mixing ?" an analysis of English-Hindi code mixing in Facebook. In *Proceedings of the First Workshop on Computational Approaches to Code Switching*, pages 116–126, Doha, Qatar, October. Association for Computational Linguistics.

Shubhanker Banerjee, Bharathi Raja Chakravarthi, and John Philip McCrae. 2020. Comparison of pretrained embeddings to identify hate speech in Indian code-mixed text. In *2nd IEEE International Conference on Advances in Computing, Communication Control and Networking –ICACCCN (ICAC3N-20)*.

Utsab Barman, Joachim Wagner, Grzegorz Chrupała, and Jennifer Foster. 2014. DCU-UVT: Word-level language classification with code-mixed data. In *Proceedings of the First Workshop on Computational Approaches to Code Switching*, pages 127–132, Doha, Qatar, October. Association for Computational Linguistics.

Pete Burnap, Gualtiero Colombo, Rosie Amery, Andrei Hodorog, and Jonathan Scourfield. 2017. Multi-class machine classification of suicide-related communication on twitter. *Online Social Networks and Media*, 2:32 – 44.

Bharathi Raja Chakravarthi, Mihael Arcan, and John P. McCrae. 2019. WordNet gloss translation for under-resourced languages using multilingual neural machine translation. In *Proceedings of the Second Workshop on Multilingualism at the Intersection of Knowledge Bases and Machine Translation*, pages 1–7, Dublin, Ireland, 19 August. European Association for Machine Translation.

Bharathi Raja Chakravarthi, Navya Jose, Shardul Suryawanshi, Elizabeth Sherly, and John Philip McCrae. 2020a. A sentiment analysis dataset for code-mixed Malayalam-English. In *Proceedings of the 1st Joint Workshop on Spoken Language Technologies for Under-resourced languages (SLTU) and Collaboration and Computing for Under-Resourced Languages (CCURL)*, pages 177–184, Marseille, France, May. European Language Resources association.

Bharathi Raja Chakravarthi, Vigneshwaran Muralidaran, Ruba Priyadharshini, and John Philip McCrae. 2020b. Corpus creation for sentiment analysis in code-mixed Tamil-English text. In *Proceedings of the 1st Joint Workshop on Spoken Language Technologies for Under-resourced languages (SLTU) and Collaboration and Computing for Under-Resourced Languages (CCURL)*, pages 202–210, Marseille, France, May. European Language Resources association.

Bharathi Raja Chakravarthi, Navaneethan Rajasekaran, Mihael Arcan, Kevin McGuinness, Noel E.O'Connor, and John P McCrae. 2020c. Bilingual lexicon induction across orthographically-distinct under-resourced Dravidian languages. In *Proceedings of the Seventh Workshop on NLP for Similar Languages, Varieties and Dialects*, Barcelona, Spain, December.

Bharathi Raja Chakravarthi. 2020. *Leveraging orthographic information to improve machine translation of under-resourced languages*. Ph.D. thesis, NUI Galway.

Edward C. Chang. 1998. Hope, problem-solving ability, and coping in a college student population: Some implications for theory and practice. *Journal of Clinical Psychology*, 54(7):953–962.

Yi-Ling Chung, Elizaveta Kuzmenko, Serra Sinem Tekiroglu, and Marco Guerini. 2019. CONAN - COunter NArratives through nichesourcing: a multilingual dataset of responses to fight online hate speech. In *Proceedings of the 57th Annual Meeting of the Association for Computational Linguistics*, pages 2819–2829, Florence, Italy, July. Association for Computational Linguistics.

Jae Eun Chung. 2013. Social networking in online support groups for health: How online social networking benefits patients. *Journal of Health Communication*, 19(6):639–659, April.

Isobelle Clarke and Jack Grieve. 2017. Dimensions of abusive language on twitter. In *Proceedings of the First Workshop on Abusive Language Online*, pages 1–10, Vancouver, BC, Canada, August. Association for Computational Linguistics.

Rob Cover. 2013. Queer youth resilience: Critiquing the discourse of hope and hopelessness in lgbt suicide representation. *M/C Journal*, 16(5).

Thomas Davidson, Debasmita Bhattacharya, and Ingmar Weber. 2019. Racial bias in hate speech and abusive language detection datasets. In *Proceedings of the Third Workshop on Abusive Language Online*, pages 25–35, Florence, Italy, August. Association for Computational Linguistics.

Kris Gowen, Matthew Deschaine, Darcy Gruttadara, and Dana Markey. 2012. Young adults with mental health conditions and social networking websites: Seeking tools to build community. *Psychiatric Rehabilitation Journal*, 35(3):245–250.

Deepak Gupta, Pabitra Lenka, Asif Ekbal, and Pushpak Bhattacharyya. 2018. Uncovering code-mixed challenges: A framework for linguistically driven question generation and neural based question answering. In *Proceedings of the 22nd Conference on Computational Natural Language Learning*, pages 119–130, Brussels, Belgium, October. Association for Computational Linguistics.

Adeep Hande, Ruba Priyadharshini, and Bharathi Raja Chakravarthi. 2020. KanCMD: Kannada codemixed dataset for sentiment analysis and offensive language detection. In *Proceedings of the Third Workshop on Computational Modeling of People's Opinions, Personality, and Emotions in Social Media*, Barcelona, Spain, December.

Henning Herrestad and Stian Biong. 2010. Relational hopes: A study of the lived experience of hope in some patients hospitalized for intentional self-harm. *International Journal of Qualitative Studies on Health and Well-being*, 5(1):4651. PMID: 20640026.

Navya Jose, Bharathi Raja Chakravarthi, Shardul Suryawanshi, Elizabeth Sherly, and John P. McCrae. 2020. A survey of current datasets for code-switching research. In *2020 6th International Conference on Advanced Computing and Communication Systems (ICACCS)*.

Vanessa Kitzie. 2018. "i pretended to be a boy on the internet": Navigating affordances and constraints of social networking sites and search engines for lgbtq+ identity work. *First Monday*, 23(7), Jul.

Klaus Krippendorff. 1970. Estimating the reliability, systematic error and random error of interval data. *Educational and Psychological Measurement*, 30(1):61–70.

Klaus Krippendorff. 2011. Computing krippendorff's alpha-reliability.

Amar Krishna, Joseph Zambreno, and Sandeep Krishnan. 2013. Polarity Trend Analysis of Public Sentiment on YouTube. In *Proceedings of the 19th International Conference on Management of Data*, COMAD '13, page 125–128, Mumbai, Maharashtra, IND. Computer Society of India.

Younghun Lee, Seunghyun Yoon, and Kyomin Jung. 2018. Comparative studies of detecting abusive language on twitter. In *Proceedings of the 2nd Workshop on Abusive Language Online (ALW2)*, pages 101–106, Brussels, Belgium, October. Association for Computational Linguistics.

Edison Marrese-Taylor, Jorge Balazs, and Yutaka Matsuo. 2017. Mining fine-grained opinions on closed captions of YouTube videos with an attention-RNN. In *Proceedings of the 8th Workshop on Computational Approaches to Subjectivity, Sentiment and Social Media Analysis*, pages 102–111, Copenhagen, Denmark, September. Association for Computational Linguistics.

Binny Mathew, Punyajoy Saha, Hardik Tharad, Subham Rajgaria, Prajwal Singhania, Suman Kalyan Maity, Pawan Goyal, and Animesh Mukherjee. 2019. Thou shalt not hate: Countering online hate speech. *Proceedings of the International AAAI Conference on Web and Social Media*, 13(01):369–380, Jul.

Harvey Milk. 1997. The hope speech. *We are everywhere: A historical sourcebook of gay and lesbian politics*, pages 51–53.

David N. Milne, Glen Pink, Ben Hachey, and Rafael A. Calvo. 2016. CLPsych 2016 shared task: Triaging content in online peer-support forums. In *Proceedings of the Third Workshop on Computational Linguistics and Clinical Psychology*, pages 118–127, San Diego, CA, USA, June. Association for Computational Linguistics.

Skanda Muralidhar, Laurent Nguyen, and Daniel Gatica-Perez. 2018. Words worth: Verbal content and hirability impressions in YouTube video resumes. In *Proceedings of the 9th Workshop on Computational Approaches to Subjectivity, Sentiment and Social Media Analysis*, pages 322–327, Brussels, Belgium, October. Association for Computational Linguistics.

Cicero Nogueira dos Santos, Igor Melnyk, and Inkit Padhi. 2018. Fighting offensive language on social media with unsupervised text style transfer. In *Proceedings of the 56th Annual Meeting of the Association for Computational Linguistics (Volume 2: Short Papers)*, pages 189–194, Melbourne, Australia, July. Association for Computational Linguistics.

Nedjma Ousidhoum, Zizheng Lin, Hongming Zhang, Yangqiu Song, and Dit-Yan Yeung. 2019. Multilingual and multi-aspect hate speech analysis. In *Proceedings of the 2019 Conference on Empirical Methods in Natural Language Processing and the 9th International Joint Conference on Natural Language Processing (EMNLP-IJCNLP)*, pages 4675–4684, Hong Kong, China, November. Association for Computational Linguistics.

Shriphani Palakodety, Ashiqur R KhudaBukhsh, and Jaime G Carbonell. 2020a. Hope speech detection: A computational analysis of the voice of peace. In *Proceedings of the 24th European Conference on Artificial Intelligence - ECAI 2020*.

Shriphani Palakodety, Ashiqur R KhudaBukhsh, and Jaime G Carbonell. 2020b. Voice for the voiceless: Active sampling to detect comments supporting the rohingyas. In *Proceedings of the AAAI Conference on Artificial Intelligence*, volume 34, pages 454–462.

Marcelo O. R. Prates, Pedro H. Avelar, and Luís C. Lamb. 2020. Assessing gender bias in machine translation: a case study with google translate. *Neural Computing and Applications*, 32(10):6363–6381, May.

Ruba Priyadharshini, Bharathi Raja Chakravarthi, Mani Vegupatti, and John P. McCrae. 2020. Named entity recognition for code-mixed Indian corpus using meta embedding. In *2020 6th International Conference on Advanced Computing and Communication Systems (ICACCS)*.

Laura Robinson, Jeremy Schulz, Grant Blank, Massimo Ragnedda, Hiroshi Ono, Bernie Hogan, Gustavo S. Mesch, Shelia R. Cotten, Susan B. Kretchmer, Timothy M. Hale, Tomasz Drabowicz, Pu Yan, Barry Wellman, Molly-Gloria Harper, Anabel Quan-Haase, Hopeton S. Dunn, Antonio A. Casilli, Paola Tubaro, Rod Carvath, Wenhong Chen, Julie B. Wiest, Matías Dodel, Michael J. Stern, Christopher Ball, Kuo-Ting Huang, and Aneka Khilnani. 2020. Digital inequalities 2.0: Legacy inequalities in the information age. *First Monday*, 25(7), Jun.

Anna Schmidt and Michael Wiegand. 2017. A survey on hate speech detection using natural language processing. In *Proceedings of the Fifth International Workshop on Natural Language Processing for Social Media*, pages 1–10, Valencia, Spain, April. Association for Computational Linguistics.

Anne-Marie Di Sciullo, Pieter Muysken, and Rajendra Singh. 1986. Government and code-mixing. *Journal of Linguistics*, 22(1):1–24.

Aliaksei Severyn, Alessandro Moschitti, Olga Uryupina, Barbara Plank, and Katja Filippova. 2014. Opinion mining on YouTube. In *Proceedings of the 52nd Annual Meeting of the Association for Computational Linguistics (Volume 1: Long Papers)*, pages 1252–1261, Baltimore, Maryland, June. Association for Computational Linguistics.

Gudbjartur Ingi Sigurbergsson and Leon Derczynski. 2020. Offensive language and hate speech detection for Danish. In *Proceedings of The 12th Language Resources and Evaluation Conference*, pages 3498–3508, Marseille, France, May. European Language Resources Association.

Charles R Snyder, Kevin L Rand, and David R Sigmon. 2002. Hope theory: A member of the positive psychology family.

Tony Sun, Andrew Gaut, Shirlyn Tang, Yuxin Huang, Mai ElSherief, Jieyu Zhao, Diba Mirza, Elizabeth Belding, Kai-Wei Chang, and William Yang Wang. 2019. Mitigating gender bias in natural language processing: Literature review. In *Proceedings of the 57th Annual Meeting of the Association for Computational Linguistics*, pages 1630–1640, Florence, Italy, July. Association for Computational Linguistics.

Rachael Tatman. 2017. Gender and dialect bias in YouTube's automatic captions. In *Proceedings of the First ACL Workshop on Ethics in Natural Language Processing*, pages 53–59, Valencia, Spain, April. Association for Computational Linguistics.

Serra Sinem Tekiroğlu, Yi-Ling Chung, and Marco Guerini. 2020. Generating counter narratives against online hate speech: Data and strategies. In *Proceedings of the 58th Annual Meeting of the Association for Computational Linguistics*, pages 1177–1190, Online, July. Association for Computational Linguistics.

Giuliano Tortoreto, Evgeny Stepanov, Alessandra Cervone, Mateusz Dubiel, and Giuseppe Riccardi. 2019. Affective behaviour analysis of on-line user interactions: Are on-line support groups more therapeutic than twitter? In *Proceedings of the Fourth Social Media Mining for Health Applications (#SMM4H) Workshop & Shared Task*, pages 79–88, Florence, Italy, August. Association for Computational Linguistics.

Eva Vanmassenhove, Christian Hardmeier, and Andy Way. 2018. Getting gender right in neural machine translation. In *Proceedings of the 2018 Conference on Empirical Methods in Natural Language Processing*, pages 3003–3008, Brussels, Belgium, October-November. Association for Computational Linguistics.

Zijian Wang and David Jurgens. 2018. It's going to be okay: Measuring access to support in online communities. In *Proceedings of the 2018 Conference on Empirical Methods in Natural Language Processing*, pages 33–45, Brussels, Belgium, October-November. Association for Computational Linguistics.

Zeerak Waseem, Thomas Davidson, Dana Warmsley, and Ingmar Weber. 2017. Understanding abuse: A typology of abusive language detection subtasks. In *Proceedings of the First Workshop on Abusive Language Online*, pages 78–84, Vancouver, BC, Canada, August. Association for Computational Linguistics.

Michael Wiegand, Josef Ruppenhofer, and Thomas Kleinbauer. 2019. Detection of Abusive Language: the Problem of Biased Datasets. In *Proceedings of the 2019 Conference of the North American Chapter of the Association for Computational Linguistics: Human Language Technologies, Volume 1 (Long and Short Papers)*, pages 602–608, Minneapolis, Minnesota, June. Association for Computational Linguistics.

Mengzhou Xia, Anjalie Field, and Yulia Tsvetkov. 2020. Demoting racial bias in hate speech detection. In *Proceedings of the Eighth International Workshop on Natural Language Processing for Social Media*, pages 7–14, Online, July. Association for Computational Linguistics.

Andrew Yates, Arman Cohan, and Nazli Goharian. 2017. Depression and self-harm risk assessment in online forums. In *Proceedings of the 2017 Conference on Empirical Methods in Natural Language Processing*, pages 2968–2978, Copenhagen, Denmark, September. Association for Computational Linguistics.

Carolyn M. Youssef and Fred Luthans. 2007. Positive organizational behavior in the workplace: The impact of hope, optimism, and resilience. *Journal of Management*, 33(5):774–800.

Marcos Zampieri, Shervin Malmasi, Preslav Nakov, Sara Rosenthal, Noura Farra, and Ritesh Kumar. 2019a. Predicting the type and target of offensive posts in social media. In *Proceedings of the 2019 Conference of the North American Chapter of the Association for Computational Linguistics: Human Language Technologies, Volume 1 (Long and Short Papers)*, pages 1415–1420, Minneapolis, Minnesota, June. Association for Computational Linguistics.

Marcos Zampieri, Shervin Malmasi, Preslav Nakov, Sara Rosenthal, Noura Farra, and Ritesh Kumar. 2019b. SemEval-2019 task 6: Identifying and categorizing offensive language in social media (OffensEval). In *Proceedings of the 13th International Workshop on Semantic Evaluation*, pages 75–86, Minneapolis, Minnesota, USA, June. Association for Computational Linguistics.

KanCMD: Kannada CodeMixed Dataset for Sentiment Analysis and Offensive Language Detection

Adeep Hande[1], Ruba Priyadharshini[2], Bharathi Raja Chakravarthi[3]

[1] Indian Institute of Information Technology Tiruchirappalli, Tamil Nadu, India
[2] ULTRA Arts and Science College, Madurai, Tamil Nadu, India
[3] Insight SFI Research Centre for Data Analytics, National University of Ireland Galway
`adeeph18c@iiitt.ac.in`, `rubapriyadharshini.a@gmail.com`,
`bharathi.raja@insight-centre.org`

Abstract

We introduce Kannada CodeMixed Dataset (KanCMD), a multi-task learning dataset for sentiment analysis and offensive language identification. The KanCMD dataset highlights two real-world issues from the social media text. First, it contains actual comments in code mixed text posted by users on YouTube social media, rather than in monolingual text from the textbook. Second, it has been annotated for two tasks, namely sentiment analysis and offensive language detection for under-resourced Kannada language. Hence, KanCMD is meant to stimulate research in under-resourced Kannada language on real-world code-mixed social media text and multi-task learning. KanCMD was obtained by crawling the YouTube, and a minimum of three annotators annotates each comment. We release KanCMD 7,671 comments for multitask learning research purpose.

1 Introduction

A surge in the active users on social media has given rise to people's engagement in expressing their opinions in the form of comments and reviews on social media platforms such as Facebook, YouTube and Twitter (Severyn et al., 2014; Clarke and Grieve, 2017; Tian et al., 2017). We see a lot of informal texts which do not follow any grammatical rules, sometimes code-mixed and even written in non-native scripts (Bali et al., 2014; Jose et al., 2020; Chakravarthi et al., 2020a). These texts can be offensive and may be directed towards an individual or community to show their dissent. Thus offensive language identification is essential for social media platforms to minimise these activities (Bohra et al., 2018). Sentiment analysis is used to interpret and classify emotions from text data after analysing it with various existing techniques (Pang and Lee, 2008). It has received a lot of interest in industry and research for identifying customer satisfaction on products and services, but there is no dataset available for code-mixed Kannada language. Code-mixing refers to the pairing of linguistic units from two or more languages into a single conversation (Pratapa et al., 2018; Priyadharshini et al., 2020). Code-mixed sentiment analysis and offensive language identification when succeed trained on code-mixed data while regular monolingual sentiment analysis might prove ineffective due to the large variations in the text (Banerjee et al., 2020).

Kannada language (ISO 639-3:kan) belong to Dravidian language family (Chakravarthi et al., 2019b; Chakravarthi, 2020), spoken predominantly by the people of Karnataka State in south India. Kannada language uses Kannada script also called Caranese which is derived from Bhattiprolu Brahmi script (Chakravarthi et al., 2020c). It is a phonemic adugida written from left to right (Chakravarthi et al., 2019a). We observed six combinations among code-mixed sentences such as no-code-mixing only Kannada written in Kannada script or Kannada written in the Latin script, inter-sentential code-mixing, code-switching at morphological level, intra-sentential code-mixing, inter-sentential and intra-sentential mix. Most comments were written in Kannada script either with Kannada grammar with English lexicon or English grammar with Kannada lexicon. Some comments were written in Kannada script with English expressions in between. Figure 1 illustrate the different level of code-mixing in our dataset.

Proceedings of the Third Workshop on Computational Modeling of PEople's Opinions, PersonaLity, and Emotions in Social media, pages 54–63
Barcelona, Spain (Online), December 13, 2020.

Code Switching Type	EXAMPLE	Translation
No-code-mixing: Only Kannada (written in Kannada Script only)	ಎನ್ ಗುರು ಎನ್ ಲಿರಿಕ್ ಎನ್ ಮ್ಯೂಸಿಕ್ ನಮ್ಮ ಮನೆಯಲ್ಲಿ ಈ ಹಾಡಿಗೆ ಫುಲ್ ಫೀದ ಆಗಿದರೆ.	Great lyrics and music mate, Everyone in my home is obsessed with this song.
Inter-sentential code-mixing: Mix of English and Kannada (Kannada written in Kannada script only)	My favorite song in 2019 is Taaja samachara ಸಾಹಿತ್ಯ ಪ್ರಿಯರೇ ಒಮ್ಮೆ ಈ ಹಾಡು ಕೇಳಿದ್ರೆ ಕೇಳ್ತಾನೆ ಇಬೇಕು ಅನ್ನುತ್ತೆ.... Everybody watch this.	My favourite song in 2019 is Taaja samachara. If it is heard by literary lovers, they would want to hear it again. Everybody watch this.
Only Kannada (written in Latin Script)	Neevu varshkke ondu cinema madru supper 1 varshkke 3-4 cinema madobadalige intha ondu cinema saku.	If you make one movie a year it's super, instead of doing 3-4 movies a year, one movie of this type is enough.
Code-switching at morphological level: (written in both Kannada and Latin script)	Nanage ಅನ್ನುತ್ತೆ ಈ ವೀಡಿಯೋ ವನ್ನು ರಶ್ಮಿಯ ಮಂದಣ್ಣ ಫ್ಯಾನ್ಸ್ deslike ಮಾಡಿರೆಬಹುದು.	I feel that this video has been disliked by the fans of Rashmika Mandana.
Intra-sentential mix of English and Kannada (written in Latin Script only)	Wonderful song daily 5/6 kelalill Andre eno miss madakodante.	A wonderful song, if I don't hear this song 5-6 times a day, I feel like I am missing something.
Inter-sentential and intra-sentential mix. (Kannada written in both Latin and Kannada script)	ಗೊತ್ತಿಲ ರಕ್ಷಿತ್ ಶೆಟ್ಟು ನಟನೆಗೆ ನಾನು ಫಿದಾ .. ಬಾಸ್ waiting for ಮೂವಿ.... caritre bareyo ಎಲ್ಲ ಲಕ್ಷಣ ಇದೆ.. All The best your bright ಫ್ಯೂಚರ್.	Don't know why, I am obsessed with Rakshit Shetty's acting. waiting for your movie, expecting it to be a blockbuster. All the best for your bright future.

Figure 1: Examples of code mixing in our dataset.

In multitask learning, the objective is to utilize the process of learning multiple tasks in order to improve the performance of the system (Martínez Alonso and Plank, 2017). Sentiment analysis and offensive language identification are related and has common aspects between them. Having the model to learn both tasks would be advantages to utilise some cues from one task to improve the other. Since Kannada is morphologically rich and under-resourced language (Prabhu et al., 2020) to improve the performance of the classification system, we annotate dataset for multitask learning. To detect customer satisfaction and eliminate offensive language in these platforms, we release KanCMD, a dataset of YouTube video comments in code-mixed Kannada-English.

2   Related Work

Sentiment analysis has become one of the primary areas of research with applications across many trades and industries(such as finance, online marketing, political science) (Severyn et al., 2014). Over the last 20 years, social media networks have contributed immensely to the availability of rich data sources for analysis of sentiment (Clarke and Grieve, 2017; Tian et al., 2017). This combined with efforts directed towards the compilation of sentiment lexicons (Turney, 2002; Lal et al., 2019) have resulted in this branch of natural language processing maturing out. In the early years of research, n-grams were used for classification of sentiments carried by the datasets. Recently, these methods have been replaced by neural model architectures. However, sentiment analysis in Kannada (Hegde and Padma, 2015; Kumar et al., 2015) has not achieved this.

Aggression identification in social media (Kumar et al., 2018) and offensive language identification (Zampieri et al., 2019) shared task has been conducted to improve the research in this area. Offensive language identification dataset was released for Greek (Pitenis et al., 2020). However, offensive language identification has not been made for the Kannada language. For language identification (LID) systems in code-mixed Languages, a Kannada-English dataset containing English, Kannada and several word-level code-mixed words was created by Sowmya Lakshmi and Shambhavi (2017). A stance detection system was employed to detect stance in Kannada social media code-mixed text using sentence embeddings. Machine learning models such as logistic regression and a distributed memory model for

55

sentence vectors were among the models to experiment (Skanda et al., 2017). Distributed representations of texts through neural networks method has experimented for sentiment analysis on Kannada-English code-mixed dataset, which had three tags, Positive, Negative and Neutral (Shalini et al., 2018). However, the dataset for Kannada was not easily available for research purpose. Following (Chakravarthi et al., 2020a), we downloaded the YouTube comments for Kannada and annotated. In our research, we release code-mixed dataset for under-resourced Kannada for sentiment analysis and offensive language identification as multi-task learning dataset.

3 Dataset Construction

We create a dataset for two tasks, namely, sentiment analysis and offensive language identification. We collected comments from YouTube using YouTube Comment Scrapper [1]. We collected comments from 18 videos on different topics ranging from movie trailers, current trends about the ban on mobile apps in India, India-China border issue, Mahabharata, and Transgenders. We used these keywords to find the video and then from the videos we collected the comments. This was collected between Feburary, 2020 and August, 2020.

3.1 Sentiment Analysis

For sentiment analysis, we adopted the approach taken by Chakravarthi et al. (2020b), and a minimum of three annotators annotated each sentence according to the following schema:

- **Positive state:** Comment contains an explicit or implicit clue in the text suggesting that the speaker is in a positive state.

- **Negative state:** Comment contains an explicit or implicit clue in the text suggesting that the speaker is in a negative state.

- **Mixed feelings:** Comment contains an explicit or implicit clue in both positive and negative feeling.

- **Neutral state:** Comment does not contain an explicit or implicit indicator of the speaker's emotional state.

- **Not in intended language:** For Kannada if the sentence does not contain Kannada written in Kannada script or Latin script then it is not Kannada.

3.2 Offensive Language Identification

We constructed offensive language identification for the Kannada language at different levels of complexity following Zampieri et al. (2019) work. More generally it expands to three-level hierarchical annotation schema. To simplify, we have split it into six labels.

- **Not Offensive**: Comments does not contain offence or profanity.

- **Offensive Untargeted**: Comments contain offence or profanity without any target. These are comments which contain unacceptable languages that do not target anyone.

- **Offensive Targeted Individual**: Comments contains offence or profanity which targets the individual.

- **Offensive Targeted Group**: Comments contains offence or profanity which targets the group.

- **Offensive Targeted Other**: Comments contains offence or profanity which does not belong to any of the previous two categories(e.g., a situation, an issue, an organization or an event).

- **Not in indented language**: Comments not in the Kannada language.

---

[1] https://github.com/philbot9/youtube-comment-scraper-cli

Gender	Male	2
	Female	3
Higher Education	Undegraduate	1
	Graduate	2
	Postgraduate	2
Medium of Schooling	English	4
	Kannada	1
Total		5

Table 1: Annotators

Language pair	Kannada-English
Number of Tokens	64,997
Vocabulary Size	20,667
Number of Posts	7,671
Number of Sentences	8,472
Average number of Tokens per post	8
Average number of sentences per post	1

Table 2: Dataset statistics

3.3 Annotators

We created Google forms to collect annotations from annotators. Gender, education background, medium of schooling was collected to know the diversity of the annotator. The annotators were warned that comments might have offensive language and abusive text. The annotator was given a choice to stop annotation if they find it disturbing or could not handle. Annotators were asked not to be biased to a particular person, situation or event during the annotation of comments. Each form was annotated by a minimum of three annotators and maximum of 5 annotators. From the Table 1, we can see that majority of the annotators' medium of schooling is English even though their mother tongue is Kannada and they were from Karnataka state in India where Kannada is the official language of the state. Krippendorff's alpha for sentiment analysis annotation was 0.73, and offensive language identification was 0.78.

Class	Kannada-English
Positive	3,518
Negative	1,484
Mixed feelings	691
Neutral	842
Other language	1,136
Total	7,671

Table 3: Sentiment Analysis Dataset Distribution

4 Data Statistics and Analysis

After performing annotations using google forms for both of the tasks, sentiment analysis and offensive language detection, all of the responses were converted into .csv format and then combined to a single dataset containing all the annotations. Our goal is to analyse the multitask dataset and perform experiments with several machine learning algorithms to establish benchmark results.

Table 3 and Table 4 shows the dataset statistics of the Kannada-English code-mixed dataset. As shown on the table, this huge dataset has 64,997 tokens, where the vocabulary size is 20,667. There are 7,671 comments and 8,472 distinct sentences in our code-mixed dataset. On average, there are eight tokens

Class	Kannada-English
Not Offensive	4,336
Offensive Untargeted	278
Offensive Targeted Individual	626
Offensive Targeted Group	416
Offensive Targeted Others	152
Other language	1,863
Total	7,671

Table 4: Offensive language Identification Dataset Distribution.

per sentence, and there is at least one sentence per post. As described earlier, the whole dataset was categorised into two tasks, sentiment analysis and offensive language detection.

The first task performed on the dataset was sentiment analysis. It was categorised into five groups, such as positive, negative, neutral, mixed-feelings, other languages. As mentioned in table 3, the distribution is as follows. Out of 7,671 posts, 3,518 have a positive polarity, being the most frequent category in this task of sentiment analysis. The second-largest category was a negative state, accounting to 1,484 comments of the whole code-mixed dataset. The absence of a speaker's emotional state relating to the subject in a post was considered as a neutral state. We split the dataset retaining ten percentage of the dataset, that is, 768 for the test, ten percentage for validation, being 767 and the remaining for training.

The second task performed on the dataset was offensive language detection. It was categorised into six groups such as not offensive, offensive untargeted, offensive targeted individual, offensive targeted group, offensive targeted other, other languages. Since the same code-mixed dataset was used for this task, the dataset statistics would be the same here. Out of 7,671 posts, 4338 of them were not considered to be offensive, which was the most frequent category in this task. We similarly split the dataset to what was done for the task of sentiment analysis.

5 Benchmark Systems

In order to provide a simple baseline, we applied several traditional machine learning algorithms such as Logistic Regression (LR), Support Vector Machine (SVM), Multinomial Naive Bayes (MNB), K-Nearest Neigbours (KNN), Decision Trees (DT), Random Forest (RF) separately, for both of the tasks, sentiment analysis and offensive language detection on KanCMD, the code-mixed Kannada-English dataset.

5.1 Experiments Setup

5.1.1 Logistic Regression (LR):

We evaluate the Logistic Regression model with L2 regularization. The input features are the Term Frequency Inverse Document Frequency (TF-IDF) values of up to 3 grams. This approach results in the model being trained only on this dataset without taking any pre-trained embeddings.

5.1.2 Support Vector Machine (SVM):

We evaluate the SVM model with L2 regularization. The features are the same as in LR. The main objective of SVM classifier is to find a hyperplane in an N-dimensional space that distinctly classifies the data points.

5.1.3 Multinomial Naive Bayes (MNB):

We evaluate a Naive Bayes classifier for multinomially distributed data, which is derived from Bayes Theorem that finds the probability of a future event to the given occurred event. Laplace smoothing is performed using $\alpha = 1$ to solve the problem of zero probability and then evaluate the MNB model with TF-IDF vectors.

5.1.4 K-Nearest Neighbour (KNN):

We use KNN for classification with 3,4,5, and 9 neighbours by applying uniform weights.

Decision Tree (DT)

Class	Precision	Recall	F1-score	Support	Class	Precision	Recall	F1-score	Support
Positive	0.59	0.73	0.66	363	NO	0.64	0.78	0.70	417
Negative	0.61	0.48	0.54	162	OU	0.21	0.09	0.13	33
Mixed	0.21	0.19	0.20	57	OTI	0.57	0.51	0.54	75
Neutral	0.39	0.14	0.21	83	OTG	0.29	0.18	0.22	44
Other	0.45	0.47	0.46	103	OTO	0.25	0.07	0.11	14
					OL	0.56	0.45	0.50	185
accuracy			0.54	768	accuracy			0.60	768
M-Avg	0.45	0.40	0.41	768	M-Avg	0.42	0.35	0.37	768
W-Avg	0.53	0.54	0.52	768	W-Avg	0.57	0.60	0.58	768

Random Forest (RF)

Class	Precision	Recall	F1-score	Support	Class	Precision	Recall	F1-score	Support
Positive	0.59	0.87	0.70	363	NO	0.65	0.89	0.75	417
Negative	0.70	0.48	0.57	162	OU	0.00	0.00	0.00	33
Mixed	0.45	0.06	0.11	57	OTI	0.71	0.35	0.47	75
Neutral	0.48	0.18	0.27	83	OTG	0.43	0.08	0.14	44
Other	0.53	0.50	0.52	103	OTO	1.00	0.06	0.11	14
					OL	0.67	0.54	0.60	185
accuracy			0.59	768	accuracy			0.66	768
M-Avg	0.55	0.42	0.43	768	M-Avg	0.58	0.32	0.34	768
W-Avg	0.58	0.59	0.55	768	W-Avg	0.63	0.66	0.61	768

Logistic Regression (LR)

Sentiment Analysis					Offensive Language Detection				
Class	Precision	Recall	F1-score	Support	Class	Precision	Recall	F1-score	Support
Positive	0.70	0.69	0.70	363	NO	0.77	0.76	0.77	417
Negative	0.60	0.51	0.55	162	OU	0.04	0.03	0.04	33
Mixed	0.24	0.26	0.25	57	OTI	0.63	0.59	0.61	75
Neutral	0.38	0.36	0.37	83	OTG	0.25	0.23	0.24	44
Other	0.45	0.55	0.50	103	OTO	0.22	0.29	0.25	14
					OL	0.64	0.71	0.68	185
accuracy			0.57	768	accuracy			0.66	768
M-Avg	0.47	0.48	0.47	768	M-Avg	0.43	0.43	0.43	768
W-Avg	0.58	0.57	0.57	768	W-Avg	0.66	0.66	0.66	768

Table 5: Tasks: Sentiment Analysis and Offensive language detection.Precision,Recall,F1-score and support for DT and RF. Class : NO(Not Offensive), OU(Offensive Untargeted), OTI(Offensive Targeted Individual), OTG(Offensive Targeted Group), OTO(Offensive Targeted Others), OL(Other Language), M-Avg (Macro Average), W-Avg (Weighted Average)

5.1.5 Decision Tree (DT):

Decision tree classification works by generating a tree structure, where each node corresponds to a feature name, and the branches correspond to the feature values. The leaves of the tree represent the classification labels. After sequentially choosing alternative decisions, each node is recursively split again, and finally, the classifier defines some rules to predict the result. We used it to classify for the two tasks as shown Table 5 for baseline. Maximum depth was 800, and minimum sample splits were 5 for DT. The criteria were Gini and entropy.

5.1.6 Random Forest (RF):

Random Forest is an ensemble classifier that makes its prediction based on the combination of different decision trees. We evaluate the RF model with the same features as DT.

Support Vector Machine (SVM)									
Class	Precision	Recall	F1-score	Support	Class	Precision	Recall	F1-score	Support
Positive	0.47	1.00	0.64	363	NO	0.55	1.00	0.71	417
Negative	0.00	0.00	0.00	162	OU	0.00	0.00	0.00	33
Mixed	0.00	0.00	0.00	57	OTI	0.00	0.00	0.00	75
Neutral	0.00	0.00	0.00	83	OTG	0.00	0.00	0.00	44
Other	0.00	0.00	0.00	103	OTO	0.00	0.00	0.00	14
					OL	0.00	0.00	0.00	185
accuracy			0.47	768	accuracy			0.55	768
M-Avg	0.09	0.20	0.13	768	M-Avg	0.09	0.17	0.12	768
W-Avg	0.22	0.47	0.30	768	W-Avg	0.30	0.55	0.39	768
Multinomial Naive Bayes (MNB)									
Class	Precision	Recall	F1-score	Support	Class	Precision	Recall	F1-score	Support
Positive	0.54	0.99	0.70	363	NO	0.60	0.98	0.74	417
Negative	0.82	0.36	0.50	162	OU	0.00	0.00	0.00	33
Mixed	1.00	0.02	0.03	57	OTI	0.86	0.33	0.48	75
Neutral	0.75	0.04	0.07	83	OTG	0.00	0.00	0.00	44
Other	0.74	0.14	0.23	103	OTO	0.00	0.00	0.00	14
					OL	0.78	0.22	0.34	185
accuracy			0.57	768	accuracy			0.62	768
M-Avg	0.77	0.31	0.31	768	M-Avg	0.37	0.26	0.26	768
W-Avg	0.68	0.57	0.48	768	W-Avg	0.60	0.62	0.54	768
K-Nearest Neighbour (KNN)									
Class	Precision	Recall	F1-score	Support	Class	Precision	Recall	F1-score	Support
Positive	0.51	0.91	0.65	363	NO	0.61	0.93	0.73	417
Negative	0.67	0.10	0.17	162	OU	0.00	0.00	0.00	33
Mixed	0.44	0.07	0.12	57	OTI	0.78	0.19	0.30	75
Neutral	0.50	0.05	0.09	83	OTG	0.67	0.09	0.16	44
Other	0.55	0.41	0.47	103	OTO	0.00	0.00	0.00	14
					OL	0.66	0.34	0.45	185
accuracy			0.52	768	accuracy			0.61	768
M-Avg	0.53	0.31	0.30	768	M-Avg	0.45	0.26	0.27	768
W-Avg	0.54	0.52	0.43	768	W-Avg	0.60	0.61	0.55	768

Table 6: Tasks: Sentiment Analysis and Offensive language detection.Precision,Recall,F1-score and support for LR, SVM, MNB and KNN. Class : NO(Not Offensive), OU(Offensive Untargeted), OTI(Offensive Targeted Individual), OTG(Offensive Targeted Group), OTO(Offensive Targeted Others), OL(Other Language). M-Avg (Macro Average), W-Avg (Weighted Average)

5.2 Experiment Results

The results of the experiments performed for both of the tasks of sentiment analysis and Offensive language detection using different methods are shown in terms of Precision, Recall, F1-score and support in Table 6 and Table 5. We used sklearn[2] to develop the models. A macro-average will compute the metrics (precision, recall, F1-score) independently for each of the classes and then take the average. Thus this metric treats all classes equally, and it does not take the attribute of class imbalance into account. A weighted average takes the metrics from each class just like a macro average, but the contribution of each class to the average is weighted by the number of examples available for it. The value counts of different classes for both the tasks areas listed in support in Table 6 and Table 5.

For sentiment analysis, all the classification algorithms perform inadequately to average on the code-

---

[2]https://scikit-learn.org/stable/

mixed dataset. Logistic regression, random forest classifiers and decision trees were the ones that fared comparatively better across all sentiment classes. To our surprise, we see that SVM performs very bad, having a bad heterogeneity than the other methods. The precision, recall and F1-score are higher for the "Positive" class followed by the "Negative" class. All of the other classes performed very poorly. One of the reasons being the nature of the dataset as the classes "Mixed feelings" and "Neutral" are challenging to annotate for the annotators due to several factors behind its reasoning.

For offensive language detection, all the classification algorithms perform poorly. We see that logistic regression and random forest are the ones that performed relatively better than the others. The precision, recall and F1-score are higher for the "Not Offensive" class followed by the "Offensive Targeted Individual" and "OL" classes. The reasons for the poor performance of other classes are as same as sentiment analysis. From Table 6 and Table 5, we see that the classification algorithms have performed better on the task of sentiment analysis in comparison to their performance on the task of offensive language detection. One of the main reasons could be the differences in the distributions of the classes among the two different tasks. Out of the total of 7,671 sentences, 46% and 19 % belong to the "Positive" and the "Negative" classes respectively while the other classes share 9%,11% and 15% respectively for sentiment analysis. This distribution is relatively better when compared to offensive language detection task where 56% belong to "Not Offensive", while the other class share a low distribution of 4%,8%,6%,2%,24%.

6 Conclusion

In this paper, we presented KanCMD, a multi-task learning dataset for sentiment analysis and offensive language identification in under-resourced Kannada language. The dataset consists of 7,671 YouTube comments annotated by a minimum of three annotators and had 0.73 for sentiment analysis annotation, and 0.78 for offensive language identification in terms of Kripendorffs alpha inter-annotator agreement. We believe this dataset will allow future work in under-resourced Kannada language to progress in multi-task learning of the code-mixed real-world data. We have created computational models to set the benchmark for this dataset. We aim to promote research in the Kannada language and to encourage future investigations into multi-task learning for under-resourced languages in general and how it can be used to improve performance for under-resourced languages.

7 Acknowledgments

The author Bharathi Raja Chakravarthi was supported in part by a research grant from Science Foundation Ireland (SFI) under Grant Number SFI/12/RC/2289_P2 (Insight_2), co-funded by the European Regional Development Fund as well as by the EU H2020 programme under grant agreement 825182 (Prêt-à-LLOD), and Irish Research Council grant IRCLA/2017/129 (CARDAMOM-Comparative Deep Models of Language for Minority and Historical Languages) for his postdoctoral period at National University of Ireland Galway.

References

Kalika Bali, Jatin Sharma, Monojit Choudhury, and Yogarshi Vyas. 2014. "I am borrowing ya mixing ?" an analysis of English-Hindi code mixing in Facebook. In *Proceedings of the First Workshop on Computational Approaches to Code Switching*, pages 116–126, Doha, Qatar, October. Association for Computational Linguistics.

Shubhanker Banerjee, Bharathi Raja Chakravarthi, and John Philip McCrae. 2020. Comparison of pretrained embeddings to identify hate speech in Indian code-mixed text. In *2nd IEEE International Conference on Advances in Computing, Communication Control and Networking –ICACCCN (ICAC3N-20)*.

Aditya Bohra, Deepanshu Vijay, Vinay Singh, Syed Sarfaraz Akhtar, and Manish Shrivastava. 2018. A dataset of Hindi-English code-mixed social media text for hate speech detection. In *Proceedings of the Second Workshop on Computational Modeling of People's Opinions, Personality, and Emotions in Social Media*, pages 36–41, New Orleans, Louisiana, USA, June. Association for Computational Linguistics.

Bharathi Raja Chakravarthi, Mihael Arcan, and John P. McCrae. 2019a. Comparison of Different Orthographies for Machine Translation of Under-Resourced Dravidian Languages. In Maria Eskevich, Gerard de Melo,

Christian Fäth, John P. McCrae, Paul Buitelaar, Christian Chiarcos, Bettina Klimek, and Milan Dojchinovski, editors, *2nd Conference on Language, Data and Knowledge (LDK 2019)*, volume 70 of *OpenAccess Series in Informatics (OASIcs)*, pages 6:1–6:14, Dagstuhl, Germany. Schloss Dagstuhl–Leibniz-Zentrum fuer Informatik.

Bharathi Raja Chakravarthi, Mihael Arcan, and John P. McCrae. 2019b. WordNet gloss translation for under-resourced languages using multilingual neural machine translation. In *Proceedings of the Second Workshop on Multilingualism at the Intersection of Knowledge Bases and Machine Translation*, pages 1–7, Dublin, Ireland, 19 August. European Association for Machine Translation.

Bharathi Raja Chakravarthi, Navya Jose, Shardul Suryawanshi, Elizabeth Sherly, and John Philip McCrae. 2020a. A sentiment analysis dataset for code-mixed Malayalam-English. In *Proceedings of the 1st Joint Workshop on Spoken Language Technologies for Under-resourced languages (SLTU) and Collaboration and Computing for Under-Resourced Languages (CCURL)*, pages 177–184, Marseille, France, May. European Language Resources association.

Bharathi Raja Chakravarthi, Vigneshwaran Muralidaran, Ruba Priyadharshini, and John Philip McCrae. 2020b. Corpus creation for sentiment analysis in code-mixed Tamil-English text. In *Proceedings of the 1st Joint Workshop on Spoken Language Technologies for Under-resourced languages (SLTU) and Collaboration and Computing for Under-Resourced Languages (CCURL)*, pages 202–210, Marseille, France, May. European Language Resources association.

Bharathi Raja Chakravarthi, Navaneethan Rajasekaran, Mihael Arcan, Kevin McGuinness, Noel E.O'Connor, and John P McCrae. 2020c. Bilingual lexicon induction across orthographically-distinct under-resourced Dravidian languages. In *Proceedings of the Seventh Workshop on NLP for Similar Languages, Varieties and Dialects*, Barcelona, Spain, December.

Bharathi Raja Chakravarthi. 2020. *Leveraging orthographic information to improve machine translation of under-resourced languages*. Ph.D. thesis, NUI Galway.

Isobelle Clarke and Jack Grieve. 2017. Dimensions of abusive language on twitter. In *Proceedings of the First Workshop on Abusive Language Online*, pages 1–10, Vancouver, BC, Canada, August. Association for Computational Linguistics.

Y. Hegde and S. K. Padma. 2015. Sentiment analysis for "kannada" using mobile product reviews: A case study. In *2015 IEEE International Advance Computing Conference (IACC)*, pages 822–827.

Navya Jose, Bharathi Raja Chakravarthi, Shardul Suryawanshi, Elizabeth Sherly, and John P. McCrae. 2020. A survey of current datasets for code-switching research. In *2020 6th International Conference on Advanced Computing and Communication Systems (ICACCS)*.

K. M. Anil Kumar, N. Rajasimha, Manovikas Reddy, A. Rajanarayana, and Kewal Nadgir. 2015. Analysis of users' sentiments from kannada web documents. *Procedia Computer Science*, 54:247 – 256. Eleventh International Conference on Communication Networks, ICCN 2015, August 21-23, 2015, Bangalore, India Eleventh International Conference on Data Mining and Warehousing, ICDMW 2015, August 21-23, 2015, Bangalore, India Eleventh International Conference on Image and Signal Processing, ICISP 2015, August 21-23, 2015, Bangalore, India.

Ritesh Kumar, Atul Kr. Ojha, Shervin Malmasi, and Marcos Zampieri. 2018. Benchmarking aggression identification in social media. In *Proceedings of the First Workshop on Trolling, Aggression and Cyberbullying (TRAC-2018)*, pages 1–11, Santa Fe, New Mexico, USA, August. Association for Computational Linguistics.

Yash Kumar Lal, Vaibhav Kumar, Mrinal Dhar, Manish Shrivastava, and Philipp Koehn. 2019. De-mixing sentiment from code-mixed text. In *Proceedings of the 57th Annual Meeting of the Association for Computational Linguistics: Student Research Workshop*, pages 371–377, Florence, Italy, July. Association for Computational Linguistics.

Héctor Martínez Alonso and Barbara Plank. 2017. When is multitask learning effective? semantic sequence prediction under varying data conditions. In *Proceedings of the 15th Conference of the European Chapter of the Association for Computational Linguistics: Volume 1, Long Papers*, pages 44–53, Valencia, Spain, April. Association for Computational Linguistics.

Bo Pang and Lillian Lee. 2008. Opinion mining and sentiment analysis. *Found. Trends Inf. Retr.*, 2(1–2):1–135, January.

Zesis Pitenis, Marcos Zampieri, and Tharindu Ranasinghe. 2020. Offensive language identification in Greek. In *Proceedings of The 12th Language Resources and Evaluation Conference*, pages 5113–5119, Marseille, France, May. European Language Resources Association.

Suhan Prabhu, Ujwal Narayan, Alok Debnath, Sumukh S, and Manish Shrivastava. 2020. Detection and annotation of events in Kannada. In *16th Joint ACL - ISO Workshop on Interoperable Semantic Annotation PROCEEDINGS*, pages 88–93, Marseille, May. European Language Resources Association.

Adithya Pratapa, Gayatri Bhat, Monojit Choudhury, Sunayana Sitaram, Sandipan Dandapat, and Kalika Bali. 2018. Language modeling for code-mixing: The role of linguistic theory based synthetic data. In *Proceedings of the 56th Annual Meeting of the Association for Computational Linguistics (Volume 1: Long Papers)*, pages 1543–1553, Melbourne, Australia, July. Association for Computational Linguistics.

Ruba Priyadharshini, Bharathi Raja Chakravarthi, Mani Vegupatti, and John P. McCrae. 2020. Named entity recognition for code-mixed Indian corpus using meta embedding. In *2020 6th International Conference on Advanced Computing and Communication Systems (ICACCS)*.

Aliaksei Severyn, Alessandro Moschitti, Olga Uryupina, Barbara Plank, and Katja Filippova. 2014. Opinion mining on YouTube. In *Proceedings of the 52nd Annual Meeting of the Association for Computational Linguistics (Volume 1: Long Papers)*, pages 1252–1261, Baltimore, Maryland, June. Association for Computational Linguistics.

K. Shalini, H. B. Ganesh, M. A. Kumar, and K. P. Soman. 2018. Sentiment analysis for code-mixed indian social media text with distributed representation. In *2018 International Conference on Advances in Computing, Communications and Informatics (ICACCI)*, pages 1126–1131.

V. S. Skanda, M. A. Kumar, and K. P. Soman. 2017. Detecting stance in kannada social media code-mixed text using sentence embedding. In *2017 International Conference on Advances in Computing, Communications and Informatics (ICACCI)*, pages 964–969.

B. S. Sowmya Lakshmi and B. R. Shambhavi. 2017. An automatic language identification system for code-mixed english-kannada social media text. In *2017 2nd International Conference on Computational Systems and Information Technology for Sustainable Solution (CSITSS)*, pages 1–5, Dec.

Ye Tian, Thiago Galery, Giulio Dulcinati, Emilia Molimpakis, and Chao Sun. 2017. Facebook sentiment: Reactions and emojis. In *Proceedings of the Fifth International Workshop on Natural Language Processing for Social Media*, pages 11–16, Valencia, Spain, April. Association for Computational Linguistics.

Peter Turney. 2002. Thumbs up or thumbs down? semantic orientation applied to unsupervised classification of reviews. In *Proceedings of the 40th Annual Meeting of the Association for Computational Linguistics*, pages 417–424, Philadelphia, Pennsylvania, USA, July. Association for Computational Linguistics.

Marcos Zampieri, Shervin Malmasi, Preslav Nakov, Sara Rosenthal, Noura Farra, and Ritesh Kumar. 2019. Predicting the type and target of offensive posts in social media. In *Proceedings of the 2019 Conference of the North American Chapter of the Association for Computational Linguistics: Human Language Technologies, Volume 1 (Long and Short Papers)*, pages 1415–1420, Minneapolis, Minnesota, June. Association for Computational Linguistics.

Contextual Augmentation of Pretrained Language Models for Emotion Recognition in Conversations

Jonggu Kim   **Hyeonmok Ko**   **Seoha Song**   **Saebom Jang**   **Jiyeon Hong**

Samsung Research

Seoul, Republic of Korea

{jonggu88.kim, felix.ko, seoha.song, saebom.jang, ji-yeon.hong}@samsung.com

Abstract

Since language model pretraining to learn contextualized word representations has been proposed, pretrained language models have made success in many natural language processing tasks. That is because it is helpful to use individual contextualized representations of self-attention layers as to initialize parameters for downstream tasks. Yet, unfortunately, use of pretrained language models for emotion recognition in conversations has not been studied enough. We firstly use ELECTRA which is a state-of-the-art pretrained language model and validate the performance on emotion recognition in conversations. Furthermore, we propose contextual augmentation of pretrained language models for emotion recognition in conversations, which is to consider not only previous utterances, but also conversation-related information such as speakers, speech acts and topics. We classify information based on what the information is related to, and propose position of words corresponding to the information in the entire input sequence. To validate the proposed method, we conduct experiments on the DailyDialog dataset which contains abundant annotated information of conversations. The experiments show that the proposed method achieves state-of-the-art F1 scores on the dataset and significantly improves the performance.

1   Introduction

As voice assistants are widely used, emotion recognition is also emerging as an important technique to provide a rich user experience. Considering that it can detect the emotion state of speakers in real-time in an on-going conversation, it can be utilized in a variety of applications to generate more diverse and appropriate responses. As if to reflect this proliferation, detecting emotional state and emotion change in conversations has been widely studied. However, there is no significant progress in this research area. Previous studies focus extensively on emotion detecting using groups of words and/or utterances representing emotion, but those are not sufficient to detect the emotion state change that varies depending on dialogue subject or speaker in given conversations.

The proposed system in this paper models each conversation to contain two different levels of information (Fig. 1). Conversation-level information is effective in distinguishing conversations that show different aspect of emotion changes. Given the specific type of conversation, utterance-level information is used to recognize speaker's emotion. Basically, our research is based on the hypothesis that even if it's the same conversation there will be very different results depending on what previous or current conversations relate to and/or who is the speaker now. They so far have not considered essential information enough, but our results show the model trained with the essential information outperforms the state-of-the-art.

Various networks that could capture features that fit our hypothesis were considered, our evaluation results show that the Transformer (Vaswani et al., 2017) encoder family, which consists of multi-layers of self-attention and fully-connected layer, generally shows better performance. A self-attention model learns to generate representations for each token based on the context of the token. That is, the information mentioned above can be incorporated as each token representing fragments of information.

Proceedings of the Third Workshop on Computational Modeling of PEople's Opinions, PersonaLity, and Emotions in Social media, pages 64–73
Barcelona, Spain (Online), December 13, 2020.

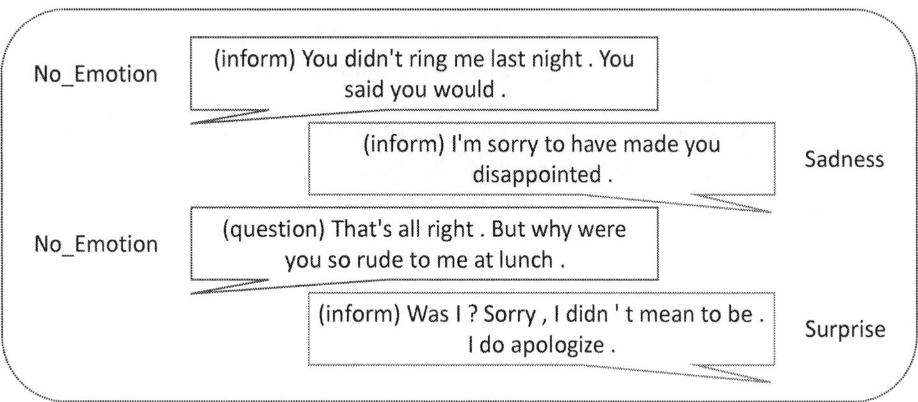

Figure 1: An example of conversation-level information and utterance-level information in DailyDialog. Topics like "attitude_and_emotion" belong to the conversation-level information, and speech acts like "inform" and "question" belong to the utterance-level information. Speakers also belong to the utterance-level information, which are regularly changed.

In this paper, we use ELECTRA (Clark et al., 2020) which is a state-of-the-art pretrained language model based on the Transformer encoder. Our experiments with the DailyDialog dataset (Li et al., 2017) containing enough annotated information of English conversations show the proposed model significantly improves the F1 scores comparing to the previous studies. Also, we thoroughly analyze effectiveness of incorporating each type of information as words in ELECTRA and different context lengths and present the result.

2   Related Work

Convolutional neural networks (CNN) and recurrent neural networks (RNN) have traditionally been used for emotion recognition. DialogueRNN (Majumder et al., 2019) has been proposed to model a speaker, a context from the preceding utterances and an emotion of the preceding utterances. DialogueGCN (Ghosal et al., 2019) has been proposed to model a conversation using directed graph to propagate the speaker's dependency information. Contextual information among distant utterances is propagated through two consecutive convolution operations by providing a convolutional network with the graph (Defferrard et al., 2016). Attention gated hierarchical memory network (AGHMN) (Jiao et al., 2020) has been proposed for real-time emotion recognition with an hierarchical memory network (HMN), a bidirectional gated recurrent unit (BiGRU) as the utterance reader and a BiGRU fusion layer for interaction between historical utterances; this network includes an attention gated recurrent unit (GRU) to update internal state and a bidirectional variant GRU to keep a balance between the contextual information from recent memories and that from distant memories. Recently, a generalized neural tensor block followed by a two-channel classifier is designed to perform contextual compositionality which obtains context information and incorporates the context into utterance representation and sentiment classification simultaneously (Li et al., 2020b).

Many natural language processing (NLP) tasks have applied Transformer (Vaswani et al., 2017) to capture long context information and enrich text representations. Knowledge-enriched Transformer (KET) (Zhong et al., 2019) uses hierarchical self-attention for exploiting contextual information and dynamically refers to external commonsense knowledge. HiTransformer-s (Li et al., 2020a) uses a hierarchical Transformer network with speaker embeddings to capture the contextual information and the interaction of speakers.

There are many studies on how to use various data such as visual expression, voice, and text to improve the performance of emotion recognition. Each type of data can be used alone in the emotion classification task, and when used together, better performance is observed empirically. This multimodal technique simply uses text and voice related to the speech (Ho et al., 2020), or additionally uses visual information such as the speaker's expression that occurs at the same time as the speech (Zadeh et al., 2018; Mittal et al., 2020; Delbrouck et al., 2020). Models that consider multimodality combine and use data of different properties for one target task. Among the studies for emotion recognition, there are studies that perform classification by hierarchically combining the relations between modals (Zadeh et al., 2018), or to select valid features using relations between modals (Mittal et al., 2020). Attention mechanisms, which are showing good performance in recent years, have also been used in several studies to find the relationship between modals (Ho et al., 2020; Delbrouck et al., 2020).

In sum, previous studies also use pretrained models and do not only concentrate on improving performance with neural networks, but incorporates a large deal of varying contextual information. Likewise, we propose and validate a method to improve performance in this paper. However, compared to the previous studies, our proposed approach has a relative strength: it is easy to incorporate the approach to finetune state-of-the-art pretrained language models.

3   Background

Pretrained language models like BERT (Devlin et al., 2019), XLNet (Yang et al., 2019) and ELECTRA (Clark et al., 2020) use the encoder of Transformer (Vaswani et al., 2017) that consists of multi-layers of self-attention and fully-connected layer. Attention can be defined using three terms, Q (queries), K (keys) and V (values). Self-attention is an attention method where Q, K and V are the same or generated from the same source. Given a sequence of vectors $[y_1, y_2, ..., y_{N_{token}}]$ whose length N_{token} is the same.

Performing projections of the queries, keys and values respectively to d_q, d_k and d_v dimensions N_{head} times[1] is empirically more effective than a single linear projection, and this method is called multi-head attention. Because the given sequence of vectors can be packed into a single matrix $X \in \mathbb{R}^{N_{token} \times d_x}$, the produced sequence of vectors can also be represented as a matrix $Y \in \mathbb{R}^{N_{token} \times d_y}$. Given X, Y is computed in the multi-head attention way as:

$$Q_i = X^T W_i^Q, \tag{1}$$

$$K_i = X^T W_i^K, \tag{2}$$

$$V_i = X^T W_i^V, \tag{3}$$

$$head_i = \text{Softmax}(Q_i K_i^T) V_i, \tag{4}$$

$$Y = \text{Concat}(head_1, ..., head_{N_{head}}) W^O, \tag{5}$$

where $[\cdot]^T$ is transpose of $[\cdot]$, $W_i^Q \in \mathbb{R}^{N_{token} \times d_q}$, $W_i^K \in \mathbb{R}^{N_{token} \times d_k}$, $W_i^V \in \mathbb{R}^{N_{token} \times d_v}$ and $W^O \in \mathbb{R}^{N_{head} \times d_{model}}$ are trainable weight matrices.

In each layer, a fully-connected layer is used to linearly transform the output of the self-attention layer, and layer normalization is used after the two outputs of self-attention and fully-connected layer are added. By stacking the layer L times, the entire model is built.

By (pre)training on a large amount of text data, a self-attention model learns to generate representations for each token based on the context of the token. Then the pretrained model learns to generate task-specific answers by finetuning. For example, by finetuning, ELECTRA can learn to recognize the emotion of the given utterance or to classify the polarity of individual words in the utterance.

ELECTRA that we used for the experiments is different from other pretrained language models in that it uses not the generator, but an additional model, a discriminator, which consists of the encoder of Transformer as the same described above. The difference between them is about details for pretraining, not finetuning, so we omit the explanation. Details of the model related to our proposed method is introduced in the next section.

---

[1] $d_k = d_v = d_{model}/N_{head}$ is generally used.

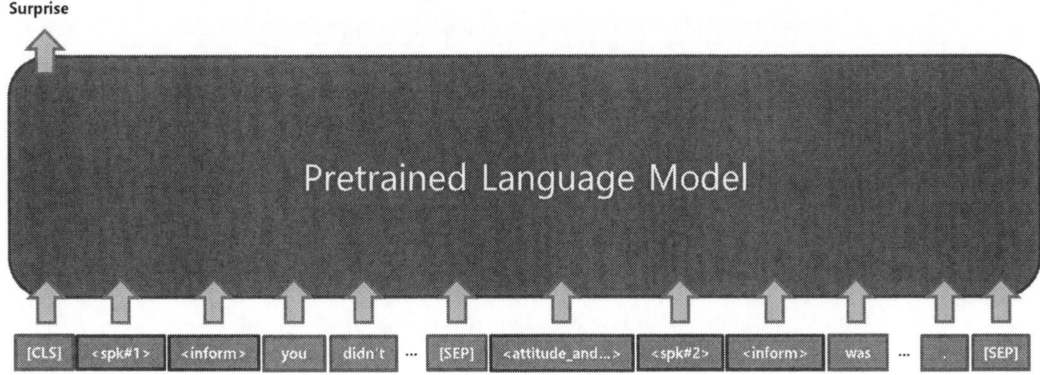

Figure 2: An example of input/output for contextual augmentation of pretrained language models.

4 Proposed Method

By finetuning on a downstream task, pretrained language models are optimized for the task. Two types of input form are generally used, and which type is used depends on the downstream task. The two types are "[CLS] seg_A [SEP]" and "[CLS] seg_A [SEP] seg_B [SEP]", where [CLS] is a special symbol and [SEP] is a special separator token.

In this paper, emotion recognition in conversations is considered, which is a task that when given T-th utterance and the context (previous utterances), the model recognizes the emotion implicit in the T-th utterance. For this task, we segment all utterances into two parts, a part for the T-th utterance and a part for the context.

Specifically, the T-th utterance is decomposed into a sequence of N_T words $[w_1^T, w_2^T, ..., w_{N_T}^T]$, where $N_{[.]}$ is the number of words of the $[.]$-th utterance. We put them all into seg_B. On the other hand, words of the previous utterances $[w_1^{T-M}, w_2^{T-M}, ..., w_{N_{T-1}}^{T-1}]$ are put into seg_A, where M is the context length. In sum, the input form is "[CLS] w_1^{T-M} w_2^{T-M} ... $w_{N_{T-1}}^{T-1}$ [SEP] w_1^T w_2^T ... $w_{N_T}^T$ [SEP]".

Each type of information is converted into words, and then put into appropriate positions of the information. Then the model will consider all the information together.

We can think of two levels of information, utterance-level and conversation-level. In DailyDialog (Li et al., 2017), for example, there are speakers, speech acts and topics, so they can be respectively mapped to one of the information levels: speakers and speech acts are mapped to utterance-level information, and topics are mapped to conversation-level information.

We add UTT_{TYPE} and CON_{TYPE} to the input sequence, encoding utterance-level and conversation-level information. For utterance-level information, we add a symbol of the information of the t-th utterance UTT_{TYPE}^t in front of the utterance. Thus, we add a symbol of the speaker of the t-th utterance UTT_{spk}^t in front of it for the speaker information. In the same way, we add a symbol of the speech act of the t-th utterance UTT_{act}^t in front of the utterance for the speech act information.

For conversation-level information, we add a symbol of the information CON_{TYPE} in front of seg_B. For example, to incorporate a topic of the conversation, we add a symbol of the topic CON_{topic} in front of the T-th utterance.

As a result, the full input form for DailyDialog is "[CLS] UTT_{spk}^{T-M} UTT_{act}^{T-M} w_1^{T-M} w_2^{T-M} ... $w_{N_{T-M}}^{T-M}$ UTT_{spk}^{T-1} UTT_{act}^{T-1} w_1^{T-1} w_2^{T-1} ... $w_{N_{T-1}}^{T-1}$ [SEP] CON_{topic} UTT_{spk}^T UTT_{act}^T w_1^T w_2^T ... $w_{N_T}^T$ [SEP]". The model then generates an emotion label at the position of [CLS] at the last layer (Fig. 2). As the input is fed to ELECTRA, we expect the model to consider and relate the information to all tokens in the utterance via multi-layers of self-attention for emotion recognition.

Table 1: The number of utterances for emotion types in DailyDialog.

Split	Anger	Disgust	Fear	Happiness	Sadness	Surprise	No_Emotion
train	827	303	146	11,182	969	1,600	72,143
valid	77	3	11	684	79	107	7,108
test	118	47	17	1,019	102	116	6,321
total	1,022	353	174	12,885	1,150	1,823	85,572

Table 2: The number of utterances for speech act types in DailyDialog.

Speech Act	train	valid	test	total
Inform	39,873	3,125	3,534	46,532
Question	24,974	2,244	2,210	29,428
Directive	14,242	1,775	1,278	17,295
Commissive	8,081	925	718	9,724

5 Experiments

5.1 Settings

We use the DailyDialog dataset (Li et al., 2017) for the experiments. DailyDialog is a human-written conversation dataset that reflects our daily communication way in various topics on our daily life. The dataset consists of 13,118 dialogues and the dialogues include 102,979 utterances. A dialog has a manually-labeled topic and an utterance has manually-labeled intention (speech act) and emotion information. In DailyDialog, emotions to be recognized are decomposed into seven categories (Anger, Disgust, Fear, Happiness, Sadness, Surprise and No_Emotion) (Table 1). Speech acts that the proposed model uses are decomposed into four categories (Inform, Question, Directive and Commissive) (Table 2), and topics are decomposed into 10 categories (Ordinary Life, School Life, Culture & Education, Attitude & Emotion, Relationship, Tourism, Health, Work, Politics and Finance) (Table 3). For fair comparison with state of the art models (Poria et al., 2017; Majumder et al., 2019; Zhong et al., 2019; Hazarikaa et al., 2021), we use the same training dataset, the same validation dataset and the same test dataset[2]: 11,118 dialogs (87,170 utterances) for training, 1000 dialogs (8,069 utterances) for validation and 1000 dialogs (7,740 utterances) for test.

We finetune and use pretrained ELECTRA-Base as a baseline model for emotion recognition. ELECTRA-Base has 12 layers, 768 hidden dimensions and 12 heads. We use batch size of 4, learning rate of 0.0001, maximum sequence length of 100 and 512 and Adam optimizer (Kingma and Ba, 2015) with 1 epoch to finetune all models[3]. As an evaluation metric, we mainly use the micro-averaged F1 score excluding the majority class, No_Emotion, because of the imbalanced class distribution, which is the same metric as in the previous work (Zhong et al., 2019). To compare with TL-ERC (Hazarikaa et al., 2021), we use the weighted macro F1 score. We use a one tailed t-test to validate the significance of improvements. Also in the comparison, we ran each model five times, and report their average scores.

We use ground-truth labels of all information. For speaker labels, we use turn numbers to distinguish a speaker from a listener because the current speaker is not explicitly given, the speaker is changed turn by turn. Then we map the numbers to specific expressions existing in the vocabulary of ELECTRA. Specifically, if the turn number is odd, we used "[unused1]"; otherwise, we used "[unused2]". For acts and topics, we used names of the labels enclosed by "<" and ">". e.g., "<question>" and "<ordinary_life>".

We compare our model with the state-of-the-art emotion recognition models. Note that all scores of

---

[2]The split can be found at `https://github.com/declare-lab/conv-emotion`.

[3]Maximum sequence length of 100 was used for fair comparison with BERT reported in previous work (Zhong et al., 2019) (Table 4). In the other cases, maximum sequence length of 512 was used (Table 5 and Fig. 3).

Table 3: The number of utterances for topic types in DailyDialog.

Topic	train	valid	test	total
Ordinary Life	23,587	3,507	2,162	29,256
School Life	4,257	0	299	4,556
Culture & Education	469	0	55	524
Attitude & Emotion	3,683	40	344	4,067
Relationship	29,713	512	2,582	32,807
Tourism	6,822	1,040	642	8,504
Health	1,969	458	205	2,632
Work	11,889	1,809	1,104	14,802
Politics	1,295	156	132	1,583
Finance	3,486	547	215	4,248

the state-of-the-art models are the scores reported in previous work (Zhong et al., 2019). The models are described as follows:

CNN (Kim, 2014): A single-layer of convolutional neural networks for the current utterance. The model does not use contextual information.

CNN + cLSTM (Poria et al., 2017): A contextual LSTM (cLSTM) to capture contextual information at utterance level after a CNN layer.

BERT (Devlin et al., 2019): A Base version of BERT finetuned on emotion recognition. The difference from ELECTRA is the method of pretraining.

DialogueRNN (Majumder et al., 2019): A customized RNN model to capture speakers and context information. Several GRUs are used to track global/party state and speaker information after feature extraction from utterances by CNN. For DailyDialog, two speakers are distinguished using a turn number of each utterance.

KET (Zhong et al., 2019): A hierarchical self-attention model to encode hierarchical conversation representations. Also, the model retrieves related commonsense knowledge from external knowledge base and exploits the knowledge.

TL-ERC (Hazarikaa et al., 2021): A transfer learning-based approach. A Transformer encoder is first trained to generate multi-turn conversations, and the trained model is trained again to generate an emotion in conversations.

5.2 Results

In comparison with state-of-the-art models, ELECTRA achieves state-of-the-art F1 scores on DailyDialog (Table 4). Even if the model is similar in the model structure, obtains an F1 score higher than BERT (Devlin et al., 2019). This result shows that ELECTRA is better than BERT in emotion recognition also.

Incorporating information as words significantly improves micro/weighted F1 scores. ELECTRA with contextual augmentation achieves micro F1 of 57.97 % and weighted F1 of 55.73 % while ELECTRA achieves micro F1 of 55.13 % and weighted F1 of 51.63 %. The F1 scores of ELECTRA with contextual augmentation are the state-of-the-art F1 scores on DailyDialog.

6 Discussion

We analyze effectiveness of the proposed method in detail in this section. In the proposed model, because we use three kinds of information, speaker, act and topic, we separate them to validate effectiveness of each type of information (Table 5). In this analysis, we find which information is the most effective on DailyDialog and how different results are according to emotion categories.

Table 4: Comparison with state-of-the art models on the test dataset of DailyDialog. **: $p < 0.01$ compared to ELECTRA.

Model	micro F1	weighted F1
CNN (Kim, 2014)	49.34	-
CNN + cLSTM (Poria et al., 2017)	49.90	-
BERT (Devlin et al., 2019)	53.12	-
DialogueRNN (Majumder et al., 2019)	50.65	-
KET (Zhong et al., 2019)	53.37	-
TL-ERC (Hazarikaa et al., 2021)	-	48.00
ELECTRA	55.13	51.63
ELECTRA with Contextual Augmentation	**57.97****	**55.73****

Table 5: F1 score of incorporating speaker (S), act (A) and topic (T) as words for each emotion type on the test dataset of DailyDialog.

#	Information Type	Anger	Disgust	Fear	Happiness	Sadness	Surprise	micro F1 All
1	none	28.14	0.00	0.00	62.25	1.88	50.76	54.67
2	S	25.75	2.40	0.00	63.66	0.38	50.24	55.70
3	A	29.71	**3.87**	0.00	63.35	0.00	49.43	55.31
4	T	30.01	1.51	0.00	65.82	34.53	50.49	58.57
5	S,A	28.67	0.00	0.00	63.89	0.00	50.47	55.82
6	S,T	29.28	2.10	0.00	**66.90**	34.80	51.23	**59.20**
7	A,T	29.11	2.36	0.00	66.27	29.73	**51.28**	58.64
8	S,A,T	**29.69**	0.00	0.00	66.53	**36.15**	50.80	58.99

Additionally, we conduct experiments to evaluate performance of the model with respect to the context length that is the number of previous utterances considered. The context length is helpful information in understanding of conversations, and in guessing the emotion more correctly. We analyze how effective different context lengths are, and at the same time, how different the performance in incorporation of different information types is.

6.1 Effectiveness of Incorporating Speaker, Act and Topic

To validate effectiveness of incorporating speaker, act and topic as words, we conduct ablation study for emotion classes (Table 5). In this study, we found a few tendencies with respect to what kind of information is used.

First, all models with incorporation of topic achieve F1 scores higher than 58.0 % (row 4, 6, 7 and 8) while the others do not. This result means that incorporation of topic is effective to improve performance of emotion recognition. In analysis on F1 score for each emotion type, we found a tendency that all models with incorporation of topic achieved higher F1 scores for Happiness and Sadness than those for the other emotions. We interpret this result as a topic is implicitly related to the emotion of happiness or sadness of the speakers in the dataset. Also, we found that these gains drove micro F1 scores to being higher. All the models obtain F1 scores of 0.00 % on Fear, we ascribe this result to low distribution (146/87,170) of the emotion type in the training dataset.

Compared to the baseline method (row 1), incorporating speaker or act also obtains improvements of F1 score (row 2, 3, 5, 6, 7 and 8); however, they are not outstanding. Specifically, in the case of DailyDailog, incorporating speaker information is not helpful as it only indicates change of turn, and does not include any personalized information. This limits the improvements on this dataset, but incorporation of speaker information could help on other datasets where personalized speaker information is available.

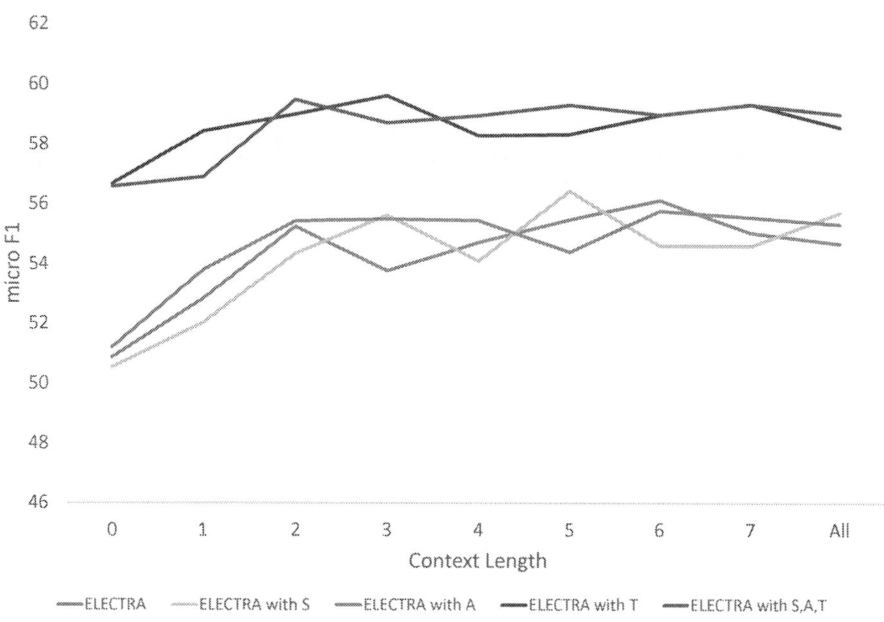

Figure 3: F1 score of incorporating speaker (S), act (A) and topic (T) for different context length on the test dataset of DailyDialog.

6.2 Effectiveness of Different Context Length with Incorporation of Different Information

What kind of help would the context length bring to emotion recognition? We analyze the effectiveness of context length with incorporation of different information (Fig. 3). Note that we use average of F1 scores after 5 runs for all context, whereas we use F1 scores after a single run for the other context lengths (0 to 7).

We found a tendency that in every model, the longer context length is used, the higher F1 score is achieved. In every model, the lowest micro F1 score is obtained using context length of 0. F1 scores are gradually improved when context length becomes longer up to 2. F1 scores of all models using context length from 2 to all are similar, but do not degrade.

7 Conclusion

We employ a state-of-the-art pretrained language model, ELECTRA, to emotion recognition in conversations. Because ELECTRA is a powerful NLP model by itself, we do not propose to modify the structure. Instead, we explore and propose an effective method of providing the model with extra information as words to improve performance of emotion recognition.

In this paper, we consider three kinds of information, speaker, act and topic, and propose a method to incorporate the information in pretrained language models. By incorporating the information, pretrained language models are expected to consider and relate the information to all tokens in the utterance via multi-layers of self-attention for emotion recognition.

Our experiments show that the proposed method improves performance of emotion recognition with large margin, and that the gain margin depends on how important the provided information is. On the DailyDialog dataset, when given the topic as words, performance of the model is highly improved. This result means that if the information provided with the proposed method is closely related to the emotion, the performance of emotion recognition is highly improved. In other words, leveraging state-of-the-art pretrained language models by simply augmenting the features with meta-information leads to large improvements, without needing to resort to more complex modeling.

References

Kevin Clark, Minh-Thang Luong, Quoc V. Le, and Christopher D. Manning. 2020. Electra: Pre-training text encoders as discriminators rather than generators. In *International Conference on Learning Representations (ICLR)*.

Michaël Defferrard, Xavier Bresson, and Pierre Vandergheynst. 2016. Convolutional neural networks on graphs with fast localized spectral filtering. In *Advances in Neural Information Processing Systems 29*, pages 3844–3852.

Jean-Benoit Delbrouck, Noé Tits, Mathilde Brousmiche, and Stéphane Dupont. 2020. A transformer-based joint-encoding for emotion recognition and sentiment analysis. In *Second Grand-Challenge and Workshop on Multimodal Language (Challenge-HML)*, pages 1–7.

Jacob Devlin, Ming-Wei Chang, Kenton Lee, and Kristina Toutanova. 2019. BERT: Pre-training of deep bidirectional transformers for language understanding. In *Proceedings of the 2019 Conference of the North American Chapter of the Association for Computational Linguistics: Human Language Technologies, Volume 1 (Long and Short Papers)*, pages 4171–4186.

Deepanway Ghosal, Navonil Majumder, Soujanya Poria, Niyati Chhaya, and Alexander Gelbukh. 2019. DialogueGCN: A graph convolutional neural network for emotion recognition in conversation. In *Proceedings of the 2019 Conference on Empirical Methods in Natural Language Processing and the 9th International Joint Conference on Natural Language Processing (EMNLP-IJCNLP)*, pages 154–164.

Devamanyu Hazarikaa, Soujanya Poria, Roger Zimmermanna, and Rada Mihalcea. 2021. Conversational transfer learning for emotion recognition. *Information Fusion*, 65:1 – 12.

N. Ho, H. Yang, S. Kim, and G. Lee. 2020. Multimodal approach of speech emotion recognition using multi-level multi-head fusion attention-based recurrent neural network. *IEEE Access*, 8:61672–61686.

Wenxiang Jiao, Michael R Lyu, and Irwin King. 2020. Real-time emotion recognition via attention gated hierarchical memory network. In *The Thirty-Fourth AAAI Conference on Artificial Intelligence (AAAI-20)*.

Yoon Kim. 2014. Convolutional neural networks for sentence classification. In *Proceedings of the 2014 Conference on Empirical Methods in Natural Language Processing (EMNLP)*, pages 1746–1751.

Diederik P. Kingma and Jimmy Ba. 2015. Adam: A method for stochastic optimization. In *3rd International Conference on Learning Representations (ICLR)*.

Yanran Li, Hui Su, Xiaoyu Shen, Wenjie Li, Ziqiang Cao, and Shuzi Niu. 2017. DailyDialog: A manually labelled multi-turn dialogue dataset. In *Proceedings of the Eighth International Joint Conference on Natural Language Processing (Volume 1: Long Papers)*, pages 986–995.

Qingbiao Li, Chunhua Wu, Zhe Wang, and Kangfeng Zheng. 2020a. Hierarchical transformer network for utterance-level emotion recognition. *Applied Sciences*, 10(13):4447.

Wei Li, Wei Shao, Shaoxiong Ji, and E. Cambria. 2020b. Bieru: Bidirectional emotional recurrent unit for conversational sentiment analysis. *ArXiv*, abs/2006.00492.

Navonil Majumder, Soujanya Poria, Devamanyu Hazarika, Rada Mihalcea, Alexander Gelbukh, and Erik Cambria. 2019. Dialoguernn: An attentive rnn for emotion detection in conversations. In *The Thirty-Third AAAI Conference on Artificial Intelligence (AAAI-19)*, pages 6818–6825.

Trisha Mittal, Uttaran Bhattacharya, Rohan Chandra, Aniket Bera, and Dinesh Manocha. 2020. M3ER: multiplicative multimodal emotion recognition using facial, textual, and speech cues. In *The Thirty-Fourth AAAI Conference on Artificial Intelligence (AAAI-20)*, pages 1359–1367.

Soujanya Poria, Erik Cambria, Devamanyu Hazarika, Navonil Majumder, Amir Zadeh, and Louis-Philippe Morency. 2017. Context-dependent sentiment analysis in user-generated videos. In *Proceedings of the 55th Annual Meeting of the Association for Computational Linguistics (Volume 1: Long Papers)*, pages 873–883.

Ashish Vaswani, Noam Shazeer, Niki Parmar, Jakob Uszkoreit, Llion Jones, Aidan N Gomez, Ł ukasz Kaiser, and Illia Polosukhin. 2017. Attention is all you need. In I. Guyon, U. V. Luxburg, S. Bengio, H. Wallach, R. Fergus, S. Vishwanathan, and R. Garnett, editors, *Advances in Neural Information Processing Systems 30*, pages 5998–6008.

Zhilin Yang, Zihang Dai, Yiming Yang, Jaime Carbonell, Russ R Salakhutdinov, and Quoc V Le. 2019. Xlnet: Generalized autoregressive pretraining for language understanding. In *Advances in Neural Information Processing Systems 32*, pages 5753–5763.

Amir Zadeh, Paul Pu Liang, Jonathan Vanbriesen, Soujanya Poria, Edmund Tong, Erik Cambria, Minghai Chen, and Louis-Philippe Morency. 2018. Multimodal language analysis in the wild: CMU-MOSEI dataset and interpretable dynamic fusion graph. In *Proceedings of the 56th Annual Meeting of the Association for Computational Linguistics (Volume 1: Long Papers)*, pages 2236–2246.

Peixiang Zhong, Di Wang, and Chunyan Miao. 2019. Knowledge-enriched transformer for emotion detection in textual conversations. In *Proceedings of the 2019 Conference on Empirical Methods in Natural Language Processing and the 9th International Joint Conference on Natural Language Processing (EMNLP-IJCNLP)*, pages 165–176.

Social Media Unrest Prediction during the COVID-19 Pandemic: Neural Implicit Motive Pattern Recognition as Psychometric Signs of Severe Crises

Dirk Johannßen
MIN Faculty
Dept. of Informatics
Universität Hamburg
& Nordakademie

Chris Biemann
MIN Faculty
Dept. of Informatics
Universität Hamburg
22527 Hamburg, Germany

http://lt.informatik.uni-hamburg.de/
{biemann, johannssen}@informatik.uni-hamburg.de

Abstract

The COVID-19 pandemic has caused international social tension and unrest. Besides the crisis itself, there are growing signs of rising conflict potential of societies around the world. Indicators of global mood changes are hard to detect and direct questionnaires suffer from social desirability biases. However, so-called implicit methods can reveal humans intrinsic desires from e.g. social media texts. We present psychologically validated social unrest predictors and replicate scalable and automated predictions, setting a new state of the art on a recent German shared task dataset. We employ this model to investigate a change of language towards social unrest during the COVID-19 pandemic by comparing established psychological predictors on samples of tweets from spring 2019 with spring 2020. The results show a significant increase of the conflict-indicating psychometrics. With this work, we demonstrate the applicability of automated NLP-based approaches to quantitative psychological research.

1 Introduction

The COVID-19 pandemic and the reactions to it have led to growing social tensions. Guitérrez-Romero (2020) studied the effects of social distancing and lockdowns on riots, violence against civilians, and food-related conflicts in 24 African countries. The author found that the risk of riots and violence have increased due to lockdowns. Resistance against national health regulations such as the duty to wear masks are partially met with resistance by movements such as anti-maskers or anti-obligation demonstrations.[1] Even anti-democratic alterations of e.g. services offered by the US Postal Service (USPS) of delivering mail-in ballots for the US presidential elections 2020, which are essential for social distancing measures amidst the pandemic, are being utilized amidst this international crisis and foster social unrest and potential outbursts of violence, civil disobedience or uprisings.[2]

Social media has become an important reflection of nationally and internationally discussed topics, and is a predictor of e.g. stock markets, disease outbreaks or political elections (Kalampokis et al., 2013). The majority of human-produced data exists in textual form and broadly in social media and thus, an the investigation of social unrest and conflict situations from social media becomes a worthwhile application area for natural language processing (NLP) problem (Gentzkow et al., 2019).

When speaking about such global phenomena such as a rise in international social unrest and possible occurrences of conflict reflected in text, the detection of specific keywords or utterances have not been successful in past research. Mueller et al. (2017) utilized Laten Dirichlet Allocation (LDA, (Blei et al., 2003)) topic modelling on war-related newspaper items and were not able to improve predictability from other multi-factor models that take into account e.g. GDP figures, mountainous terrain or ethnic

---

[1]https://firstdraftnews.org/latest/coronavirus-how-pro-mask-posts-boost-the-anti-mask-movement/

[2]https://www.businessinsider.com/trump-walks-back-threat-block-covid-relief-over-usps-funding-2020-8?r=DE&IR=T

Proceedings of the Third Workshop on Computational Modeling of PEople's Opinions, PersonaLity, and Emotions in Social media, pages 74–86
Barcelona, Spain (Online), December 13, 2020.

polarization. Furthermore, Chadefaux (2012) showed that news reports on possible war situations alone did not function as good predictors but identified sharp frequency increases before war emerged, possibly helping with just-in-time safety measures but likely failing to avoid war situations altogether.

Alternatively, the risks of escalation could be determined based on politician's personalities and the current mood and tone of utterances (Schultheiss and Brunstein, 2010, p. 407). However, intrinsic desires and personality can hardly be measured directly (see Section 3). Intrinsic or subconscious desires and motivation would more likely correlate with personalities, tone, and thus possibly social unrest.

We hypothesize that the frequency of social unrest predictors have significantly changed in social media textual data during the COVID-19 pandemic drawn from the Twitter 1 percent stream[3] in early 2019 and 2020, whilst linguistic features stay comparably stable and unchanged. With this, we aim to demonstrate a possible transition from laborsome manual psychological research to automated NLP approaches.

After presenting and discussing related work in Section 2, we will first introduce the concept of implicit motives and self-regulating levels in more details in Section 3 and the social unrest predictors thereafter in Section 4. The data utilized for experiments is described in Section 5 and the methodology in Section 6. Thereafter, we will present the results in Section 7 and discuss their impacts in Section 8. Lastly, we will draw a conclusion in Section 9.

2 Related Work

Conflict predictions from natural language are rarely encountered applications and have mainly been about content analysis and less about crowd psychology. Kutuzov et al. (2019) used one-to-X analogy reasoning based on word embeddings for predicting previous armed conflict situations from printed news. Johansson et al. (2011) performed named entity recognition (NER) and extracted events via Hidden Markov Models (HMM) and neural networks, which were combined with human intelligence reports to identify current global areas of conflicts, that, in turn, were utilized mainly for world map visualizations.

Investigation of personality traits has mainly been focussing on so-called explicit methods. For these, questionnaires are filled out either by interviewers, through observations, or directly by participants. One of the most broadly utilized psychometrics is the Big Five inventory, even though its validity is controversial (Block, 1995). The five-factory theory of personality (later named Big Five) identifies five personality traits, namely *openness to experiences, conscientiousness, extraversion, agreeableness* and *neuroticism* (McCrae and Costa Jr., 1999; Goldberg, 1981). This Big Five inventory was utilized by Tighe and Chegn (2018) for analyzing these five traits of Filipino speakers.

Some studies perform natural language processing (NLP) for investigating personality traits. Lynn et al. (2020) utilized an attention mechanism for deciding upon important parts of an instance when assigning the five-factor inventory classes. The Myers-Briggs Type Indicator (MBTI) is a broadly utilized adaption of the Big Five inventory, which Yamada et al. (2019) employed for asserting the personality traits within tweets.[4]

The research field of psychology has moved further towards automated language assertions during the past years. One standard methodology is the utilization of the tool linguistic inquiry and word count (LIWC), developed by Pennebaker et al. (1999). The German version of LIWC was developed by Wolf et al. (2008). It includes 96 target classes, some of which are rather simple linguistic features (word count, words longer than six characters, frequency of punctuation), and psychological categories such as anxiety, familiarity, or occupation. Even though the tool appears rather simple from an NLP point of view, it has a long tradition to be utilized for content research in the field of behavioral psychology. Studies utilizing LIWC have shown that function words are valid predictors for long-term developments such as academic success (Pennebaker et al., 2014). Furthermore, it has been shown that LIWC corre-lates with the Big Five inventory (McCrae and Costa Jr., 1999). Importantly, the writing style of people can be considered a trait, as it has shown high stability over time, which means that it is not dependent on

---

[3]`https://developer.twitter.com/en/docs/labs/sampled-stream/overview`

[4]A *Tweet* is a short message from the social network microblogging service Twitter (`https://www.twitter.com/`) and consists of up to 240 characters.

one's current mood, the time of day, or other external conditions (Pennebaker and King, 2000). Hogen-raad (2003) utilized an implicit motive (see Section 3) dictionary approach to automatically determine risks of war outbreaks from different novels and historic documents, identifying widening gaps between the so-called power motive and affiliation motive in near-war situations.

Overall, the work on automated classification of implicit motive data or the use of NLP for the assertion of psychological traits in general is rather sparse or relies on rather outdated methods, as this application domain can be considered a niche (Schultheiss and Brunstein, 2010; Johannßen and Biemann, 2019; Johannßen and Biemann, 2018; Johannßen et al., 2019). One recent event in this area was the GermEval 2020 Task 1 on the Classification and Regression of Cognitive and Motivational Style from Text (Johannßen et al., 2020). The best participating team reached a macro f1 score of 70.40 on the task of classifying implicit motives combined with self-regulating levels, resulting in 30 target classes. However, behavioral outcomes from automatically classified implicit motives have – to our knowledge – not yet been researched.

3 Implicit Motives and Self-regulatory Levels

Implicit motives can reveal intrinsic, unconscious human desires, and thus avoid social desirability biases, which usually are present when utilizing direct questionnaires. They originated from the Thematic Apperception Test (TAT) by Murry et al (1943). Participants are confronted with ambiguous images of multiple people that interact with each other as displayed in Figure 1, and are asked to answer four questions: i) who is the main person, ii) what does that person feel? iii) why does the person feel that way, and iv) how does the story end? From these questions, trained psychologists can assign one of five motives: affiliation (A), freedom (F), achievement (L), power (M), and zero (0). The psychologists follow some rules, one being the so-called primacy rule, where the very first identifiable motive determines the whole instance, despite what follows (Scheffer and Kuhl, 2013). These motives have shown to be behavioral predictors and allow for long-term statements of e.g. group dynamics or success (McClelland and Boyatzis, 1982; Schultheiss and Brunstein, 2010). Implicit motives have been broadly utilized in the 1980s but at the cost of laborsome manual annotating processes. It takes about 20 hours of training for an annotator to encode one of the implicit motives. Skilled human annotators take up to 50 hours per 100 participants. This costly annotating process has hampered this once-promising psychometric (Schultheiss and Brunstein, 2010, p. 140).

Whilst the classification performance of implicit motive models have been explored and achieved high results (e.g. (Johannßen and Biemann, 2019; Johannßen et al., 2020)), behavioral consequences and mass phenomena from automated labeled textual instances have barely been researched.

In addition to the implicit motives, the data set from the GermEval20 Task 1 comes with so-called levels per textual instance. The levels were developed by Kuhl (2001). They describe the self-regulatory enactment in five dimensions. According to Scheffer and Kuhl (2013) the 1st level is the ability to self-regulate a positive affect, the 2nd is the sensitivity for positive incentives, the 3rd self-regulates a negative affect, the 4th is the sensitivity for negative incentives and the 5th level describes the passive coping with fears. In other words, these levels help to identify the type of the participant's emotional response according to the identified implicit motive.

As with many psychometrics, the reliability of implicit motives, and especially their predecessor (the TAT) is controversial. One main point of criticism is that implicit motives do not correlate significantly with so-called explicit motives. Whilst implicit motives try to measure intrinsic desires indirectly by asking participants associative questions, explicit motives try to measure desires via direct questionnaires. In psychology, reliability means, that personality traits revealed by one measure may not conflict with personality traits measured by other, well-established measures. Since the measured desires of implicit and explicit motives generally do not match, the reliability of implicit motives is said to be weak.

Schultheiss et al. (2010) explain this lack of reliability and correlation with the fact that explicit implicit motives are by definition of different measurements that can not be directly compared. Whilst implicit motives measure intrinsic desires that are subconscious, explicit motives are more influenced by a social expectation bias (i.e. what do participants think is a socially sound and accepted answer to a question) and thus are closer connected to behaviorism. Nonetheless, reliability in psychological research demands different observable results of metrics to be coherent (Reuman, 1982) when the descriptions of what a psychometric is supposed to measure matches (i.e. desires).

Another point of criticism is the way the TAT images are selected. They emerge from an empirical study, where participants are shown different images. Only when past frequencies of motives are achieved with an image, this image gets added to the available testing stock. With this, however, the very first selected implicit motive images could not have been validated. Nowadays, many scholars argue that the amounts of positive evidence legitimize this methodology, but it has yet to be resolved (Hibbard, 2003).

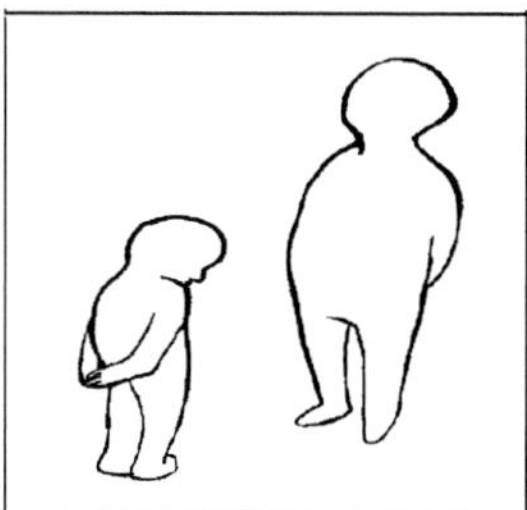

Figure 1: Exemplary image to be interpreted by participants utilized for the operant motive test (OMT). Identifiable motives are the affiliation motive (A), the power motive (M), achievement (L), and freedom (F). A 0 represents the unassigned motive (Kuhl and Scheffer, 1999).

The transition from natural language to intrinsic desires and motivation is not trivial, as humans do not express intrinsic and unconscious desires unfiltered and directly. As soon as a direct questionnaire is involved, social desirability biases (i.e. thoughts of publicly expected answers) alter an uninfluenced introspection (Brunstein, 2008). Such direct questionnaires are called explicit methods, in contrast to implicit methods, such as e.g. the TAT and subsequent tests produced by image descriptions.

4 Social Unrest Predictors

Times of severe social unrest are reflected by distinct patterns of implicit motives and linguistic features. Winter (2007) surveyed multiple prior studies, identifying three main predictors: *responsibility*, *activity inhibition*, and *integrative complexity*, displayed in Table 1. In this study, the author identified and analyzed 8 occurrences of crises and social unrest by examining influential political speeches of this time. Thereafter, the outcomes of these crises – whether they ended peacefully or in conflict – were projected on indicators from earlier research.

Winter and Barenbaum (1985) found that the power motive (M) has a moderating effect of responsibility. In other words, responsibility determines, how vast amounts of power motivated expressions are behaviorally enacted. If a high responsibility score is measurable, power motivated individuals act pro-social. On the contrary, if the responsibility score is low, aggression and lack of leadership are to be expected.

Activity inhibition is reflected, according to by McClelland et al. (1972) as the frequency of "not" and "-n't" contradictions in TAT or other verbal texts. Activity inhibition functions as motivational and emotional regulation. The authors identified a negative correlation between activity inhibition and male alcohol consumption. Combined with a high power motive (M) and low affiliation motive (A), subsequent research by McClelland and his colleagues revealed a so-called leadership motive pattern (LMP) (McClelland and Boyatzis, 1982; McClelland, 1988). The higher this LMP, the more responsible leaders act. As for *integrative complexity* it was observed, that the lower the frequency of utterances in accordance to the 7-point score was (see Table 1), the more likely escalations became.

Category	Measure	Example or Explaination
Responsibility		
i) moral standards	observable, if people, actions, or things are described with either morality or legality	'she wants to do the right thing'
ii) obligation	means, that a character in a story is obliged to act because of a rule or regulation	'he broke a rule'
iii) concern for others	emerges, when a character helps or intends to help others or when sympathy is shown or thought	'the boss will understand the problem and will give the worker a raise'
iv) concerns about consequences	can be identified when a character is anxious or reflects upon negative outcomes	'the captain is hesitant to let the man on board, because of his instructions'
v) self-judgment	scores when a character critically judges his or her value, morals, wisdom, self-control, etc. and has to be intrinsic	'the young man realizes he has done wrong'
Activity inhibition		
linguistic negation	in English terms, the authors describe activity inhibition as the frequency of "not" and "-n't"	responsibility measure, e.g. a variable negatively correlated with male alcohol consumption
leadership motive pattern (LMP)	combined with a high power motive (M) and low affiliation motive (A)	predicts responsible leadership power behaviors instead of profligate impulsive expressions of power
Integrative complexity		
7-point continuum range score from simplicity to	1: no sign of conceptual and differentiation or integration can be observed	only one solution is considered to be legitimate
differentiation and integration	7: overreaching	viewpoints are expressed, involving different relationships between alternate perspectives

Table 1: According to Winter (2007), some distinct psychometrics and their combinations predict social unrest – namely responsibility, activity inhibition, and integrative complexity. The table shows their categories, measurements and offer examples or explanations. Responsibility is measured with a dedicated TAT, activity inhibition (AI) and integrative complexity is determined via content analysis. Especially the combination of low responsibility, high activity inhibition and little integrative complexity (e.g. high frequency of the power motive combined with the self-regulatory 4th level) predict situations of social unrest with negative escalatory outcomes.

5 Training and experimental data

For testing the proposed hypothesis (Section 1), we first train a classification model and utilize this model for testing social network textual data. In this section, we will describe the two different data sources for training and the experiments.

5.1 Model Training Data

The data utilized for training models were made available by the organizers of the *GermEval-2020 Task 1 on the Classification and Regression of Cognitive and Motivational Style from Text.*[5][6] (Johannßen et al., 2020) The training set consists of 167,200 unique answers, given by 14,600 participants of the OMT (see Section 3. The training data set is imbalanced. The power motive (M) is the most frequent class, covering 41.02% of data points. The second most frequent class, achievement (L) only accounts for 19.63% and thus is half as frequent as M. The training data was assembled and annotated by the University of Trier, reaching a pairwise annotator intraclass correlation of r = .85. With only 22 words on average per training instance (i.e. a participant's answer) and a standard deviation of 12 words, training a classifier on this data is a short text classification task (Johannßen et al., 2020).[7]

5.2 Experimental Data

The experimental data was collected before this work by crawling the Twitter API and fetching 1 percent of the worldwide traffic of this social network (Gerlitz and Rieder, 2013). We sample posts over the time window from March to May of both, 2019 and 2020. There are no apparent linguistic differences between the two samples. The average word count, part-of-speech (POS) tags, sentence length, etc. are comparable.

Thereafter, we extracted the *text* and *date time* fields of posts marked as German. From those files hashtags, name references (starting with '@'), corrupted lines, and any post shorter than three content words were removed. The resulting files for 2019 and 2020 contained more than 1 million instances. Lastly, the instances were randomly shuffled. We drew and persisted 5,000 instances per year for the experiments, as this data set size is large enough for producing statistically significant results. The posts on average consist of 11.97 (2019) and 11.8 (2020) words per sentence, and thus are very short. During the experiments, further pre-processing steps were undertaken, which are described in Section 6. By stretching out the data collection time window and by comparing the same periods in two subsequent years, we aim to reduce any bias effect that might impact Twitter user behavior over short periods, e.g. the weather, any sports event, or short-lived political affairs.

6 Methodology for Implicit Motive Classification Social Unrest Prediction

For constructing a model of sufficient quality to test our hypothesis, we follow Johannßen and Biemann (2019) and train a long short-term memory network (LSTM, (Hochreiter and Schmidhuber, 1997)) combined with an attention mechanism.

An LSTM is a special type of recurrent neural network (RNN). An RNN not only has connections between units from layer to layer but also between units of the same layer. Furthermore an LSTM also has a mechanism called the *forget gate*, allowing the structure to determine which to keep and which information to forget during the training process. The attention mechanism (Young et al., 2018) can capture the intermediate importance of algorithmic decisions made by the network. It can be employed for enhanced results but also investigated for researching algorithmic decisions. However, it is debated upon, whether this algorithmic importance can serve as an explanation. Even though oftentimes, the algorithmic importance is correlated with an explanation for the task (i.e. does a model for image recognition of animals *look* at the animals or the backgrounds of the images?), there are cases, where algorithmic importance and explanation for the task differ (Jain and Wallace, 2019; Wiegreffe and Pinter, 2019)). Since automatically labeling implicit motives is a sequential problem revolving around identifying the first verbal enactment of a motive (see Section 3, we decided to employ a Bi-LSTM with an attention mechanism (Schuster and Paliwal, 1997).

---

[5]GermEval is a series of shared task evaluation campaigns that focus on Natural Language Processing for the German language.

[6]https://www.inf.uni-hamburg.de/en/inst/ab/lt/resources/data/germeval-2020-cognitive-motive.html

[7]The data can be retrieved via https://www.inf.uni-hamburg.de/en/inst/ab/lt/resources/data/germeval-2020-cognitive-motive.html

We decided against additional features such as part of speech (POS) tags or LIWC features like in our previous work (Johannßen and Biemann, 2019), as we did not reach the best results with these additional features. The maximum token length was set to 20, as determined by preliminary experiments (Johannßen and Biemann, 2019), and reflects the primacy rule of the implicit motive theory described in Section 3. The average answer length of the training data set was 22 tokens (see Section 5). With this decision to limit the considered tokens, we aim to closely replicate the implicit motive coding practices manually performed by trained psychologists (Kuhl and Scheffer, 1999). Accordingly, it is preferable to assign the 0 motive (i.e. no clear motive could be identified) than to falsely assign a motive that is not the very first one in the sequence.

Some standard pre-processing steps were applied to reduce noise, which was to remove the Natural Language Toolkit (NLTK) German corpus stop words[8], to lowercase the text, remove numbers, normalize special German letters (i.e. umlaute). Emojis were removed as well, since Twitter offers a selection of a 3,348 emojis[9] , that in turn mainly do not capture sufficient informational gain per textual answer for the task at hand. To remove stop words has to be an informed choice when it comes to performing NLP on psychological textual data. For example, function words are said to predict academic success (see Section 2). However, during our experiments, we saw an increase in model performance when stop words were removed.

After the training, we utilize the model on the two sampled data sets described in Subsection 5.2. According to our hypothesis in Section 1 and following the theories in Section 4, investigate the frequency of the power motive with the self-regulatory level 4, which we expect to be higher. At the same time, we will also analyze the other motives and levels to see which ones are now less frequent and to what extent. Furthermore, we compare different linguistic features and statistics from 2019 to 2020 to see, if any of these show differences that might indicate possible biases in the data.

Our Bi-LSTM model was set to be trained within 3 epochs and with a batch size of 32 instances. The model was constructed having 3 hidden layers and utilized pre-trained fasttext embeddings (Bojanowski et al., 2017), as this character-based or word fragment-based language representation has shown to be less prone to noisy data and words that have not been observed yet like e.g. spelling mistakes or slang – both often observable in social media data. The fasttext embeddings had 300 dimensions and were trained on a Twitter corpus, ideally matching the task at hand.[10] Explorative experiments with different parameter combinations have shown that a drop-out rate of .3 and step width of .001 produced good results.

The cross-entropy loss was reduced rather quickly and oscillated at 1.1 when we stopped training early during the second epoch. After each epoch, the model was evaluated on a separate development test. After the training was finished, the model was tested once on the GermEval20 Task 1 test data and with the official evaluation script. This provides the chance to compare the achieved results with the best-participating team. Schütze et al. (2020) achieved a macro f1 score of 70.40, which our Bi-LSTM model was able to outperform with an f1 score of 74.08, setting a new state of the art on this dataset.

7 Results

After having trained the Bi-LSTM model and sampled the experimental data, we will describe the results and findings of the conducted Twitter COVID-19 experiments in this section. An overview of all results is displayed in Table 2.

To investigate the main predictor for social unrest *activity inhibition* (see Section 4), the power motive (M) in combination with level 4 was counted. The self-regulatory level 4 describes the sensitivity for negative incentives (see Section 3). These measures are collected for all four data sets. Our Bi-LSTM model assigned power 4 in 33.76% of all cases for the Twitter sample from March to May of 2019, making this the most frequent label. However, for the data sample from 2020, power 4 is as frequent as

---

[8]The Natural Language Toolkit (NLTK) is a collection of python libraries for NLP `https://www.nltk.org/`.

[9]`https://emojipedia.org/twitter/twemoji-13.0.1/`

[10]The fasttext model was obtained from Spinningbytes at `http://spinningbytes.ch/resources/wordembeddings`

Metric	2019	2020	Percentage delta	Significance
Activity inhibition and responsibility				
Power 4	33.76	37.40	10.97	p<.01***
LIWC Family	.08	.05	-37.60	p<.05*
LIWC insight	.23	.17	-26.09	p<.05*
Implicit motives				
Power motive	65.84	68.24	3.64	p<.01***
Freedom motive	20.28	17.72	-12.63	p<.01***
Achievement motive	6.80	7.00	2.94	p>.05
Affiliation motive	2.00	1.86	-7.00	p>.05
Null motive	5.10	5.10	.00	p>.05
Self-regulatory levels				
Level 1	6.50	6.01	-7.54	p>.05
Level 2	2.76	3.26	18.12	p>.05
Level 3	27.20	25.58	-5.96	p<.01***
Level 4	42.78	45.20	5.67	p<.01***
Level 5	15.86	14.92	-5.93	p<.05*
Linguistic statistics				
Average words	11.97	11.80	-1.42	p>.05
Verbs	1.19	1.22	2.52	p>.05
Adjectives	.43	.43	.00	p>.05
Words >6 letters	38.65	38.86	.54	p>.05

Table 2: Overview of the different psychometric and statistical results. * represents significant results, *** represents highly significant results. All combinations of motives and levels have been examined. Note that most motives, levels, and statistical values stay constant. However, power 4 is more frequent, whilst the freedom motive is less. As the linguistic statistic metrics stay relatively stable, this indicates no observable sampling bias.

37.4%, making this an increase of 10.97%. For calculating the significance of this rise, we perform a t-test on the label confidences for the power motive with self-regulatory level 4 for both, 2019 and 2020 with the 5,000 samples from each year (see Section 5).

The two-sample t-test on the confidence levels shows, that the rise in frequency is statistically significant ($p < 0.05$ with $\bar{x}_1 = .27$, $\bar{x}_2 = .29$, $\sigma_1 = .28$, $\sigma_2 = .28$, $N_1 = 5,000$ and $N_2 = 5,000$).

The affiliation motive (A) is barely classified, covering only 2% (2019) and 1.89% (2020) of all instances. The slight decrease is not statistically significant ($p > .05$). The frequency of self-regulatory level 4 is elevated by 6.7%. The whole of all assigned power motive labels has only risen by 3.64%, both having risen less than the combination of the power motive and level 4 combined. The strongest decline in frequency can be measured for the freedom motive with -12.63%. The other motives of affiliation, achievement, and null have barely changed in comparison to 2019 with 2020. The same holds for the average amounts of words per sentence, verbs, adjectives, and words containing at least 6 letters, all of which have barely changed, not indicating sampling biases. An overview of the class frequencies is provided in Table 3.

Since both, responsibility and integrative complexity can only be measured by employing a specific TAT and a questionnaire, which would have to be performed with each Twitter user, we can only investigate activity inhibition as a combination of the power motive with the self-regulatory level 4. However, we will review some psychological LIWC categories, that follow a close description as the five categories

Implicit motive	Frequency	Self-regulatory level	Frequency
		2019	
Power	3,251	1	492
Affiliation	141	2	193
Achievement	414	3	1,487
Freedom	9622	4	1,872
Zero	232	5	724
		0	232
		2020	
Power	3,433	1	316
Affiliation	90	2	151
Achievement	203	3	1,259
Freedom	923	4	2,233
Zero	761	5	780
		0	261

Table 3: Overview of the class frequencies.

of Winter's responsibility scoring system (Winter and Barenbaum, 1985). Relevant LIWC categories for the responsibility is the combination of *family*, which are terms connected to expressions like 'son' or 'brother', and *insight*, which contain expressions such as 'think' or 'know', representing self-aware introspection. Family shows a significant decrease from 2019 (0.08) to 2020 (0.05) of -37.5%. The frequency of insight terms fell from 2019 (.23) to 2020 (.17) by -26%, all of which are statistically significant changes ($p < 0.05$ for both categories).

8 Discussion

We hypothesized that the social unrest predictors by Winter (2007), namely *activity inhibition, responsibility*, and *integrative complexity* are automatable and reveal changes in natural language and signs of social unrest observable through the use of social media textual data connected to the COVID-19 pandemic.

The main research objective of this work is to find novel approaches to automatically provide the community with red flags for growing tensions and signs of social unrest via social media textual data. For this, *activity inhibition* is the main predictor. It consists of a distinct shift in implicit motives. It is present when the frequency of the power motive with the self-regulating level 4 (sensitivity for negative incentives, see Section 3) is elevated and the affiliation motive is suppressed – even though Winter (2007) did not find clear evidence of the latter. The comparable rise by 10.97% ($p < 0.01$) is an indicator of the social tension of COVID-19 related social media posts.

Since other linguistic statistics, such as the average amounts of adjectives, verbs, words per sentence, or words containing at least 6 letters have barely changed, this indicates that the measurable differences in social unrest predictors are content-based and not due to linguistic biases.

It is remarkable, that whilst the power motive has been labeled more frequently, the frequency of the labeled freedom motive has declined by -12.63% from 2019 to 2020. This freedom motive has barely been researched yet but has a close connection to the power motive. Whilst power-motivated individuals desire control over their fellow humans and their direct surrounding for the sake of control, freedom-motivated individuals seek to express themselves and want to avoid any restraining factors. Motives are said to be rather stable but can change over time (Schultheiss and Brunstein, 2010). This change in motive direction could indicate a roughening of verbal textual content and interpersonal communication. Example utterances classified as freedom and power from 2019 compared with 2020 are displayed in Table 4.

The change of responsibility, as reflected in LIWC categories, retreated by roughly 30% from 2019 to 2020. This responsibility indicates a personal involvement in topics and decisions, that we feel are relevant for our surroundings. If this involvement diminishes, our interest in participating in constructive solutions to problems does as well.

```
M 'RT @FrauLavendel: ist es wahr          M Corona-Regeln im Saarland sind zum
  dass schulleitungen den                   Teil absurd und unverhältnismäßig
  schüler*innen drohen                    F RT @kattascha: In den USA bekommen
F RT @UteWeber: Nach einem relativ          viele Menschen keine Lohnfortzahlung
  unfeierlichen,                            im Krankheitsfall. Das bedeutet:
  regionalen Offline-Tag aufs Sofa          Selbst bei Verdacht auf #COVID19 w...
  sinken, wie von der Tarantel            A Wer einen Discord-Server sucht,
  gestochen aufspringen und zur...          um entspannt mit seinen Kollegen
A Weltbestseller "P.S. Ich liebe            zu zocken oder gemeinsam abzuhängen
  dich" bekommt einen zweiten Teil          ist hier genau...
  https://t.co/9If15CrNAP                 ------- Translation -----
------- Translation -----               M the Corona rules for the Saarland
M 'RT @FrauLavendel: is it true that        are partially absurd and dis-
  principals threatens students             proportionate
F RT @UteWeber: after a relatively      F RT @kattascha: in the US a lot
  un-celebrational, regional offline        of people don't receive continued
  day, as bitten by a tarantula             pay in case of illness. That means:
  jumping up                                even in case of suspected #COVID19
A world best-selling book "P.S. Ich     A Whoever is looking for a Discord
  liebe dich" gets a second part           server for enjoyably game with
  https://t.co/9If15CrNAP                  their colleagues or chill together,
                                           is in the right place...
```

Table 4: Some example tweets from 2019 (left) compared with 2020 (right). Whilst the power motive (M) is more frequent in 2020, the freedom motive (F) became less frequent. The affiliation motive (A) was very infrequent in both, 2019 and 2020. This signature indicates increased social unrest in 2020 in comparison with 2019.

9 Conclusion and Outlook

With this work, we conducted a first attempt at automating psychometrics for investigating social unrest in social media textual data. The Bi-LSTM model combined with an attention mechanism of this work achieved an f1 score of 74.08 on 30 target classes, making it state of the art on a respective recent shared task dataset. With this model, we measured a statistically significant rise in the power motive with self-regulating level 4, which reflects the social unrest predictor of *activity inhibition* in the direct comparison of the samples from March to May of 2019 vs. 2020.

Furthermore, we investigated *responsibility*, which shows significant reductions during the COVID-19 pandemic, hinting at negative outcomes of interpersonal and verbal communication on the social media platform Twitter.

This first approach most likely does not qualify for a real-world social prediction system. Predictions of such a system can not yet be reliable enough for deriving necessary actions from them. On the upside, implicit motives do not only qualify for examining general socio-economic tensions, but can be applied on an individual or small group scale. As an example, detecting tensions within a small group can help to shape the group and guiding it into a better fit. Furthermore, we advocate for combining implicit motives with sufficiently many complementary psychometrics and content-based analysis e.g. sentiment analysis, topic modeling, or emotion detection.

Besides those combinations with other information sources for future work, different sampling approaches and larger data set sizes should be utilized for reproducing findings and research correlations with other social unrest predictors and indicators. In this work, we have made the first steps towards understanding the automation of psychological findings. Since only 5,000 samples were drawn from a single social network platform, we advocate for broadening this approach to include many more samples from wider time windows paired with mixing the data sources. In addition to that, deeper investigations into the linguistic variances between times of so-called social unrest and more peaceful times should be performed, as those could reveal patterns and characteristics of time-specific utterances.

Even though this work is only introductory, the observed correlations and social unrest patterns are in line with an intuitive assumption of how language in social media data changes amid a pandemic. Future work arises in the application of this methodology on other events and crises, eventually providing a quantitative basis for implicit motive research.

References

David M. Blei, Andrew Y. Ng, and Michael I. Jordan. 2003. Latent dirichlet allocation. *Journal of machine Learning research*, 3(Jan):993–1022.

Jack Block. 1995. A contrarian view of the five-factor approach to personality description. *Psychological Bulletin*, 117(2):187–215.

Piotr Bojanowski, Edouard Grave, Armand Joulin, and Tomas Mikolov. 2017. Enriching Word Vectors with Subword Information. *Transactions of the Association for Computational Linguistics*, 5:135–146.

Joachim C. Brunstein. 2008. Implicit and explicit motives. *Motivation and Action*, pages 227–246.

Thomas Chadefaux. 2012. Early Warning Signals for War in the News. *Journal of Peace Research*, 51(1).

Matthew Gentzkow, Bryan Kelly, and Matt Taddy. 2019. Text as Data. *Journal of Economic Literature*, 57(3):535–574.

Carolin Gerlitz and Bernhard Rieder. 2013. Mining One Percent of Twitter: Collections, Baselines, Sampling. *M/C Journal*, 16(2), nr.620.

Lewis R. Goldberg. 1981. Language and individual differences: The search for universals in personality lexicons. *Review of personality and social psychology*, 2(1):141–165.

Roxana Gutiérrez-Romero. 2020. Conflict in Africa during COVID-19: social distancing, food vulnerability and welfare response. *SSRN Electronic Journal*. ID 3616421.

Stephen Hibbard. 2003. A critique of Lilienfeld et al.'s (2000) "The scientific status of projective techniques". *Journal of Personality Assessment*, 80(3):260–271.

Sepp Hochreiter and Jürgen Schmidhuber. 1997. Long Short-term Memory. *Neural computation*, 9:1735–1780.

Robert Hogenraad. 2003. The Words that Predict the Outbreak of Wars. *Empirical Studies of the Arts*, 21:5–20.

Sarthak Jain and Byron C. Wallace. 2019. Attention is not Explanation. *arXiv:1902.10186 [cs]*.

Dirk Johannßen and Chris Biemann. 2018. Between the Lines: Machine Learning for Prediction of Psychological Traits - A Survey. In *Proceedings of the International Cross-Domain Conference*, pages 192–211, Hamburg, Germany. Springer.

Dirk Johannßen and Chris Biemann. 2019. Neural classification with attention assessment of the implicit-association test OMT and prediction of subsequent academic success. In *Proceedings of the 15th Conference on Natural Language Processing (KONVENS 2019): Long Papers*, pages 68–78, Erlangen, Germany. German Society for Computational Linguistics & Language Technology.

Dirk Johannßen, Chris Biemann, and David Scheffer. 2019. Reviving a psychometric measure: Classification of the Operant Motive Test. In *Proceedings of the Sixth Annual Workshop on Computational Linguistics and Clinical Psychology (CLPsych)*, pages 121–125, Minneapolis, MN, USA. Association for Computational Linguistics.

Dirk Johannßen, Chris Biemann, Steffen Remus, Timo Baumann, and David Scheffer. 2020. GermEval 2020 Task 1 on the Classification and Regression of Cognitive and Motivational style from Text. In *Proceedings of the GermEval 2020 Task 1 Workshop in conjunction with the 5th SwissText & 16th KONVENS Joint Conference 2020*, pages 1–10, Zurich, Switzerland (online). German Society for Computational Linguistics & Language Technology.

Fredrik Johansson, Joel Brynielsson, Pontus Hörling, Michael Malm, Christian Mårtenson, Staffan Truvé, and Magnus Rosell. 2011. Detecting Emergent Conflicts through Web Mining and Visualization. In *Proceedings - 2011 European Intelligence and Security Informatics Conference, EISIC 2011*, pages 346 – 353, Athens, Greece. Springer.

Evangelos Kalampokis, Efthimios Tambouris, and Konstantinos Tarabanis. 2013. Understanding the Predictive Power of Social Media. *Internet Research*, 23(5).

Julius Kuhl and David Scheffer. 1999. *Der operante Multi-Motiv-Test (OMT): Manual [The operant multi-motive-test (OMT): Manual]*. Impart, Osnabrück, Germany: University of Osnabrück.

Julius Kuhl. 2001. *Motivation und Persönlichkeit: Interaktionen psychischer Systeme*. Hogrefe Verlag, Göttingen, Germany.

Andrey Kutuzov, Erik Velldal, and Lilja Øvrelid. 2019. One-to-X Analogical Reasoning on Word Embeddings: a Case for Diachronic Armed Conflict Prediction from News Texts. In *Proceedings of the 1st International Workshop on Computational Approaches to Historical Language Change*, pages 196–201, Florence, Italy. Association for Computational Linguistics.

Veronica Lynn, Niranjan Balasubramanian, and Hansen A. Schwartz. 2020. Hierarchical Modeling for User Personality Prediction: The Role of Message-Level Attention. In *Proceedings of the 58th Annual Meeting of the Association for Computational Linguistics*, pages 5306–5316, Online. Association for Computational Linguistics.

David C. McClelland and Richard Boyatzis. 1982. Leadership Motive Pattern and Long-Term Success in Management. *Journal of Applied Psychology*, 67:737–743.

David C. McClelland and William N. Davis. 1972. *The Drinking Man: Alcohol and Human Motivation*. Free Press, New York.

David C. McClelland. 1988. *Human Motivation*. Cambridge University Press.

Robert R. McCrae and Paul T. Costa Jr. 1999. A Five-Factor theory of personality. In *Handbook of personality: Theory and research, 2nd ed*, pages 139–153. Guilford Press, New York, NY, US.

Hannes Mueller and Christopher Rauh. 2017. Reading Between the Lines: Prediction of Political Violence Using Newspaper Text. *American Political Science Review*, 112:1–18.

Henry A. Murray. 1943. *Thematic Apperception Test*. Harvard University Press.

James W. Pennebaker and Laura King. 2000. Linguistic styles: Language use as an individual difference. *Journal of personality and social psychology*, 77:1296–312.

James W. Pennebaker, Martha E. Francis, and Roger J. Booth. 1999. Linguistic inquiry and word count (LIWC). *Software manual*.

James W. Pennebaker, Cindy K. Chung, Joey Frazee, Gary M. Lavergne, and David I. Beaver. 2014. When Small Words Foretell Academic Success: The Case of College Admissions Essays. *PLOS ONE*, 9(12):e115844.

David A. Reuman. 1982. Ipsative behavioral variability and the quality of thematic apperceptive measurement of the achievement motive. *Journal of Personality and Social Psychology*, 43(5):1098–1110.

David Scheffer and Julius Kuhl. 2013. *Auswertungsmanual für den Operanten Multi-Motiv-Test OMT*. sonderpunkt Verlag, Münster, Germany.

Oliver C. Schultheiss and Joachim C. Brunstein. 2010. *Implicit Motives*. Oxford Univ Pr, Oxford ; New York, 1 edition.

Mike Schuster and Kuldip K. Paliwal. 1997. Bidirectional recurrent neural networks. *IEEE Transactions on Signal Processing*, 45(11):2673–2681.

Henning Schäfer, Ahmad Idrissi-Yaghir, Andreas Schimanowski, Michael R. Bujotzek, Hendrik Damm, Jannis Nagel, and Christoph M. Friedrich. 2020. Predicting Cognitive and Motivational Style from German Text using Multilingual Transformer Architecture. In *Proceedings of the GermEval 2020 Task 1 Workshop in conjunction with the 5th SwissText & 16th KONVENS Joint Conference 2020*, pages 17–22, Zurich, Switzerland (online). German Society for Computational Linguistics & Language Technology.

Edward Tighe and Charibeth Cheng. 2018. Modeling Personality Traits of Filipino Twitter Users. In *Proceedings of the Second Workshop on Computational Modeling of People's Opinions, Personality, and Emotions in Social Media*, pages 112–122, Louisiana, LA, USA. Association for Computational Linguistics.

Sarah Wiegreffe and Yuval Pinter. 2019. Attention is not not Explanation. *arXiv:1908.04626 [cs]*. arXiv: 1908.04626.

David G. Winter and Nicole B. Barenbaum. 1985. Responsibility and the power motive in women and men. *Journal of Personality*, 53(2):335–355.

David G. Winter. 2007. The Role of Motivation, Responsibility, and Integrative Complexity in Crisis Escalation: Comparative Studies of War and Peace Crises. *Journal of personality and social psychology*, 92:920–37.

Markus Wolf, Andrea B. Horn, Matthias R. Mehl, Severin Haug, James W. Pennebaker, and Hans Kordy. 2008. Computergestützte quantitative Textanalyse: Äquivalenz und Robustheit der deutschen Version des Linguistic Inquiry and Word Count. *Diagnostica*, 54(2):85–98.

Kosuke Yamada, Ryohei Sasano, and Koichi Takeda. 2019. Incorporating Textual Information on User Behavior for Personality Prediction. In *Proceedings of the 57th Annual Meeting of the Association for Computational Linguistics: Student Research Workshop*, pages 177–182, Florence, Italy. Association for Computational Linguistics.

Tom Young, Devamanyu Hazarika, Soujanya Poria, and Erik Cambria. 2018. Recent Trends in Deep Learning Based Natural Language Processing [Review Article]. *IEEE Computational Intelligence Magazine*, 13:55–75.

Topic and Emotion Development among Dutch COVID-19 Twitter Communities in the early Pandemic

Boris Marinov*, **Jennifer Spenader***, **Tommaso Caselli**⊖,
*Department of Artificial Intelligence, ⊖CLCG
⊖*University of Groningen, Groningen, The Netherlands
`boris.marinov96@gmail.com,`
`{j.k.spenader,t.caselli}@rug.nl,`

Abstract

The paper focuses on a large collection of Dutch tweets to gain insight into the perception and reactions of users during the early months of the COVID-19 pandemic. We focused on five major communities of users: government and health organizations, news media, politicians, the general public and conspiracy theory supporters, investigating differences among them in topic dominance and the expressions of emotions. Through topic modeling we monitor the evolution of the conversation about COVID-19 among these communities. Our results indicate that the focus on COVID-19 shifted from the virus itself to its impact on the economy between February and April. Surprisingly, the overall emotional public response appears to be substantially positive and expressing trust, although differences can be observed in specific groups of users.

1 Introduction

During the early COVID-19 pandemic, Twitter has played a key role in facilitating communication from government agencies and officials, but also among members of the general public. Twitter content has thus had a major influence on the public perception and sentiment surrounding the developing COVID-19 situation around the world. In this work, we conduct an exploratory study to investigate potential quantitative differences in topic dominance and emotional content between different user communities. To better focus our study, we restrict the the analysis to Dutch Twitter during the first three months of the COVID-19 pandemic.

Many individuals rely on Twitter for information. In the United States, 68% of people reported social media as their "news-outlets" (Matsa and Shearer, 2018), with a third of people also claiming that social media is an important source of health and science information (Hitlin and Olmstead, 2018). These figures are not surprising, since many official agencies, e.g. the government and health organizations, increasingly use Twitter to communicate key information to the public. This is in part because research has shown that Twitter can be particularly effective during rapidly developing events, such as disasters, political unrest, and outbreaks (Househ, 2016; LaLone et al., 2017; Daughton and Paul, 2019; Rogers et al., 2019). For example, during the 2015 Zika virus outbreak, credible organizations such as the World Health Organization (WHO) and the Center for Disease Control (CDC) used Twitter to circulate important health information (Stefanidis et al., 2017).

As there is no gate-keeping on the platform, content quality varies widely, from informal comments by private individuals to official communications from the government. Some content is made up of misinformation, rumors, and false statements, that are then massively circulated via the platform (Kumar and Geethakumari, 2014; Hamidian and Diab, 2016; Li et al., 2019). For this reason, studying the topics and emotional content of different user communities around a major public event (the COVID-19 pandemic) can give us important insights into both the public perception of the situation, the response of official agencies, and the general sentiment as the pandemic developed.

Proceedings of the Third Workshop on Computational Modeling of PEople's Opinions, PersonaLity, and Emotions in Social media, pages 87–98
Barcelona, Spain (Online), December 13, 2020.

The first case in The Netherlands was reported on the 27th of February.[1] While a growing number of papers that analyze Twitter activity during the pandemic have already come out (Ordun et al., 2020; Chen et al., 2020; Schild et al., 2020), they largely focus on the situation in the United States, or other English speaking countries. Instead, we focus primarily on tweets from The Netherlands or Belgium, only considering Dutch language data. This allows us to study the direct relation between disease spread, government response and the public sentiment on a more local scale. Dutch tweets are almost exclusively tweeted by individuals or organizations within the Netherlands, the Flemish area of Belgium, or, to a lesser extent by Dutch individuals abroad.This contrasts with English tweets which are more heterogeneous since English has a larger group of speakers and users. In particular we address the following questions:

RQ1 How varied is the discourse around COVID-19 by Dutch speaking communities? What topics dominate?

RQ2 Do different users (e.g., politicians, journalists, influencers, active and casual users, among others) focus on different topics related to the COVID-19 outbreak?

RQ3 Do different users express different emotions about the COVID-19 outbreak?

The main contributions of this paper can be summarized as follows: (1) we conduct an extensive analysis of a newly created and publicly available Dutch Twitter dataset (Caselli and Basile, 2020) covering the first three months of the COVID-19 pandemic; (2) we found commonalities across user communities, but also different identifiable focuses, and (3) we identify community differences also in the emotional spectrum. Our analysis characterizes the evolution of the discourse around COVID-19 in Dutch speaking communities between February and April 2020, both in the topics that dominated and in the emotions expressed that reflect differences across Twitter communities during this virtual national conversation.

2   Related Works

Twitter has been largely used as a proxy of natural language data for the study of different socio-demographics issues of a target population. Previous work ranges from the identification of personality traits (Plank and Hovy, 2015), expressions of emotions (Hagen et al., 2015; Dini and Bittar, 2016), language use (Blodgett et al., 2016), age (Sloan et al., 2015), gender (Rangel et al., 2017), and authorship attributions (Schwartz et al., 2013; Rangel et al., 2017), among others. Previous attempts at community detection of Twitter users have used numerous methods and classification types, categorizing users based on their tweet context (Java et al., 2007), interaction and topics in the network (Darmon et al., 2014; Bakillah et al., 2015), sentiment oriented approaches (Abel et al., 2011; Cao et al., 2015) and following-to-followers ratio (Krishnamurthy et al., 2008).

Topic modeling has been widely and successfully used as a distant reading method to explore massive amounts of data and identify clusters of information (Yang et al., 2011; Ritter et al., 2010; Sarioglu et al., 2013; Schöch, 2017). The application of these approaches to Twitter data is a challenging task due to the short nature of the texts (Hong and Davison, 2010). Previous work has mainly applied Latent Dirichlet Allocation (LDA) based methods (Blei et al., 2003) with varying degree of success. The main issue is that LDA works under the assumption that a document can belong to multiple topics, where the membership is determined by some probability over the words. Since tweets are short snippets of text communicating often one single thought, they are instead more likely to contain only a single topic (2018). For this reason, we make use of the recently proposed semantics-assisted non-negative matrix factorization method (SeaNMF), (Shi et al., 2018).

There is already a growing number of published research studies where a range of different analyses, including sentiment and public response, have been applied to COVID-19 social media (Sharma et al., 2020; Ordun et al., 2020). However, as far as we know, no research has focused in detail on a single country and its social media response.

---

[1] https://www.rivm.nl/en/novel-coronavirus-covid-19/current-information

3 Data Collection and Cleaning

We conducted our analysis on a newly created dataset, `40twene_nl` (Caselli and Basile, 2020).[2] The messages have been extracted from an on-going and continuous collection of Twitter messages in Dutch (Sang, 2011; Bouma, 2015) by means of a selection of relevant keywords. Keyword identification was done manually by monitoring a trend website [3] from February to April 2020. For each day, top trending and COVID-19 related hashtags were extracted. To ensure variability and limit biases, the selection of the keywords was conducted by considering the trends during different moments of each day (i.e., morning, afternoon, evening, night). This resulted in 39 unique keywords which have been applied to obtain the messages in the selected periods of time. The keywords are not preprocessed (e.g., lemmatization or stemming) and instead only exact matches were looked for in hashtags or messages. Retweets have been excluded since they would have added noise. The dataset contains 2,390,596 tweets and only the Twitter IDs are distributed. We have used Hydrator[4] to retrieve the texts of the tweets and all associated metadata, including the geolocalization, the user screen name, the user name, the user description, the timestamp, the number of likes, the number of retweets, the geographical coordinates, and the place. The use of keywords may have introduced bias in the selection of the data by excluding non-Dutch speaking users living in The Netherlands or Belgium. This may result in a less representative analysis of the whole populations, with some minority voices "not being heard".

3.1 Preprocessing

Basic preprocessing is conducted to prepare the data. In particular, we have cleaned the data by (1) removal of duplicate tweets and tweets that have been deleted; (2) removal of hyperlinks (3) lower casing (4) removal of all keywords used for collecting the data; (5) removal of stop words;[5] (6) lemmatization and removal of closed-class words;[6] (7) removal of numerals and user mentions.

After preprocessing, 2,390,487 tweets remained (55,600 for February, 1,396,408 for March and 938,479 for April). Figure 1 illustrates the daily frequency of the tweets in the dataset, as well as some key dates of the evolution of the pandemic in the Netherlands.[7] Peaks around key dates indicate a link between the frequency and the occurring events, with a pattern similar to that of previous studies during past outbreaks (Shin et al., 2016).

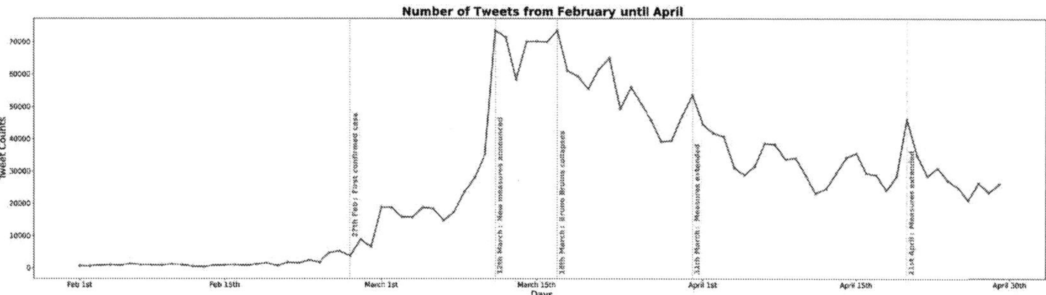

Figure 1: Daily Tweet frequencies from February to April

4 What's the Buzz About #COVID19_NL?

The `40twene_nl` collection has been specifically designed to identify messages about the COVID-19 in Dutch. The first step in our analysis is to determine whether this conversation about the pandemic has

---

[2] `https://osf.io/pfnur/?view_only=5cc01c6cadc8441eb47659459fd5db10`

[3] `https://getdaytrends.com`

[4] `https://github.com/DocNow/hydrator`

[5] We extended the original list for Dutch available in NLTK with additional data from this web-page: `https://eikhart.com/blog/dutch-stopwords-list`

[6] We used Frog (Bosch et al., 2007); closed-class words have been deleted if Frog assigned a probability higher or equal than 0.7. We did not further evaluate the quality of Frog on tweets.

[7] `https://en.wikipedia.org/wiki/COVID-19_pandemic_in_the_Netherlands#1120_March`

been characterized by the presence of different issues.

Hashtags and mentions are an important Twitter feature and can give a good initial overview into conversations on the platform. Mentions are used by users to notify others of the post, while hashtags allow for easier searching and grouping of tweets. Table 1 summarizes the top 5 hashtags and mentions for each month (hashtags containing *corona* or *covid* not included in count). For February the hashtags are more concerned with events happening outside of the Netherlands, however for March and April more relevant and local events can be seen (food hoarding, wearing of masks, working from home). The mentions for all months are largely centered around RIVM and particular politicians as one would expect. The number of mentions towards politicians does however increase in March and April compared to February, suggesting a reliance on the countries' leaders.

Table 1: Top 5 hashtags and mentions across February, March and April, with English translations\ explanations.

February		March		April	
Hashtag	English	**Hashtag**	English	**Hashtag**	English
1. #rivm	*Dutch CDC*	1. #rivm	*Dutch CDC*	1. #blifthuis	*stay home*
2. #china	*China*	2. #blifthuis	*stay home*	2. #persconferentie	*press conference*
3. #virus	*virus*	3. #hamsteren	*hoarding*	3. #rivm	*Dutch CDC*
4. #wuhan	*Wuhan*	4. #rutte	*Dutch PM*	4. #rutte	*Dutch PM*
5. #italie	*Italy*	5. #thuiswerken	*work from home*	5. #thuiswerken	*work from home*
Mention	English	**Mention**	English	**Mention**	English
1. @rivm	*Dutch CDC*	1. @rivm	*Dutch CDC*	1. @rivm	*Dutch CDC*
2. @nos	*Nat. TV News*	2. @minpres	*Prime minister*	2. @minpres	*Prime minister*
3. @telegraaf	*Nat. Newspaper*	3. @telegraf	*Nat.newspaer*	3. @telegraaf	*Nat.newspaper*
4. @nunl	*Nu.nl, News site*	4. @nos	*Nat.TV news*	4. @nos	*Dutch PM*
5. @coronanederland	*Corona Netherlands*	5. @theirrybaudet	*Right wing politician*	5. @hugodejonge	*Health minister*

4.1 Topic Modeling

We next conducted a topic modeling analysis as a method to aggregate messages and identify informative clusters of similar words, i.e., topics. Given that the keywords in `40twene_nl` are stable across time, this collection appears to be particularly suitable both for monitoring topic changes over time (i.e., from February to April 2020) and for comparing topic dominance differences between groups of users.

We apply a recently proposed method based on semantics-assisted non-negative matrix factorization (SeaNMF) (Shi et al., 2018). Existing NMF methods learn topics by decomposing the term-document matrix into lower ranked matrices, demonstrating strong performances in dimension reductions and clustering for high-dimensional data (Choo et al., 2015), with the approach being successfully applied to topic modeling (Kim et al., 2015). SeaNMF builds on top of this by leveraging word-context semantic correlations during training, overcoming the sparse problems of short texts and outperforming typically used LDA models.

Two important parameters of SeaNMF are the number of topics and the α value (weight for factorizing the word semantic correlation matrix). Setting α to 1 leads to best results,[8] while the number of topics is varied to investigate if there are differences across the three months concerning the narratives around COVID-19. Four evaluations are used to judge the fit of the model: **Average Pointwise Mutual Information (APMI)** and **Normalized PMI (NPI)** indicate how well the words in each topic relate to each other (relying on co-occurance); while **topic diversity (TD)** and **rank-biased overlap (RBO)** measure the diversity of the topics (Bianchi et al., 2020). We report in Table 2 the results of the evaluation of the SeaNMF models for each month separately. The number of topics ranges between 30 and 150, with increasing steps of 20, thus exploring different granularities of aggregation.

4.2 Topic Modeling Findings

In general, we obtain relatively high scores compared to other works on clustering twitter data (Cheng et al., 2014; Bianchi et al., 2020).We consider this as additional evidence of the homogeneity of the

---

[8]The threshold of the α value is based on evidence from literature, namely Shi et al. (2018)

Table 2: Topic modeling evaluation per month (scores for the optimal number of topics are in bold). NPI was used to finally select the optimal number of topics

Number Topics	February				March				April			
	APMI	NPMI	TD	RBO	APMI	NPMI	TD	RBO	APMI	NPMI	TD	RBO
30	3.0529	0.2589	0.9933	0.9998	2.0278	0.1637	0.8833	0.9930	2.2268	0.1752	0.9500	0.9975
50	3.3987	0.2669	0.9860	0.9997	2.1632	0.1854	0.8640	0.9938	2.4016	0.2055	0.9140	0.9954
70	3.7174	0.2719	0.9786	0.9996	2.4076	0.2111	0.8514	0.9937	2.6059	0.2242	0.9243	0.9980
90	3.9307	0.2896	0.9756	0.9997	**2.4083**	**0.2138**	**0.8389**	**0.9952**	2.6777	0.2297	0.9111	0.9984
110	**4.1662**	**0.3093**	**0.9773**	**0.9998**	2.3602	0.2059	0.8291	0.9958	**2.7358**	**0.2306**	**0.8955**	**0.9982**
130	4.1329	0.2911	0.9669	0.9997	2.3992	0.2093	0.8223	0.9964	2.7059	0.2269	0.8885	0.9983
150	4.2502	0.3016	0.9707	0.9997	2.5140	0.2177	0.8160	0.9969	2.777	0.2289	0.882	0.9985

`40twene_nl`, and as a cue that the topics we have induced are potentially indicating specific sub-topics on COVID-19 in Dutch.

The topic evaluation measures each emphasize different aspects. The scores for TD and its sister measure RBO are both high, indicating that the induced topic clusters are well differentiated from each other. However, TD has a different behavior when compared to RBO in assessing topic diversity. In February, TD and RBO substantially remained unchanged; while we observe a lowering of TD when larger numbers of topics are selected, but scores for both measures are in the range of 0.90s. A similar behavior can be observed in April, although the scores of both measures start to diverge at 110 topics, suggesting a lower quality of the generated topics. March, however, stands out. While RBO remains substantially unchanged across the number of topics, TD keeps degrading, suggesting less diversity in the topics. Similar observations hold for the scores of the APMI and NPMI. When combining all measures together, it appears that NPMI could be used to discriminate what would be an optimal number of topics for each month. In particular, as soon as the NPMI score stops increasing, we selected the corresponding number of topics as the best. For February and April we identify this threshold at 110, while for March this lies at 90.

The variation across the months is small, despite the fact that March has substantially more tweets than the other two months (1,396,408 *vs.* 55,600 for February and 938,479 for April). However, this is an indication of a variation in the way Twitter users were talking about the outbreak. Table 3 outlines the top 5 topics per month. Labels have been manually assigned by one of the authors according to the keywords. Looking at the table we see that in February, the outbreak was still perceived as something far away from the Netherlands or Belgium, with focus on China and global events. This changes in March where the situation moves from global to local, with a larger focus on the infections and dealing with the new way of life. In April, the infections are improving, with focus on the COVID-19 consequences on the economy and a renewed interest in the world-wide situation.

Table 3: Top 5 topics for each month

February	March	April
COVID-19 China: 31.26%	COVID-19 Netherlands: 15.02%	Economy: 11.58%
Early COVID-19: 20.36%	Infections: 9.79%	Government: 5.38%
Global Issues: 9.04%	Economy: 6.86%	Global Issues: 5.35%
COVID-19 Europe: 6.47%	Government: 6.64%	Measures: 5.27%
Measures: 3.97%	Global Issues: 4.73%	COVID-19 Europe: 4.94%

5 Emotional and Discourse Analysis of Users' Language

To gain better insightswe computed two emotional prior scores for the messages by means of a lexicon look up approach. The lexicon used for this was the Dutch version of the NRC Emotional Lexicon (Mohammad and Turney, 2013) that contains emotion association scores for 14,182 words for 10 different emotions, each represented by a score between 0 or 1. Two additional columns for the word lemma and stem have also been added, to increase the likelihood of finding a match.

The first emotional score, called **Polarity Score**, assigns a positive or negative score to every message on the basis of the scores associated to the entries in the NRC Lexicon. To make the score operational, emotions that in the lexicon that are deemed to be negative (e.g., "Anger", "Disgust", "Fear" and "Sadness"), have their scores inverted and ambiguous ones have been excluded. To compute this score, we go over each word in every tweet and attempt to find a match in the lexicon. If an entry is found, all associated scores for the emotional categories are added up. In case multiple entries are found, the scores are again added up and an average score is returned. This score indicates the actual emotion directionality carried by a tweet, influenced by positive and negative words within it, rather than the dominant emotion label.

The second emotional score, that we called **Emotional Load**, aims at assessing the emotional weight of the messages, i.e., how many emotions a message has. We compute the users' Emotional Load by assigning a point any time that a word in a message matches an entry in the NRC lexicon. The procedure of computing the score is similar to that of the **Polarity Score**, however the lexicon is left unchanged and negative emotions are not inverted. For each found word in a tweet, the scores in the entry are added up. Similarly as before, in case multiple entries are found, the total added scores are averaged out.

Emojis are also included in the score calculation of both measures. A different lexicon was used for this (Novak et al., 2015), with the lexicon containing sentiment scores for each emoji. For the Emotional Load, each detected emoji simply adds 1 to the score, while for the Polarity Score, the actual emotion score of the corresponding emoji is used.

We applied these measures to specific groups of users corresponding to socio-demographic categories of interest. In particular, we wanted to investigate if there are differences among five major societal actors: governmental and public health organizations, news media (i.e., TVs, radios, newspapers), politicians, the general public, and promoters/supporters of conspiracy theories. These groups have been selected as they appear to play different roles with respect to the impact of COVID-19. Governmental and public health organizations are in charge of everyday management and decisions which impact on the population; news media are responsible for setting the tone and the narratives about COVID-19; politicians represent the connecting elements between the government and the different groups of interest they represent; the general population is somehow a passive actor who undergoes the decisions of the government; conspiracy theory activists promote "alternative facts" on COVID-19, are responsible for spreading misinformation, and build narratives that directly oppose those of governments and news media.

The identification and clustering of the users in socio-demographic categories has been conducted as follows: first, we have distinguished the authors of the tweets into verified and non-verified users. User names are cleaned to only include alphabetic characters. We then conducted a semi-automatic automatic entity linking by associating the screen names to Wikipedia entry. Ideally the screen name would return a single entry with the needed information in the form of a summary page. Each retrieved Wikipedia summary is then further matched with a set of pre-defined keywords characterizing every target group extracted from the user description. In case a screen name returned multiple Wikipedia entries, a summary is taken from each and the matching process repeated. After this first pass, we manually checked that the automatically assigned labels were correct. A limitation of this strategy is that the lack of Wikipedia entry places the target users in the general population. As a strategy to compensate this potential generalization of users in the general public demographic, we further distinguished in the general population all verified accounts from the rest. Verified accounts in Twitter are used to signal the authenticity of the accounts of users of public interest. The conspiracy theory activists are found by searching for users whose messages contained the "5G" keyword.

5.1 Emotional Content Findings

Table 4 reports the percentages of tweets per user category for which, respectively, no matches, a single match, or multiple matches were found in the NRC Dutch version of the lexicon. [9] Quite surprisingly, we observe that for all user categories, between 88% to 96% of the tweets have one or more corresponding entries in the lexicon, besides some translation errors.

Table 5 illustrates the results of the Polarity Score and the Emotional Load for each category of users.

---

[9]For the General Population (Non-Verified) a random sample of 40,000 messages was selected for the scores

Table 4: Lexicon coverage per user category.

User Category	0 matches (%)	1 match (%)	> 1 matches (%)
Politicians	0.66	2.37	96.97
News Media	2.85	8.49	88.66
Government/Health Organizations	0.61	2.94	96.45
General Population (Verified)	2.5	7.3	90.20
General Population (Non-Verified)	2.14	6.24	91.62
Conspiracy Theory	1.71	5.16	93.13

Table 5: Polarity Score and Emotional Load scores for each of the selected category of users.

User Category	Number of Users	Number of Tweets	Polarity Score	Emotional Load
Politicians	150	4826	0.7387	9.0370
News Media	142	26072	-0.3051	5.7403
Government/Health Organizations	62	3101	0.9848	8.3099
General Population (Verified)	1082	43037	0.2113	6.4115
General Population (Non-Verified)	226146	2366469	0.1150	7.3628
Conspiracy Theory	8195	14291	-0.2446	7.3212

For completeness, we also report the number of identified users per category and their associated tweets.

The Polarity Score clearly indicates that there are differences in the directionality of the expressed emotions in the messages across the various categories. We can observe that Politicians and Governmental/Health Organizations express very high positive emotions with scores very near to the maximum level, i.e., 1. This clearly marks a distinctive element for both types of users: they are the main actors in the management and containment of the virus among the population. Their communication is oriented to express positive messages showing leadership, unity, and solutions to the problem. On the opposite side, we find the News Media and the Conspiracy Theory groups. In both cases, negative polarity scores are expected, although for different reasons. News Media in the time period we have considered were focused on reporting the number of new infected cases, number of death, people in intensive care units, job losses, and, more in general, the impact of the lockdown on the Dutch society. Although there were also positive messages, the majority of the news events that were covered is associated with negative emotions, boosting an already existing trend of News Media on bad news (Thompson et al., 2017). One of the main activities of conspiracy theories is counteract the official narratives. In this specific case, their messages have an opposite tone with respect to the Politicians and Governmental/Health Organizations. Indeed, a recurrent theme is accusing both these categories of lying and having creating this crisis to increase their control on the population. The remaining two categories, expression of the population at large, are associated with a positive Polarity Score. For both groups the scores are the lowest when compared to the other user groups, and with the verified account being higher than the non-verified ones (0.2113 *vs.* 0.1150, respectively). It thus appears that verified accounts have contributed to promote a positive attitude in the time of the crisis, in line with the communication of other public figures such as Politicians and Government/Health Organizations. Such a positive attitude is also mirrored, although with lesser intensity, by the population at large (i.e., the non-verified accounts).

Table 6 reports the distribution of the polarity per class (i.e., scores are not summed) and the average polarity values.

Table 6: Polarity Scores: percentages of tweets per polarity class and average polarity per class for each of the user categories.

User Category	% Positive	Average score positive	% Negative	Average score negative
Politicians	50.27	3.54	30.33	-3.44
News Media	33.38	2.81	40.49	-3.07
Government/Health Organizations	52.11	3.70	28.64	-3.30
General Population (Verified)	41.01	3.14	34.17	-3.15
General Population (Non-Verified)	40.72	3.30	34.89	-3.52
Conspiracy Theory	37.26	3.16	39.54	-3.60

We observe that the averages for both the positive and negative Polarity Scores are roughly similar across all user categories, with the News Media being a slight exception with the lowest positive average of 2.81. The lower Polarity Scores observed in Table 5 is due to the distribution of the messages in the positive and negative classes, indicating that contrasting emotions are at play and tends to compensate in our computation of the Polarity Score.

The only analysis to which we make a tentative comparison with our results is EmoItaly[10], a study that quantified emotions in Italy from January to May 2020. EmoItaly uses a similar approach to automatically identify the emotions, i.e., dictionary lookup using the Italian version of the NRC lexicon. However, it differs from our method because it computes the global "amount" for each emotion label (i.e., a weight for each emotion, rather than a dominant emotion). Besides this difference, on the basis of the reported results, it appears that the general population in Italy had a much more negative attitude than in the Netherlands during the same period.

When focusing on the Emotional Load, quite surprisingly Politicians and Governmental/Health Organizations are the groups of users that tend to have high levels of emotions in their messages. On the other hand, News Media accounts are least emotionally loaded. However, this low level of emotions, which may reflect specific lexical choices in the framing of news, is not mirrored in low levels of Polarity Scores. In contrast, the remainder of the user groups have comparable scores. However, the connection between Emotional Load and Polarity Score can be used to get additional insights on the behavior of these category of users. Given the way the Polarity Score is computed, these low values (all ranging between 0.24 and 0.10) should also be read as cues of conflicting emotions.

To better assess the differences across the categories we ran two statistical tests. First, we used a Kruskal-Wallis test across all groups. The results indicates that both for the Polarity Score (Chi square = 3047, DF = 5, p-value<0.05) and the Emotional Load (Chi square = 3047, DF = 5, p-value<0.05), the differences are statistically significant. Further we ran a pairwise comparison using a Wilcoxon rank sum test. The results show that both for the Polarity Score and the Emotional Load, the differences across the groups are significant (p-value<0.05), with the exception of the pair General Population (Non-Verified) and Conspiracy Theory (p-value>0.05).

5.2 Top Emotions and Topics Across User Groups

We further investigated two additional aspects connected with the selected groups, namely the dominant emotion and the associated topics, and their evolution in the selected time period. The emotion labels correspond to prior values, obtained by means of a dictionary look-up approach using the NRC Dutch Lexicon. Results are illustrated in Table 7.

As far as the topics are concerned, the patterns we have already observed in Table 3 is actually mirrored by the users. In February, COVID-19 is still perceived as something that is not affecting the Netherlands. Politicians mention COVID-19 as something that is related to China but are still concerned with other, more generic, issues (e.g., Politics, News Outlets, and Global Issues). On the other hand, COVID-19 is already quite central in the discussions of all the other groups. News Media are reporting potential early cases of COVID-19 and are initiating a discussion on the economic impact of the disease. The General Population (Non-Verified) discusses the spread of the disease across Europe and also about the measures being adopted to limit the spreading. This latter aspect is also present in the Conspiracy Theory group, although it represents a larger number of messages than in all other groups (i.e., 7.37%), showing a bigger sensitivity to the topic. Governmental and Health Organizations both stress that COVID-19 is a Chinese issue. However, we can observe that a portion of the messages are also dedicated to the discussion of measures against COVID-19 and its impact in the country. After the onset of the outbreak, March sees big changes in all groups. References to China have basically disappeared from the public conversation. The focus now is on the Netherlands and in Europe. With the exception of Politicians, all other groups are mainly concerned about the number of daily infections. Governmental/Health Organizations also appear to be mainly concerned about making the population aware of the measures to control the spreading (i.e., wash your hand frequently and remain at home as much as possible). Politicians, on the other hand, are mainly concerned with the economic impact of COVID-19. April shows a further change in

---

[10]http://corpora.ficlit.unibo.it/EmoItaly/

Table 7: Top 5 dominant topics and emotions for each user category.

User Category	February Topics		February Emotions		March Topics		March Emotions		April Topics		April Emotions	
Politicians	COVID-19 China	49.3%	Trust	25.35%	Economy	14.93%	Trust	30.22%	Economy	22.07%	Trust	29.44%
	Early COVID-19	18.31%	Fear	18.31%	COVID-19 NL	14.05%	Sadness	19.86%	Government	7.32%	Anticipation	20.17%
	News Outlets	5.63%	Anticipation	12.68%	Infections	9.43%	Anticipation	17.05%	Global Issues	6.21%	Sadness	19.01%
	Politics	4.23%	Disgust	11.27%	COVID-19 EU	5.27%	Fear	11.16%	COVID-19 EU	5.75%	Anger	11.87%
	Global Issues	4.23%	Sadness	9.86%	Government	5%	Anger	10.93%	Measures	5.7%	Fear	10.15%
News Media	COVID-19 China	58.6%	Sadness	19.14%	Infections	26.75%	Sadness	21.56%	Economy	20.62%	Sadness	24.10%
	Early COVID-19	11.72%	Anticipation	16.99%	Economy	13.68%	Anticipation	17.60%	Infections	7.63%	Anticipation	18.67%
	Global Issues	7.42%	Fear	15.16%	COVID-19 NL	6.92%	Trust	15.32%	Global Issues	6.69%	Trust	14.72%
	COVID-19 EU	5.05%	Disgust	15.05%	Hospitals	5.44%	Fear	12.26%	Measures	6.33%	Anger	13.4%
	Economy	3.76%	Anger	12.04%	Press Conference	4.59%	Anger	11.99%	Government	5.03%	Fear	12.33%
Governmental/Health Organizations	COVID-19 China	60.98%	Trust	21.95%	Infections	22.83%	Trust	28.64%	Economy	16.87%	Anticipation	18.67%
	Early COVID-19	16.1%	Anticipation	18.54%	COVID-19 NL	10.83%	Anticipation	23.16%	Measures	9.68%	Trust	24.36%
	Global Issues	11.22%	Anger	16.10%	Measures	9.46%	Sadness	16.50%	Life Online	5.94%	Sadness	17.83%
	Measures	2.93%	Fear	14.63%	Economy	9%	Fear	11.48%	Global Issues	5.8%	Anger	11.74%
	COVID-19 NL	2.44%	Sadness	12.68%	Government	7.18%	Anger	8.15%	Government	5.28%	Fear	9.02%
General Population (Verified)	COVID-19 China	36.47%	Sadness	17.35%	Infections	16.86%	Sadness	19.27%	Economy	16.74%	Sadness	21.49%
	Early COVID-19	18.36%	Anticipation	17.22%	COVID-19 NL	10.12%	Trust	19.25%	Measures	7.46%	Anticipation	19.98%
	Global Issues	11.13%	Fear	15.74%	Economy	9.44%	Anticipation	18.59%	Global Issues	6.76%	Trust	18.33%
	COVID-19 EU	7.72%	Disgust	12.87%	Government	7.01%	Anger	11.96%	Government	5.22%	Anger	12.61%
	Sports	4.39%	Trust	12.15%	Measures	5.2%	Fear	11.87%	COVID-19 EU	4.69%	Fear	11.1%
General Population (Non-Verified)	COVID-19 China	30.58%	Anticipation	17.25%	COVID-19 NL	15.06%	Trust	20.00%	Economy	11.48%	Trust	20.19%
	Early COVID-19	20.55%	Trust	16.59%	Infections	9.71%	Anticipation	18.31%	Government	5.38%	Anticipation	19.35%
	Global Issues	9.02%	Fear	15.32%	Economy	6.84%	Sadness	16.79%	Global Issues	5.32%	Sadness	18.53%
	COVID-19 EU	6.48%	Sadness	14.23%	Government	6.64%	Fear	12.1%	Measures	5.24%	Anger	11.92%
	Measures	4.07%	Anger	11.47%	WFH	4.53%	Anger	11.65%	COVID-19 EU	4.95%	Fear	11.44%
Conspiracy Theory	COVID-19 China	37.89%	Sadness	16.84%	Infections	14.77%	Trust	18.28%	Conspiracies	28.9%	Trust	21.01%
	Early COVID-19	17.37%	Anger	14.74%	COVID-19 NL	13.19%	Sadness	18.17%	Economy	6.07%	Sadness	19.00%
	COVID-19 EU	7.37%	Fear	14.74%	Economy	7.5%	Anticipation	17.74%	Environment	4.43%	Anticipation	16.91%
	Global Issues	7.37%	Anticipation	14.74%	Government	5.29%	Anger	13.3%	Global Issues	3.83%	Anger	14.75%
	Measures	7.37%	Trust	14.21%	Conspiracies	4.71%	Fear	12.27%	Measures	3.65%	Fear	12.29%

the narratives: the economic situation becomes the main issue of every group, with the exception of the Conspiracy Theory group, where it makes up only 6.07% of the messages. At the same time, it seems that information concerning the daily count of infections is not of interest anymore. The only group that basically keeps discussing these counts is the News Media.

When focusing on the emotions, a few patterns can be observed. The dominant emotion for the Politicians and Government/Health Organizations is Trust. This is actually a constant with minimal variations during the three month period. It is also interesting to observe, especially for the Politicians, how Fear has been continuously losing prominence, leaving room for Sadness, expressing sympathy for the deaths and infected, and Anticipation, an emotion expressing ane expectation of predictable future events. Sadness is, on the contrary, the prevalent emotion of the News Media users. When it comes to the General Population, the differences between the verified and non-verified accounts become minimal in March and are maintained in April. There are slightly variations in the order of the top three dominant emotions, but they remain unchanged: Trust, Sadness, and Anticipation. Finally, we conclude our analysis looking at the Conspiracy Theory group. Interestingly, the most dominant emotion for this group in March and April is Trust, a positive emotion. However, Table 5 indicates that the associated Polarity Scores for this user category are actually negative. As a sanity check and as a way to interpret this result, we manually checked all messages whose dominant emotion is Trust across all the categories of users. Our hypothesis is that for the Conspiracy Theory group, Trust has a negative reading corresponding to Mistrust. To verify our hypothesis, we calculated the number of messages containing a negation.[11]. It turns out that while for all other user categories, negations of messages labeled with Trust are 28.6% on average, for the Conspiracy Theory group the percentage jumps to 40.1%. This supports to our hypothesis that the Trust results is actually 'Mistrust' expressed as negated Trust in the messages of this group.

6 Conclusion

We examined Dutch language Twitter responses to the COVID-19 pandemic from February until April of 2020. The overall public response appears to be substantially positive, mainly expressing trust, although differences across groups of users are present. The results demonstrate the effectiveness and necessity of monitoring social media platforms in order to gauge a nation's response to such large scale events. Such findings were already documented in previous virus outbreaks, such as the MERS outbreak in 2015 (Shin

---

[11]We have used the following Dutch negation words: "niet" [not], "nooit"[never], "nimmer" [never], "nergens" [nowhere], "niemand"[none], "niks" [nothing], "geen" [no]

et al., 2016).

The trend of the most discussed topics changes from talking about COVID-19 in Europe, to focusing more on the economy and adjustments of living styles, such as working from home (**RQ1**). While different user groups mostly appear to discuss the same major issues (e.g., the development of the pandemic in the country, the measures adopted by the government, and the impact on the economy), there are differences in their priorities and the specific topics they emphasize. These differences seem to reflect the interests, the role in society, and the stance of the users during the COVID-19 pandemic (**RQ2**). Emotional differences were also observed between the user groups, both in the overall emotional content as well as their dominant emotions. The dominant emotions, like the topics, reflect the roles of the groups, with Politicians and Government and Health Organization inspiring trust, TV/Radio News outlining the sadness of the situation, the general public being worried but also feeling assured by the "people in charge", and some indication of mistrust by the users concerned with the conspiracy theories (**RQ3**).

Future work will focus on three directions: first, we want to investigate the topics and emotional reactions of more fine-grained categories of users by targeting different professions (e.g., teachers, doctors, nurses, musicians, entertainers, among others); second, we want to investigate if the emotional response is different across geographic areas of the country that have been affected differently by the COVID-19 outbreak. For instance, the Noord Brabant province was one of the major outbreak areas, while the Groningen province was minimally affected. We thus expect that messages from Noord Brabant should be characterized by more negative emotions than those from the Groningen area. Finally, in future research it would be useful to run similar studies on datasets in other European languages, in order to allow a comparison of how different national situations and governmental responses impacted public perception of the early stages of the pandemic.

Acknowledgments

The authors want to thank the three anonymous reviewers for their useful comments and suggestions.

References

Fabian Abel, Qi Gao, Geert-Jan Houben, and Ke Tao. 2011. Analyzing user modeling on twitter for personalized news recommendations. In *international conference on user modeling, adaptation, and personalization*, pages 1–12. Springer.

Mohamed Bakillah, Ren-Yu Li, and Steve HL Liang. 2015. Geo-located community detection in twitter with enhanced fast-greedy optimization of modularity: the case study of typhoon haiyan. *International Journal of Geographical Information Science*, 29(2):258–279.

Federico Bianchi, Silvia Terragni, and Dirk Hovy. 2020. Pre-training is a hot topic: Contextualized document embeddings improve topic coherence. *arXiv preprint arXiv:2004.03974*.

David M Blei, Andrew Y Ng, and Michael I Jordan. 2003. Latent dirichlet allocation. *Journal of machine Learning research*, 3(Jan):993–1022.

Su Lin Blodgett, Lisa Green, and Brendan O'Connor. 2016. Demographic dialectal variation in social media: A case study of African-American English. In *Proceedings of the 2016 Conference on Empirical Methods in Natural Language Processing*, pages 1119–1130, Austin, Texas, November. Association for Computational Linguistics.

Antal van den Bosch, Bertjan Busser, Sander Canisius, and Walter Daelemans. 2007. An efficient memory-based morphosyntactic tagger and parser for dutch. *LOT Occasional Series*, 7:191–206.

Gosse Bouma. 2015. N-gram frequencies for dutch twitter data. *Computational Linguistics in the Netherlands Journal*, 5:25–36.

Nan Cao, Lu Lu, Yu-Ru Lin, Fei Wang, and Zhen Wen. 2015. Socialhelix: visual analysis of sentiment divergence in social media. *Journal of visualization*, 18(2):221–235.

Tommaso Caselli and Valerio Basile. 2020. 40twene_nl version 1.0. DOI: 10.17605/osf.io/pfnur.

Emily Chen, Kristina Lerman, and Emilio Ferrara. 2020. Covid-19: The first public coronavirus twitter dataset. *arXiv preprint arXiv:2003.07372*.

Xueqi Cheng, Xiaohui Yan, Yanyan Lan, and Jiafeng Guo. 2014. Btm: Topic modeling over short texts. *IEEE Transactions on Knowledge and Data Engineering*, 26(1-1).

Jaegul Choo, Changhyun Lee, Chandan K Reddy, and Haesun Park. 2015. Weakly supervised nonnegative matrix factorization for user-driven clustering. *Data Mining and Knowledge Discovery*, 29(6):1598–1621.

David Darmon, Elisa Omodei, and Joshua Garland. 2014. Followers are not enough: A question-oriented approach to community detection in online social networks. *arXiv preprint arXiv:1404.0300*.

Ashlynn R Daughton and Michael J Paul. 2019. Identifying protective health behaviors on twitter: observational study of travel advisories and zika virus. *Journal of medical Internet research*, 21(5):e13090.

Luca Dini and André Bittar. 2016. Emotion analysis on Twitter: The hidden challenge. In *Proceedings of the Tenth International Conference on Language Resources and Evaluation (LREC'16)*, pages 3953–3958, Portorož, Slovenia, May. European Language Resources Association (ELRA).

Matthias Hagen, Martin Potthast, Michel Büchner, and Benno Stein. 2015. Webis: An ensemble for twitter sentiment detection. In *Proceedings of the 9th international workshop on semantic evaluation (SemEval 2015)*, pages 582–589.

Sardar Hamidian and Mona Diab. 2016. Rumor identification and belief investigation on Twitter. In *Proceedings of the 7th Workshop on Computational Approaches to Subjectivity, Sentiment and Social Media Analysis*, pages 3–8, San Diego, California, June. Association for Computational Linguistics.

Paul Hitlin and Kenneth Olmstead. 2018. The Science People see on Social Media. Pew Research Center, March 21, 2018.

Liangjie Hong and Brian D Davison. 2010. Empirical study of topic modeling in twitter. In *Proceedings of the first workshop on social media analytics*, pages 80–88.

Mowafa Househ. 2016. Communicating ebola through social media and electronic news media outlets: A cross-sectional study. *Health informatics journal*, 22(3):470–478.

Akshay Java, Xiaodan Song, Tim Finin, and Belle Tseng. 2007. Why we twitter: understanding microblogging usage and communities. In *Proceedings of the 9th WebKDD and 1st SNA-KDD 2007 workshop on Web mining and social network analysis*, pages 56–65.

Hannah Kim, Jaegul Choo, Jingu Kim, Chandan K Reddy, and Haesun Park. 2015. Simultaneous discovery of common and discriminative topics via joint nonnegative matrix factorization. In *Proceedings of the 21th ACM SIGKDD International Conference on Knowledge Discovery and Data Mining*, pages 567–576.

Balachander Krishnamurthy, Phillipa Gill, and Martin Arlitt. 2008. A few chirps about twitter. In *Proceedings of the first workshop on Online social networks*, pages 19–24.

KP Krishna Kumar and G Geethakumari. 2014. Detecting misinformation in online social networks using cognitive psychology. *Human-centric Computing and Information Sciences*, 4(1):1–22.

Nicolas LaLone, Andrea Tapia, Christopher Zobel, Cornelia Caraega, Venkata Kishore Neppalli, and Shane Halse. 2017. Embracing human noise as resilience indicator: twitter as power grid correlate. *Sustainable and Resilient Infrastructure*, 2(4):169–178.

Quanzhi Li, Qiong Zhang, Luo Si, and Yingchi Liu. 2019. Rumor detection on social media: Datasets, methods and opportunities. In *Proceedings of the Second Workshop on Natural Language Processing for Internet Freedom: Censorship, Disinformation, and Propaganda*, pages 66–75, Hong Kong, China, November. Association for Computational Linguistics.

Katerina Eva Matsa and Elisa Shearer. 2018. News use across social media platforms 2018— pew research center. *Journalism and Media*.

Saif M Mohammad and Peter D Turney. 2013. Nrc emotion lexicon. *National Research Council, Canada*, 2.

Petra Kralj Novak, Jasmina Smailović, Borut Sluban, and Igor Mozetič. 2015. Sentiment of emojis. *PloS one*, 10(12).

Catherine Ordun, Sanjay Purushotham, and Edward Raff. 2020. Exploratory analysis of covid-19 tweets using topic modeling, umap, and digraphs. *arXiv preprint arXiv:2005.03082*.

Barbara Plank and Dirk Hovy. 2015. Personality traits on Twitter—or—How to get 1,500 personality tests in a week. In *Proceedings of the 6th Workshop on Computational Approaches to Subjectivity, Sentiment and Social Media Analysis*, pages 92–98, Lisboa, Portugal, September. Association for Computational Linguistics.

Francisco Rangel, Paolo Rosso, Martin Potthast, and Benno Stein. 2017. Overview of the 5th author profiling task at pan 2017: Gender and language variety identification in twitter. *Working notes papers of the CLEF*, pages 1613–0073.

Alan Ritter, Colin Cherry, and Bill Dolan. 2010. Unsupervised modeling of Twitter conversations. In *Human Language Technologies: The 2010 Annual Conference of the North American Chapter of the Association for Computational Linguistics*, pages 172–180, Los Angeles, California, June. Association for Computational Linguistics.

Anna Rogers, Olga Kovaleva, and Anna Rumshisky. 2019. Calls to action on social media: Detection, social impact, and censorship potential. In *Proceedings of the Second Workshop on Natural Language Processing for Internet Freedom: Censorship, Disinformation, and Propaganda*, pages 36–44, Hong Kong, China, November. Association for Computational Linguistics.

Erik Tjong Kim Sang. 2011. Het gebruik van twitter voor taalkundig onderzoek. *TABU: Bulletin voor Taalwetenschap*, 39(1/2):62–72.

Efsun Sarioglu, Kabir Yadav, and Hyeong-Ah Choi. 2013. Topic modeling based classification of clinical reports. In *51st Annual Meeting of the Association for Computational Linguistics Proceedings of the Student Research Workshop*, pages 67–73, Sofia, Bulgaria, August. Association for Computational Linguistics.

Leonard Schild, Chen Ling, Jeremy Blackburn, Gianluca Stringhini, Yang Zhang, and Savvas Zannettou. 2020. " go eat a bat, chang!": An early look on the emergence of sinophobic behavior on web communities in the face of covid-19. *arXiv preprint arXiv:2004.04046*.

Christof Schöch. 2017. Topic modeling genre: An exploration of french classical and enlightenment drama. *DHQ: Digital Humanities Quarterly*, 11(2).

Roy Schwartz, Oren Tsur, Ari Rappoport, and Moshe Koppel. 2013. Authorship attribution of micro-messages. In *Proceedings of the 2013 Conference on Empirical Methods in Natural Language Processing*, pages 1880–1891.

Karishma Sharma, Sungyong Seo, Chuizheng Meng, Sirisha Rambhatla, Aastha Dua, and Yan Liu. 2020. Coronavirus on social media: Analyzing misinformation in twitter conversations. *arXiv preprint arXiv:2003.12309*.

Tian Shi, Kyeongpil Kang, Jaegul Choo, and Chandan K Reddy. 2018. Short-text topic modeling via non-negative matrix factorization enriched with local word-context correlations. In *Proceedings of the 2018 World Wide Web Conference*, pages 1105–1114.

Soo-Yong Shin, Dong-Woo Seo, Jisun An, Haewoon Kwak, Sung-Han Kim, Jin Gwack, and Min-Woo Jo. 2016. High correlation of middle east respiratory syndrome spread with google search and twitter trends in korea. *Scientific reports*, 6:32920.

Luke Sloan, Jeffrey Morgan, Pete Burnap, and Matthew Williams. 2015. Who tweets? deriving the demographic characteristics of age, occupation and social class from twitter user meta-data. *PloS one*, 10(3):e0115545.

Anthony Stefanidis, Emily Vraga, Georgios Lamprianidis, Jacek Radzikowski, Paul L Delamater, Kathryn H Jacobsen, Dieter Pfoser, Arie Croitoru, and Andrew Crooks. 2017. Zika in twitter: temporal variations of locations, actors, and concepts. *JMIR public health and surveillance*, 3(2):e22.

Paul Thompson, Raheel Nawaz, John McNaught, and Sophia Ananiadou. 2017. Enriching news events with meta-knowledge information. *Language Resources and Evaluation*, 51(2):409–438.

Tze-I Yang, Andrew Torget, and Rada Mihalcea. 2011. Topic modeling on historical newspapers. In *Proceedings of the 5th ACL-HLT Workshop on Language Technology for Cultural Heritage, Social Sciences, and Humanities*, pages 96–104.

Sentiments in Russian Medical Professional Discourse during the Covid-19 Pandemic

Irina Ovchinnikova
Sechenov First Moscow State
Medical University
Moscow, Russia
ovchinnikova.ig@1msmu.ru

Liana Ermakova
HCTI - EA 4249
Université de Bretagne
Occidentale
Brest, France
liana.ermakova@univ-brest.fr

Diana Nurbakova
LIRIS UMR 5205 CNRS
INSA Lyon - University of Lyon
Villeurbanne, France
diana.nurbakova@insa-lyon.fr

Abstract

Medical discourse within the professional community has undeservingly received very sparse researchers' attention. Medical professional discourse exists offline and online. We carried out sentiment analysis on titles and text descriptions of materials published on the Russian portal Mir Vracha (90,000 word forms approximately). The texts were generated by and for physicians. The materials include personal narratives describing participants' professional experience, participants' opinions about pandemic news and events in the professional sphere, and Russian reviews and discussion of papers published in international journals in English. We present the first results and discussion of the sentiment analysis of Russian online medical discourse. Based on the results of sentiment analysis and discourse analysis, we described the emotions expressed in the forum and the linguistic means the forum participants used to verbalise their attitudes and emotions while discussing the Covid-19 pandemic. The results showed prevalence of neutral texts in the publications since the medical professionals are interested in research materials and outcomes. In the discussions and personal narratives, the forum participants expressed negative sentiments by colloquial words and figurative language.

1 Introduction

Medical discourse exists in communication within the professional community and in doctor-patient communication. In communicative acts, a dominant participant is a healthcare professional who influences patient's social behaviour (Waitzkin, 1989). Researchers of doctor-patient communication described its institutional character, high level of bureaucratic and legislative regulation, peculiar professional ethics (Kuipers, 1989), and sensitivity to cultural diversity (Ferguson and Candib, 2002). Meanwhile, medical online discourse within the professional community has undeservingly received sparse researchers' attention. Healthcare professionals arrange communication to discuss studies and practical issues, to provide colleagues with an opinion summarizing a unique practical experience or a case study (Kuipers, 1989). The professionals communicate through online conferences, professional portals and professional CRM platforms. In professional medical communication, a free discussion and prevalence of facts over sentiments match principles of evidence-based medicine. Meanwhile, professionals are unable to avoid emotions while discussing medical subjects (Franz and Murphy, 2018). The outburst of the Covid-19 pandemics slightly changed the norms in medical professional communication motivating researchers and practitioners to publish raw data and promote a certain treatment (Bavel, 2020). Researchers' emotional involvement into scientific discussion jeopardises objectivity and independence of results and conclusions. The pandemic evokes public interest in medical professional discussions since the media spread controversial news about vaccine development and disease treatment. Due to the interest, a description of medical discourse peculiarities is of importance for communication researchers and social media.

In this paper, we characterise medical discourse within the professional community on a Russian medical portal bringing into focus sentiments and linguistic means to express emotions in medical texts

Proceedings of the Third Workshop on Computational Modeling of PEople's Opinions, PersonaLity, and Emotions in Social media, pages 99–108
Barcelona, Spain (Online), December 13, 2020.

generated by and for professional physicians. **The objective of our research** is to discover sentiments in texts published on the medical professional forum and to describe a set of linguistic means to express the sentiments and emotions in the professional communication, especially in the context of current pandemics. To the best of our knowledge, sentiments and emotions in the Russian medical professional discourse during the Covid-19 pandemics have not been described yet.

The remainder of the paper is organised as follows. We discuss the related work in Section 2. We present our data collection and the methodology in Section 3. Next, we report our results in Section 4 and provide detailed discussion in Section 5. Finally, we conclude the paper with Section 6.

2 Related Work

In this Section, we describe two groups of works closely related to our study, namely: medical discourse features and sentiment analysis of medical discourse.

2.1 Medical Discourse Features

Medical discourse is a highly regulated institutional professional discourse. It includes various genres for communication among competent professionals and conversations with healthcare customers where a biomedical model of practice co-exists with patient centeredness (Khan, 2019). The structure of the discourse provides a frame to express authority, status, social control in appropriate ways according to the professional ethics, bureaucratic procedures and institutional processes in the society (Kuipers, 1989). A set of medical discourse constituents contains concepts of scientific ideology, restrictions due to professional legal and ethical norms, peculiar genres of professional communication (surgery reports, collective intelligence case reports, medical reviews, etc.), medical semiotics (including terminology), highly structured procedures and sign systems (dress code, observation schedules, etc.), peculiar terminology and patient centeredness (Khan, 2019; Shuravina, 2013; Staiano, 2016).

The structure of texts in the discourse presupposes prerequisites to introduce a problem, a review of familiar approaches to solve it, an explanation of a new basic idea to contribute to the problem solution, and clear outcome to apply into practice (Wilce, 2009; Waitzkin, 1989). The choice of lexical formulas in professional communication depend on the objective of a message (to inform, to clarify, to discuss) and a medical domain the text belongs to (scientific research in particular area, introduction of a new drug, instruction to employ new equipment, etc.). The texts addressed to the professionals require a peculiar structure that facilitates comprehension. Nye with co-authors (Nye et al., 2018) showed the abstract semantic structure of articles published on PubMed. According to the study, the text structure of the medical research articles contains parts for data description (patients, diagnoses), for discussion of procedures (intervention) and outcome (intervention consequences), for deliberation of advantages of a new approach. The discussion part often contains explanations of diagnosis in terms of medical semiotics (Staiano, 2016). The topics of the medical professional discourse are connected to the texts semantic structure and the discourse constituents. The subjects of the texts represent categories corresponding to diagnosis, intervention, treatment, ethics, legislative and bureaucratic regulation, and research.

Sentiments and evaluation of social conflicts are avoided in communication within the professional community. Medical language generally excludes a critical appraisal of the social context (Waitzkin, 1989). The medical text structure in the professional community does not include the content of this type since the texts are produced by and for competent professional physicians (Kuipers, 1989).

A basic idea of a message in medical discourse belongs to scientific ideology because it provides a 'technical' solution to a problem (see a definition of the scientific ideology in (Habermas, 1970). The scientific ideology presupposes objectivism, analytic cognitive style, impersonalisation, generalisation. In medical professional communication, texts transmit the scientific ideology due to discussing 'technical' solutions to problems and enforcing professional domination (Habermas, 1970). While communicating with patients, health professionals follow the structure to get objective data and to solve a problem. Meanwhile, sentiments are required in medical discourse in doctor-patient communication due to its patient centeredness (Ferguson and Candib, 2002; Khan, 2019). However, it is still unclear whether sentiments penetrate into communication within the professional community.

2.2 Sentiment Analysis of Medical Discourse

The analysis of sentiments expressed by experts in medical discourse on professional portals and forums can provide valuable information about predominant subjects and the position of healthcare workers on the important topics. The analysis of sentiments allows researchers to clarify ways and means that are in use to express emotions in the professional community. The professional portal monitoring enables detection of the community attitudes to prominent events and medical abnormalities during the current pandemic. Nevertheless, the results of sentiment analysis in medical discourse are much behind those in other domains (Zunic et al., 2020). There are few domain-specific corpora and lexicons publicly available for sentiment analysis in the healthcare area (Zunic et al., 2020). However, linguistic and content features of medical discourse require a domain-specific sentiment source (Denecke and Deng, 2015). Xu et al. (Xu et al., 2015) carried out citation sentiment analysis in biomedical clinical trial papers in order to decide whether a study can be reproduced or not. Abdaoui (Abdaoui, 2016) studied forums for healthcare professionals to learn classification models used after to identify messages posted by experts in other health forums. He analysed healthcare workers' expertise and reputation and the sentiments they express (emotions and polarity). The work resulted in the construction of French lexicon of sentiments and emotions called FEEL (French Expanded Emotions Lexicon). The results of sentiment analysis are of high importance for healthcare practitioners who would like to improve doctor-patients communication according to the patients' attitudes to their diseases. Rajput (Rajput, 2020) tackles the challenge of reflecting the real mental state of a patient by applying sentiment analysis of texts gathered via various sources including social media. Alnashwan et al. (Alnashwan et al., 2019) identified a set of categories related to the Lyme disease and classified medical forum posts into those categories. Salas-Zárateand et al. (Menasalvas et al., 2017) analysed the positive or negative polarity of document aspects (a review, a piece of news, and a tweet, among others) based on ontologies in the diabetes domain.

Several works were carried out on the classification of patient-authored content into positive, negative and neutral (Ali et al., 2013; Bobicev et al., 2012; Carrillo-de Albornoz et al., 2018; Goeuriot et al., 2012)). Yadav et al. (Yadav et al., 2018) analysed the sentiment based on available information from 'patient.info' which contains opinions about medical conditions self narrated by the users. Multiple forms of medical sentiments can be inferred from users' medical condition, treatment, and medication (Denecke and Deng, 2015; Yadav et al., 2018). However, the implicit sentiment should be also considered (Denecke and Deng, 2015).

Zunic, Corcoran, and Spasic (Zunic et al., 2020) performed a systematic review of the literature about sentiment analysis in medical discourse by studying PubMed and MEDLINE. They found that the majority of data were gathered from social support platforms and social networks serving as online information exchange. In many cases, communities were created around severe and chronic health conditions and discuss treatments (medications, surgery, orthodontic services), prevention, practitioners, or a health care system in general.

To the best of our knowledge, the sentiment analysis has not been applied yet to the discussions held by Russian medical online communities. We carry out the analysis to learn the peculiarities of medical professional communication in Russian and ways to express emotions in medical professional discourse.

3 Materials and method

3.1 Data Collection

We carried out our research based on the RSS data from 29/06/2020 to 11/08/2020 from the professional portal Mir Vracha ('МирВрача'[1]: The doctor's world) which contains various materials useful for healthcare workers. Created in 2011 by a medical team, now this web resource counts more than 100,000 users. Famous national professional resources guide the portal following the principles of evidence-based medicine. The access to the portal content is restricted; however, certified professionals and medical universities students have free access to the portal and are able to publish their materials on its forum. We collected 185 entries in Russian in XML format. Each entry contains title, link, description, and

---

[1] https://mirvracha.ru

content. Texts from the fields `title`, `description`, and `content` were concatenated, lower-cased and tokenised with `nltk.word_tokenize`. The `content` includes more than 90,000 word forms. Then we manually analysed the top 10,000 frequent words w.r.t. the aspect of their semantics and correspondence to the medical discourse categories and topics described by Ney et al. (Nye et al., 2018). We excluded stop words and examined the high frequency words (50+ occurrences) to obtain reliable results. While considering categories and topics, we analysed contexts of a frequent word and then attributed the most relevant category to the word. Semantic connections within categories were examined based on the WordNet[2]. For instance, пациент 'patient' is mostly mentioned in discussions of studies including researches of drugs to treat Covid-19; therefore, it belongs to '*Research*'. Thus, the topics were selected based on the distributive analysis of the frequent words. The final number of topics was settled on according to the material represented on the portal.

3.2 Methodology

We performed sentiment analysis of titles and description with the `Dostoevsky`[3] sentiment analysis library for Python. The analysis is based on evaluation of words with emotional connotations in an input text. It takes a text as input and returns a sentiment classification of positive, negative or neutral. Dostoevsky's model is trained on the RuSentiment dataset consisting of more than 30,000 comments from the Russian social network VKontakte[4].

Thus, in this paper we analyse the material collected from the forum Mir Vracha, which contains (a) personal narratives describing participants' professional experience; (b) participants' opinions about pandemic news and events in the professional sphere; (c) Russian reviews and discussion of papers published in international journals in English. We analysed contexts of words: '*Covid-19, the coronavirus, Covid, SARS-COV-2*' attempting to reveal emotional attitude and linguistic means to express emotions. All the authors of the present paper are Russian native speakers and have a linguistic background.

4 Results

4.1 Topics of Medical Discourse Materials Published in the Forum

We discuss the semantic groups of words from the frequency list considering the top 10,000 word forms. Their frequency varies from 465 (это 'this') to 2 occurrences (2,826 words). The most frequent word in the list is пациент 'patient' (582 occurrences). Semantic analysis allows us to distribute the words (frequency 50+) among the topics of medical discourse (see Table 1). We distinguish six main topics of online medical discourse based on the discourse description in (Nye et al., 2018) and (Kuipers, 1989).

Since the portal is aimed at informing the community and providing the healthcare professionals with a platform to discuss news and issues of the current interest, '*Research*' contains more frequent words than any other topic. The '*Diagnosis*' includes names of diseases that had been discussed in the participants' narratives and reviews due to various reasons. The category '*Bureaucracy*' contains words that denote the regulation of professional communication and practice. The high frequency words from the general lexicon correspond to the outcomes of intervention. Nevertheless, Covid-19 appeared to be the most discussed issue because the topic '*Pandemic*' had been referred to by 672 frequent inflexion forms. The Covid-19 pandemic is characterised in 55 texts from 185 entries.

Thus, the topics correspond to the medical discourse constituents and ideology. The most frequent of the top 10,000 words do not refer to sentiments or emotions. Professional communication appears to discuss the prominent topics mostly avoiding emotional expressions.

4.2 Results of Sentiment Analysis

4.2.1 General Data Analysis

We carried out sentiment analysis on text titles and descriptions. The results of the analysis are shown in Table 2. A **title** was classified as *positive* or *negative* when it contains a word with a positive (as

---

[2]`https://wordnet.princeton.edu/`
[3]`https://pypi.org/project/dostoevsky/`
[4]`https://vk.com/`

Table 1: Representativeness of the medical discourse topics in the list of the frequent words

Topics	words belonging to the topic	Word frequency
Research	Author (автор), clinical (клинический), data (данные), patients (пациент) result (результат), study (исследование)	1,428
Diagnosis	Disease (заболевание), illness (болезнь), infection (инфекция), pain (боль), pregnancy (беременность), stroke (инсульт), symptom (симптом), syphilis (сифилис), virus (вирус)	682
Pandemic	Covid-19, coronavirus (коронавирус), sars-cov-2	672
Intervention	Antibodies (антитела), help (помощь врача), MRI (МРТ), therapy (терапия), treatment (лечение)	532
Bureaucracy	Doctor (врач), healthcare (здравоохранение), medical (медицинский), Ministry of Health (Министерство здравоохранения), organization (организация)	522
General lexicon	Death (смерть), health (здоровье), life (жизнь), risk (риск)	496

Table 2: Sentiment classification of the texts from the "MirVracha" portal

Classification	Positive	Negative	Neutral	Skip
Text titles	9	13	156	7
Text descriptions	1	21	160	3

улучшить 'to improve' or улыбка 'a smile') or negative emotional connotation (as опасность 'danger', смерть 'death', боль 'pain'), respectively, or as *neutral*, otherwise. The titles present the approach to the text content, which is of importance for its author. The titles are short. Due to ambiguous associations evoked by the title, it is hard to characterise the content of the text. Thus, the result of sentiment analysis on the text description does not match the classification of its title. The title 'Вымрем, как мамонты и динозавры?' ('Will we die out like mammoths and dinosaurs?') is *neutral*; nevertheless, the text description is classified as *negative* since the author doubted the vaccination efficacy and a chance to overcome the Covid-19 pandemic next year, using words with negative emotional connotations (рок 'doom', умирание 'dying', злой 'evil', etc.). Since the text descriptions include more information about the text content and therefore, represent a better candidate for the sentiment analysis algorithm, we will characterise sentiments in the descriptions.

Sentiment analysis on **text descriptions** examined initial sentences of texts and narratives published on the portal. The algorithm failed to classify 3 texts, while 160 descriptions were classified as neutral. Nevertheless, 21 texts showed negative content; one description was estimated as a text with positive content (see Table 2).

4.2.2 Analysis of Words with Emotional Connotations

Since the sentiment analysis is based mostly on lexical semantics, the words with emotional connotations contributed to classification of the text description sentiment, positive or negative. In Table 3, there is a set of words with emotional connotations that occurred in the initial sentences of the input texts; the words are arranged in alphabetical order, their frequencies are shown in brackets.

The set contains four positive words belonging to the general Russian lexicon. Among words with negative connotations, there are adjectives and nouns denoting negative feelings and emotions ('bad, grim, guilty, offended, sadness', etc.), adjectives and nouns referring to unpleasant experience ('agonizing, complaint, deception, idiotic, pain', etc.), verbs denoting sad and tragic events ('to beat, to die', etc.). Several words belong to legal discourse ('criminal, accused' ets.) since the forum participants discussed legislative regulation of medical practice; the words reveal the topic '*Bureaucracy*' where the discussions of legal issue belong. Nevertheless, in the set of words with negative connotations, words from medical

Table 3: Words with emotional connotations in the text descriptions

Positive class, # descriptions = 1
Beautiful (красивый 3), a smile (улыбка 6), sweet (милый 4), young (молодой 40)

Negative class, # descriptions = 21
Accused (обвиняемый 5), acne (угри 2), adiposity (ожирение 30), agonizing (мучительный 2), bad (плохой 11), to beat (бить 1), bleeding (кровотечение 27), complaint (жалоба 49), coronavirus (коронавирус 155, коронавирусный 93) criminal (уголовный 13), danger (опасность 32), death (смерть 100), deception (ложь 2), deceiver (обманщик 2), to die (умирать 8, умереть 44), to die out (вымирать 1), disabled teenager (подросток-инвалид 1), to disappear forever (кануть в бездну 1), disgrace (немилость 2), disease (заболевание 245), doom (рок 2), dying (умирание 1), evil (злой 1), to fall (падать 11), to get sick (болеть 2, заболеть 25), grim (мрачный 2), guilty (виноватый 10, виновен 5), horrible (жуткий 6), horror (ужас 7), idiotic (идиотский 2), illness (болезнь 93), infection (инфекция 109), infertile (бесплодный 2), lamentation (стенание 1), to lie (врать 1), loss (потеря 34), miscarriage (невынашивание 5), moribund (умирающий 2), nightmare (кошмар 3), offended (обиженный 4), pain (боль 100), prison (тюрьма 16), prohibited (запретить 4, запрещать 4), resignation (отставка 4), sadness (печаль 2), scary (страшный 24), threat (угроза 26), trouble (проблема 83), useless (бесполезный 2), to vomit (стошнить 2), worse (хуже 13)

discourse appear to be the most representative group. The group includes names of diseases and negative outcomes of treatment that may be considered as a part of the lexicon of the 'Diagnosis' theme. According to the results of sentiment analysis, the participants who shared their negative experience in personal narratives produced the descriptions with negative content. Since Covid-19 represents a new disease, the healthcare professionals have been mostly discussing research results and publications in medical journals since the pandemic outbreak.

4.3 Analysis of Texts about Covid-19

Texts about Covid-19 were classified as negative (7 texts) and neutral (48 texts). The studies did not evoke any emotional conversations on the forum since the texts devoted to consideration of the Covid-19 origin and treatment were mostly classified as neutral.

In the *neutral* texts, the forum participants used terminology (рецептор ACE2 'ACE2 receptor', гипертензивный 'hypertensive' etc.), while considering the effect of drugs on the coronavirus (азитромицин 'azithromycin', etc.). They referred to publications discussing other pandemics ('испанка' "Spanish" influenza') and the most recent articles reported a research of the coronavirus (статья в Nature Microbiology 'the article in Nature Microbiology', etc.). Thus, the content of the texts about Covid-19 reflects the basic topics of the professional medical discourse: *'Research'*, *'Diagnosis'*, *'Intervention'*, *'Outcomes'*, *'Contagion'*, *'Bureaucracy'* (including legal and ethic regulation).

In the *negative* texts, words with negative connotations denote predictions as to the outcome of the pandemic, the evaluation of the social behaviour and the bureaucratic regulation, names of disease (see Table 3). Thus, the negative content mostly covers the *'Diagnosis'* topic.

Moreover, a text with negative content includes a critical appraisal of the social context due to *'Black lives matter'* protest during the outburst of Covid-19 in New York: "An article summarising editorial articles about the link between COVID-19 and racism from Nature, Science and three leading medical journals was published on June 13. As they are all very similar in terms of meaning and content, I'll cite the most illustrative example: "*A number of people who see the protests as possible drivers of more covid-19 cases have suggested that it is hypocritical of doctors to support anti-racism protestors now when weeks earlier they denounced large crowds due to the risk of spreading covid-19. Framing anti-racism protests against the control of covid-19 is a false dichotomy.*" [5] [6]. The author explores boundaries of the medical ethics when social protests endangers people health. Healthcare professionals must follow the ethical norms regardless of their social sympathy and political opinions. Large crowds on the streets of American cities facilitate spreading the virus therefore doctors and practitioners have to condemn the protests; however, condemnation would show sympathy to racism. Words лицемерие 'hypocrisy', ругать 'to scold' manifest negative attitude to professionals who support the protesters; nevertheless, the author keeps distance from evaluating the events emotionally. However, the text shows importance of including critical appraisal of the social context during the current pandemic.

Contexts of words referring to the current Covid-19 pandemic reveal a set of linguistic means to express an attitude to the event. Nevertheless, the means rarely occurred in the publications. Direct evaluation is represented by words that denote feelings and emotions (печаль 'sadness'; пренебрежение 'disdain' etc.) or refer to a negative status, consequences, events (бездумный 'harebrained'; угроза 'threat'; немилость 'disgrace', etc.). The forum participants preferred to express irony while discussing the coronavirus (В современной медицине не бывает новостей не про COVID-19. Самые нековидные вести чуток да соприкасаются с коронавирусной заразой 'In the current medicine, all news are associated with Covid-19. Even non-Covid-19 news touches on the infection a little bit). The ironic attitude is manifested by Russian colloquial words (чуток 'just a bit', зараза 'infection' and 'bad person'). Discussing drugs and vaccine development, physicians used figurative language. Comparisons and metaphors allow diminishing the threat by emphasizing its temporal character (коронавирусная напасть 'coronavirus scourge') and associating the contagion with a fire (спичка при пожаре 'playing with fire', 'add fuel to the fire'). The idioms and tropes influence the perception of information about the virus generating cultural associations with sentiments expressed in the Russian literature masterpieces (русская рулетка 'Russian roulette'; сколько патронов в барабане 'how many cartridges are there in the cylinder').

As we have mentioned earlier, the forum participants did not intend to express emotions; they appealed to emotions and used figurative language when they were interested in attracting readers' attention to current problems in fighting the pandemic. The forum participants cited literary texts and used colloquial expressions, figurative language, and idioms. The typical attitude to the subject of the discussion, which the forum participants expressed in their texts, is ironical evaluation of the professional experience.

5 Discussion

The materials published on the Mir Vracha portal represent the medical professional discourse as it reveals itself in communication among healthcare professionals. To the best of our knowledge, we present the first results and discussion of the sentiment analysis of Russian medical discourse online. The texts published on the forum reflect the intention to consider an individual practice against the backdrop of the current research materials. Due to the interest in the research, the most frequent words belong to '*Research*' and '*Diagnosis*' discourse categories.

The topics of the physicians' publications on the professional portal differ from the popular topics in the communities on social media. Zunic et al. (Zunic et al., 2020) showed that members of communities were interested in consideration of 'Intervention' (medications, operations, etc.), while the Russian healthcare professionals are focused on the '*Research*' and '*Diagnosis*' topics. The professionals did not discuss the subjects that were the most popular themes on Twitter. Abd-Alrazaq et al. (Abd-Alrazaq et al., 2020) found out four main themes of the tweets devoted to the Covid-19 pandemic: origin of the virus; its sources; its impact on people, countries, and the economy; and ways of mitigating the risk of infection. In

---

[5]The original: "Тринадцатого июня вышла заметка, собравшая воедино редакторские статьи о связи COVID-19 и расизма, появившиеся в журналах Nature, Science и трех ведущих медицинских журналах [3]. Они довольно похожи по смыслу и содержанию, поэтому я приведу лишь самый яркий пример: "Группы людей, которые рассматривают протесты как один из возможных двигателей распространения случаев COVID-19, отмечали, что это лицемерие со стороны врачей, поддерживающих протестующих сейчас, когда лишь несколькими неделями раньше они ругали большие скопления людей за распространение COVID-19. Противопоставление между протестами против расизма и контролированием COVID-19 - ложная дихотомия"

[6]The referred article was published on BioEdge website: https://www.bioedge.org/bioethics/covid-19-driven-by-racism-say-major-journals/13469

July-August 2020, the Russian healthcare professionals had been concentrating on the virus origin and the ways to recognise and to treat the disease. The difference in the set of themes between the professional community and ordinary users of social media reveals boundaries of the medical professional discourse. Within the discourse, its semantic categories dominate in communication among competent professionals who are motivated to obtain more medical information and to offer 'technical' solutions.

The topics of the publications (see Table 1) represent the discourse categories of medical professional discourse. The discourse category contains the semantics relevant to medicine and healthcare associated with the medical professional language and the texts structure to arrange the professional communication (Wilce, 2009; Nye et al., 2018; Staiano, 2016).

Peculiar terminology including Latin terms is an essential constituent of medical discourse. Complicated connections of terms reflect interactions of concepts and references to a subject, which are to be examined and described in various conditions. Names of the diseases are the high frequency words in our materials. Other terms were also in use on the portal; however, the forum participants used different terms according to the subject they discussed, so each term occurred twice or once. Nevertheless, the terminology caused the algorithm of sentiment analysis to classify the publications on the Mir Vracha as neutral. Meanwhile, in the communities on social media, texts patients suffering from cancer received essential differences in the sentiments (emotions and polarity: see (Abdaoui, 2016)). The difference in the emotional attitude to the content between the professional community and the community of the patients reveals different communicative intentions and objectives as well as the medical discourse boundaries.

Along with the recent development of narrative medicine, the importance of professional social control brings doctor-patient communication into focus in medical discourse studies (Franz and Murphy, 2018). Meanwhile, online communication within the professional community shows patient centeredness through the frequency of words referring to patients and their experience ('patient, pain, therapy' etc.). The patient centeredness is not obvious due to the scientific ideology of medical professional discourse, which brings into focus the 'Research' category. Since the scientific ideology supports finding a solution to current and forthcoming problems, the participants of the forum on the Mir Vracha portal discussed facts and case studies preferring to avoid emotional outbursts.

Sentiment analysis results show reasonable evaluation of the texts published on the medical professional portal. Absence of emotional words in the list of high frequency words confirms the unessential contribution of the emotional expressions to the content of the medical professional discourse texts. The texts contain emotions and attitudes expressed by means of figurative language. Meanwhile, doctor-patient communication on the Internet shows instances of metaphors, metonyms, and idioms in written messages on forums (Kharitonova et al., 2019). The professionals use a similar set of linguistic means to express emotions and attitudes in their communication within the community. The physicians expressed negative emotions caused by their professional experience during the current Covid-19 pandemics appealing to irony as a tool to diminish the threat and the seriousness of the problem they must find a solution to.

6   Conclusion

We carried out sentiment analysis on titles and text descriptions of materials published on the Russian professional medical portal Mir Vracha (90,000 word forms approximately). To the best of our knowledge, we present the first results and discussion of the sentiment analysis of Russian professional online medical discourse. The texts were generated by and for physicians and reflect the peculiarities of medical professional discourse. The medical professional discourse revealed in communication within the professional community is focused on the semantic categories 'Research', 'Diagnosis', 'Intervention', 'Bureaucracy'. The categories provide linguistic means to verbalise the professional activity and bureaucratic regulation of medical practice. Based on the results of sentiment analysis and discourse analysis, we described the emotions expressed in the forum and linguistic means the forum participants used to verbalise their attitudes and emotions while discussing the Covid-19 pandemic. The attitudes and emotions show negative sentiments manifested by colloquial words and figurative language. In further research, it is necessary to widen online medical professional communication materials for sentiment analysis in order to describe a thesaurus of sentiment linguistic means.

References

Alaa Abd-Alrazaq, Dari Alhuwail, Mowafa Househ, Mounir Hamdi, and Zubair Shah. 2020. Top concerns of tweeters during the covid-19 pandemic: Infoveillance study. *J Med Internet Res*, 22(4):e19016, Apr.

Amine Abdaoui. 2016. *French Social Media Mining: Expertise and Sentiment. (Fouille des Médias Sociaux Français: Expertise et Sentiment)*. Ph.D. thesis, University of Montpellier, France.

Tanveer Ali, David Schramm, Marina Sokolova, and Diana Inkpen. 2013. Can I hear you? sentiment analysis on medical forums. In *Proceedings of the Sixth International Joint Conference on Natural Language Processing*, pages 667–673, Nagoya, Japan, October. Asian Federation of Natural Language Processing.

Rana Alnashwan, Humphrey Sorensen, Adrian O'Riordan, and Cathal Hoare. 2019. Accurate classification of socially generated medical discourse. *Int. J. Data Sci. Anal.*, 8(4):353–365.

J.J. Van et al. Bavel. 2020. Using social and behavioural science to support COVID-19 pandemic response. *Nature Human Behaviour*, 4(5):460–471, May.

Victoria Bobicev, Marina Sokolova, Yasser Jafer, and David Schramm. 2012. Learning sentiments from tweets with personal health information. In Leila Kosseim and Diana Inkpen, editors, *Advances in Artificial Intelligence - 25th Canadian Conference on Artificial Intelligence, Canadian AI 2012, Toronto, ON, Canada, May 28-30, 2012. Proceedings*, volume 7310 of *Lecture Notes in Computer Science*, pages 37–48. Springer.

Jorge Carrillo-de Albornoz, Javier Rodríguez Vidal, and Laura Plaza. 2018. Feature engineering for sentiment analysis in e-health forums. *PLOS ONE*, 13(11):1–25, 11.

Kerstin Denecke and Yihan Deng. 2015. Sentiment analysis in medical settings: New opportunities and challenges. *Artificial Intelligence in Medicine*, 64(1):17 – 27.

Warren J Ferguson and Lucy M Candib. 2002. Culture, language, and the doctor-patient relationship. *Family medicine*, 24:353–361.

Berkeley Franz and John W. Murphy. 2018. Reconsidering the role of language in medicine. *Philosophy, Ethics, and Humanities in Medicine*, 13(1), June.

Lorraine Goeuriot, Jin-Cheon Na, Wai Yan Min Kyaing, Christopher Khoo, Yun-Ke Chang, Yin-Leng Theng, and Jung-Jae Kim. 2012. Sentiment lexicons for health-related opinion mining. In *Proceedings of the 2nd ACM SIGHIT International Health Informatics Symposium*, IHI '12, page 219–226, New York, NY, USA. Association for Computing Machinery.

J. Habermas. 1970. Technology and science as 'ideology.'. In J. Habermas, editor, *Toward a Rational Society*, pages 79 – 126. Boston: Beacon.

Munir Khan. 2019. The perspective of medical communication on the biomedical model of practice and patient centeredness: A review of the language of medical case presentation genre. *International Journal of Linguistics, Literature, and Translation*, 2:71–80.

N.V. Kharitonova, S.V. Baryshnikova, and O.V. Monastyretskaya. 2019. Peculiarity of lexical component of professionally oriented discourse in the internet (based on medical forum). *Philology. Theory and Practice*, 12:331–334.

Joel C. Kuipers. 1989. "medical discourse" in anthropological context: Views of language and power. *Medical Anthropology Quarterly*, 3(2):99–123.

Ernestina Menasalvas, María del Pilar Salas-Zárate, José Medina-Moreira, Katty Lagos-Ortiz, Harry Luna-Aveiga, Miguel Ángel Rodríguez-García, and Rafael Valencia-García. 2017. Sentiment analysis on tweets about diabetes: An aspect-level approach. *Computational and Mathematical Methods in Medicine*, 2017.

Benjamin Nye, Junyi Jessy Li, Roma Patel, Yinfei Yang, Iain Marshall, Ani Nenkova, and Byron Wallace. 2018. A corpus with multi-level annotations of patients, interventions and outcomes to support language processing for medical literature. In *Proceedings of the 56th Annual Meeting of the Association for Computational Linguistics (Volume 1: Long Papers)*, pages 197–207, Melbourne, Australia, July. Association for Computational Linguistics.

Adil Rajput. 2020. Chapter 3 - natural language processing, sentiment analysis, and clinical analytics. pages 79 – 97.

Ludmila Sergeevna Shuravina. 2013. Medical discourse as a type of institutional discourse. *Journal of Health and Social Behavior*, 328(37):65–67.

K.V. Staiano. 2016. *Interpreting Signs of Illness: A Case Study in Medical Semiotics*. Approaches to Semiotics [AS]. De Gruyter.

Howard Waitzkin. 1989. A critical theory of medical discourse: Ideology, social control, and the processing of social context in medical encounters. *Journal of Health and Social Behavior*, 30(2):220–239.

James M. Wilce. 2009. Medical discourse. *Annual Review of Anthropology*, 38(1):199–215.

Jun Xu, Yaoyun Zhang, Yonghui Wu, Jingqi Wang, Xiao Dong, and Hua Xu. 2015. Citation sentiment analysis in clinical trial papers. *AMIA ... Annual Symposium proceedings. AMIA Symposium*, 2015:1334—1341.

Shweta Yadav, Asif Ekbal, Sriparna Saha, and Pushpak Bhattacharyya. 2018. Medical sentiment analysis using social media: Towards building a patient assisted system. In *Proceedings of the Eleventh International Conference on Language Resources and Evaluation (LREC 2018)*, Miyazaki, Japan, May. European Language Resources Association (ELRA).

Anastazia Zunic, Padraig Corcoran, and Irena Spasic. 2020. Sentiment analysis in health and well-being: Systematic review. *JMIR Med Inform*, 8(1):e16023, Jan.

Multilingual Emoticon Prediction of Tweets about COVID-19

Stefanos Stoikos
Pomona College
st.stoikos@gmail.com

Mike Izbicki
Claremont Mckenna College
mike@izbicki.me

Abstract

Emojis are a widely used tool for encoding emotional content in informal messages such as tweets, and predicting which emoji corresponds to a piece of text can be used as a proxy for measuring the emotional content in the text. This paper presents the first model for predicting emojis in highly multilingual text. Our `BERTmoticon` model is a fine-tuned version of the multilingual BERT model (Devlin et al., 2018), and it can predict emojis for text written in 102 different languages. We trained our `BERTmoticon` model on 54.2 million geolocated tweets sent in the first 6 months of 2020, and we apply the model to a case study analyzing the emotional reaction of Twitter users to news about the coronavirus. Example findings include a spike in sadness when the World Health Organization (WHO) declared that coronavirus was a global pandemic, and a spike in anger and disgust when the number of COVID-19 related deaths in the United States surpassed one hundred thousand. We provide an easy-to-use and open source python library for predicting emojis with `BERTmoticon` so that the model can easily be applied to other data mining tasks.

1 Introduction

The COVID-19 pandemic has caused intense emotional reactions on social media. Some tweets are sad:

> *This Corona stuff is no joke. Watching people get laid off at work today really made me open my eyes. Wish it was all over.*

And other tweets are angry:

> *I saw that bottles of Purell were selling for $149! Go away price gougers and go away coronavirus!*

What both of these tweets have in common is that their emotional content is captured by emojis present in the tweet's text. Emojis are often used in informal tweets sent between friends (Danesi, 2016), but most tweets do not contain emojis. For example, the following tweet by the BBC (a major British newspaper) is clearly meant to help us find joy amidst the stress of COVID-19:

> *Father dresses as Transformers character Bumblebee to surprise his son on his first day back at school after lockdown.*

But there are no emojis in the text to indicate that the tweet is joyful. One possible emoji for this tweet would be the "grinning face", but more subtle emojis like "grinning face with tongue" or "grinning face with smiling eyes" would also be appropriate and convey slightly different emotions. The goal of this paper is to automatically annotate these emoji-less tweets with appropriate emojis in order to better understand the emotional content in online discussions of COVID-19.

Proceedings of the Third Workshop on Computational Modeling of PEople's Opinions, PersonaLity, and Emotions in Social media, pages 109–118
Barcelona, Spain (Online), December 13, 2020.

language	tweet	emoji prediction (top 5)
English	Washington sick man Is 1st in US to Catch Newly Discovered Dangerous Pneumonia. Get out your face masks folks! #coronavirus #wuhan #mask	
French	Un homme malade de Washington est le premier aux États-Unis à attraper une pneumonie dangereuse nouvellement découverte. Sortez vos masques! #coronavirus #wuhan #mask	
German	Der kranke Mann aus Washington ist der erste in den USA, der an einer neu entdeckten gefährlichen Lungenentzündung erkrankt. Holen Sie sich Ihre Gesichtsmasken Leute! #coronavirus #wuhan #mask	
Hebrew	אזהרה בוושינגטון הוא הראשון בארה"ב כדי לתפוס דלקת ריאות מסוכנת שהתגלתה לאחרונה. תוציאו את המסכות בפנים שלכם, חבר'ה! נגיף הקורונה ווהאן מסכה	
Indonesian	Orang sakit Washington adalah yang pertama di AS untuk Menangkap Pneumonia Berbahaya yang Baru Ditemukan. Keluarkan masker wajah kalian! #coronavirus #wuhan #mask	
Italian	Un malato di Washington è il primo negli Stati Uniti a contrarre una polmonite pericolosa scoperta di recente. Tira fuori le tue maschere per il viso, gente! #coronavirus #wuhan #mask	
Japanese	ワシントンの病人は新しく発見された危険な肺炎を捕まえるために米国で最初です。フェイスマスクの人を出してください！＃コロナウイルス＃武漢＃マスク	
Portuguese	Homem doente em Washington é o primeiro nos Estados Unidos a pegar pneumonia perigosa recém-descoberta. Tirem suas máscaras, pessoal! #coronavirus #wuhan #mask	
Spanish	Un enfermo de Washington es el primero en los Estados Unidos en contraer una neumonía peligrosa recién descubierta. ¡Saquen sus mascarillas, amigos! #coronavirus #wuhan #mascara	
Tagalog	Ang taong may sakit sa Washington ay Ika-1 sa Estados Unidos upang Makuha ang Bagong Nakatuklas na Mapanganib na pneumonia. Lumabas ang iyong mga maskara sa mukha mga kamag-anak! #coronavirus #wuhan #mask	

Figure 1: BERTmoticon predicts good emojis in a wide variety of languages. All non-English text above was translated from the English using Google Translate.

Prior work on predicting emojis from the text of a tweet (Barbieri et al., 2017, Felbo et al., 2017, Zhang et al., 2019) has focused only on English language tweets. Models submitted for the SemEval 2018 Task 2 (Barbieri et al., 2018) are the most multilingual emoji prediction models currently published, but this task considered only English and Spanish tweets. Because COVID-19 is a worldwide phenomenon, however, to understand emotional responses to COVID-19, we must be able to predict emojis in all languages used on Twitter. We therefore introduce the first highly multilingual model for emoji prediction, which we call BERTmoticon. Our model is based on fine-tuning the multilingual BERT model (Devlin et al., 2018), which was trained on a dataset of 102 distinct languages. Figure 1 shows the output of our model on a tweet translated into ten different languages.

A large body of work has emerged analyzing tweets about COVID-19. One prominent line of research attempts to identify how misinformation about the disease spreads online (Elhadad et al., 2020, Kouzy et al., 2020, Prabhakar Kaila et al., 2020, Sharma et al., 2020, Yang et al., 2020). An important subcategory of this research investigates the spread of racist (Budhwani and Sun, 2020, Schild et al., 2020) and ageist (Jimenez-Sotomayor et al., 2020) misinformation. Other research more similar to our own investigates the sentiment of tweets about the coronavirus. Some of this research focuses on specific locations such as Belgium (Kurten and Beullens, 2020), Paris (Saire and Cruz, 2020), Poland (Jarynowski et al., 2020) or India (Das and Dutta, 2020). Other research studies English-language tweets (Rajput et al., 2020, Yin et al., 2020) over wider geographic areas. Our research stands out from this prior work in two important ways. First, we do not consider a subset of tweets about COVID-19, we consider all tweets, written in all languages, sent from anywhere in the world. This is a significantly more challenging technical problem than previous research addressed, but it is also much more useful. Second, we are the first paper to consider the more general emoji prediction problem rather than the sentiment prediction problem. In sentiment prediction, the goal is to assign a positive or negative sentiment to each tweet, and for the coronavirus topic it can be difficult to decidedly assign one sentiment. Tweets about COVID-19 can express negative sentiments because the disease has killed millions of people and forced us to make drastic changes to our lifestyles but also can contain funny, uplifting content exhibiting a positive sentiment such as:

Happy #NationalCatDay from my beautiful adopted pandemic pet!

In the emoji prediction task, we are able to get a more fine-tuned emotional understanding of tweets. For example, we can answer questions like: is the tweet sad? angry? joyful?

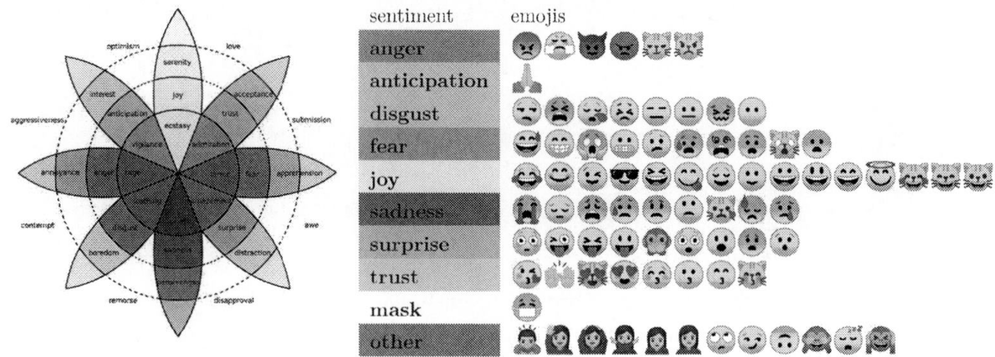

Figure 2: (*Left*) The Plutchik wheel of emotions. (*Right*) We have grouped the emoticons into 10 different categories: 8 emotional categories from the Plutchnik wheel, 1 category for the "face with medical mask" emoticon, and 1 category for all other emoticons that represent emotions that are not clearly in the Plutchik wheel.

Our contributions are as follows. In Section 2 we introduce the first dataset for training highly multilingual emoji prediction models, `TwitterEmoticon`. We then use this dataset to train the first highly multilingual emoticon prediction model, `BERTmoticon`. Our model is open source and has an easy to use PyPi package.[1] In Section 3, we introduce the first highly multilingual dataset of tweets about COVID-19, called `TwitterCOVID`. To generate the dataset, we introduce a novel dataset generation method combining the Twitter API, Bing Translate, and the `spaCy` tokenization library (Honnibal and Montani, 2017). We then apply the `BERTmoticon` model to the `TwitterCOVID` dataset to map how Twitter users across the world have emotionally responded to a variety of COVID-19 news events. This is the first highly multilingual emotion analysis of tweets in any language, and by far the most comprehensive analysis to-date specifically about the COVID-19 pandemic.

2 The `BERTmoticon` Model

In this section, we first describe the emoticons we are trying to predict and present the `TwitterEmoticon` dataset that the `BERTmoticon` model was trained on. Then we describe our training procedure and model evaluation results. We take particular care to ensure that the `TwitterEmoticon` dataset is sampled from a similar distribution to the `TwitterCOVID` dataset analyzed in Section 3 below in order to ensure that the `BERTmoticon` model will transfer well to this unlabeled dataset.

2.1 The Target Emoticons

Emojis were first added to the Unicode standard in 2010, and the current version of the standard (12.1.0) defines 3304 different emojis (The Unicode Consortium, 2019). Prior work on emoji prediction has limited itself to predicting only a subset of the available emojis. For example, Barbieri et al. (2017) consider only the 20 most commonly used emoji, and DeepMoji (Felbo et al., 2017) considers only 64 emoji. There are two primary reasons for only considering a subset of emoji. First, emoji-usage follows a power law distribution where the top 1% of most used emoji account for over 99% of all emoji usage.[2] There is therefore very little training data for the less popular emojis, and so we cannot expect a classifier to have high prediction accuracy for these emoji. Second, many emoji (e.g. the Greek Flag emoji 🇬🇷) do not contain emotional information, and so the ability to predict these emoji does not help us understand the emotional content of text.

We follow previous work and focus on predicting only a limited set of emoji. Specifically, we focus on the original 80 emoji defined in the Unicode standard's emoticon code block (code points `0x1f600`

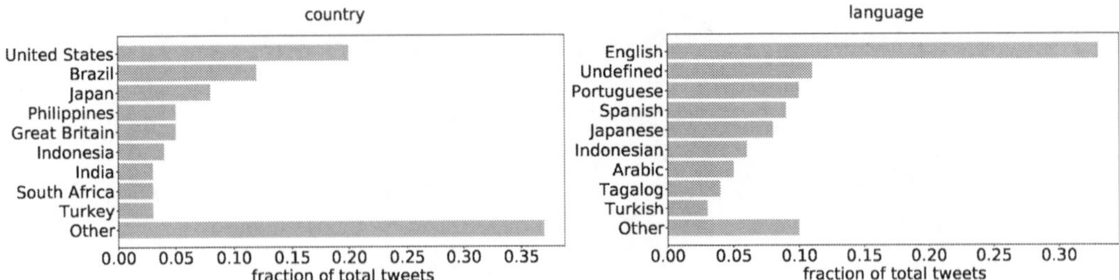

Figure 3: Stats on the most common countries of origin (*left*) and languages (*right*) for tweets in the `TwitterEmoticon` dataset. Languages are determined using Twitter's API, which has official support for 66 languages. It is known, however, that more than 100 language are actively used on Twitter (Hong et al., 2011), and our `BERTmoticon` model supports all of these languages. All prior work on emoji prediction has focused on only 1 or 2 languages.

$- 0x1f650$). In common usage, the words *emoji* and *emoticon* are interchangeable, but in this paper we adopt the Unicode Standard's definitions of these terms. By these definitions, an *emoji* is any one of 3304 pictographs that are not part of any written language, and an *emoticon* is one of the original 80 emoji defined in the code block specified above. We limit our analysis to emoticons for three reasons. First, they are the most commonly used emoji on twitter, so we can expect to achieve relatively high accuracy. Second, each emoticon represents an emotion (emoticon is a portmanteau of emotion and icon). Third, the emoticon block contains the "face with medical mask" emoji (☺), which is important for our case study analyzing emotional responses to the coronavirus.

Figure 2 shows the 80 emoticons and a mapping from these emoticons to the Plutchik wheel of emotions (Plutchik, 1991). The Plutchik wheel is a standard psychological model for encoding emotions that has been highly influential in emotion prediction systems (e.g. Kant et al., 2018, Liu et al., 2019, Suttles and Ide, 2013). It has 8 primary emotional categories (anger, anticipation, disgust, fear, joy, sadness, surprise, and trust). These emotions are arranged spatially so that similar emotions (e.g. joy, trust) appear near each other, and dissimilar emotions (e.g. joy, sadness) appear opposite each other. Furthermore, each emotional category is broken down into sub-categories that encode the strength of the emotion (e.g. ecstasy is an extreme form of joy, and serenity is a mild form of joy).

There is currently no standard mapping from emoticons onto the Plutchik wheel, and in Figure 2 (*right*) we provide a suggested mapping. To generate this mapping, we manually assigned each emoticon to an emotion based on the description of the emoticon on the website `emojipedia.org`. The mapping is not perfect. The category joy has many emoticons representing different facets of joy, but the category anticipation has only a single emoticon. We emphasize that our `BERTmoticon` model will predict raw emoticons directly, but we present the mapping onto the Plutchnik wheel emotions to help make the wide array of emoticon emotions more easily understandable.

2.2 The `TwitterEmoticon` Dataset

The `TwitterEmoticon` dataset is designed for training a classifier that takes as input a tweet and outputs an emoticon that represents the emotion of the tweet. To generate the dataset, we collected all geolocated[3] tweets sent over the six month period between January and June, 2020. Approximately 400 million tweets meet this criteria. Then we filtered these tweets so that only tweets containing one of our 80 target emoticons were included, and any retweets were removed. In total, the `TwitterEmoticon` dataset contains 64.2 million tweets sent by 4.2 million users. The tweets are written in 66 different languages and were sent from 246 different countries. Figure 3 shows the total number of tweets per

---

[3]Twitter users can adjust their privacy settings to include different amounts of geolocation metadata. In particular, they can include the exact GPS coordinate that a tweet was sent from, an approximate location (for example, the city that the tweet was sent from), or no location information at all. We say that a tweet is *geolocated* if any of this metadata is included about the tweet. Approximately 1% of all tweets are geolocated.

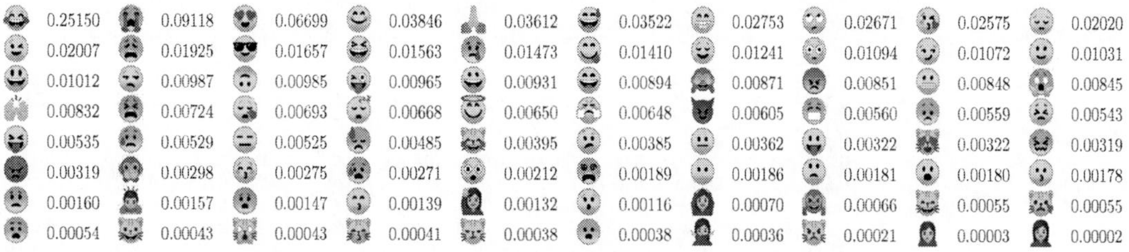

Figure 4: The 80 target emoticons we are trying to predict, and their fraction of all emoticons in the `TwitterEmoticon` dataset. The distribution follows a power law.

language, and Figure 4 shows the frequency of each emoticon in the dataset.

We preprocess each tweet by replacing all user mentions with a special token `<mention>` and all URLs with a special token `<url>` and deleting all emojis. We decided to keep all hashtags because hashtags can contain potentially valuable emotional content useful for emoticon prediction. Finally, we delete all emoticons from the tweet, and use the emoticons as the tweet's classification label. Most tweets have only a single emoticon label, but some tweets have multiple emoticons. This is a problem because standard multi-class classification techniques require only a single label per data point. We address the issue by following the procedure established by (Felbo et al., 2017). If a tweet has multiple emoticons, then we duplicate it in the training data once for each emoticon, with each instance being labeled by a single one of the emoticons.

We carefully split the `TwitterEmoticon` dataset into training, validation, and test sets ensuring that no user is present in more than one set in order to prevent data leakage. In particular we assign 80% of users to the training set, 10% to the validation set, and 10% to the test set. The tweets contained in each set are then the tweets sent by each of the users in the set.

2.3 Training Protocol

Our `BERTmoticon` model is the multilingual BERT model (Devlin et al., 2018) fine-tuned on the `TwitterEmoticon` dataset. The multilingual BERT model is a popular model for fine-tuning because it achieves state-of-the-art performance on a wide variety of natural language tasks. It was trained on data from 102 distinct languages, and the language of each training sample need not be known for either training or inference. Followup research has shown that the multilingual BERT model has language-independent internal representations that allow it to encode information from languages it has not seen during training time (Pires et al., 2019, Wu et al., 2019). Feng et al. (2020) recently released a more advanced version of the multilingual BERT model that achieves better performance on standard NLP tasks and uses 109 training languages. We would expect better performance on our emoticon-prediction task using this more advanced multilingual BERT model, but we did not use this model because all of our experiments were completed before this model was publicly released.

We followed a two step fine-tuning procedure. First, we trained only the last layer of the model, generating a model we call `BERTmoticon-LL`. Then, we trained all parameters to generate the `BERTmoticon` model, warm starting from `BERTmoticon-LL`. We used the validation set to select optimal hyperparameters for both models. `BERTmoticon-LL` was trained using Adam (Kingma and Ba, 2014) with a learning rate of 10^{-4}, and `BERTmoticon` was trained using Adam with a learning rate of 10^{-5}. Both models used a batch size of 64. A single epoch on the `TwitterEmoticon` dataset took approximately 6 days to run on one NVidia GeForce RTX 2080 GPU. We trained both models on a single epoch, but found that the model converged before the epoch was finished.

2.4 Model Evaluation

The `BERTmoticon-LL` model achieves a Macro-F1 score of 0.159 on the test set and the `BERTmoticon` model achieves a Macro-F1 score of 0.210. Table 1 shows a performance breakdown by emoji and by language. Prediction performance on each language varies dramatically because each

113

	😂	🙏	😍	😷	😭	😊	😴	😒	😮	😔	😡	😌	Macro-F1
Model													
BERTmoticon-LL	0.440	0.226	0.190	0.111	0.111	0.185	0.018	0.111	0.049	0.008	0.011	0.007	0.159
BERTmoticon	**0.479**	**0.361**	**0.309**	**0.256**	**0.249**	**0.244**	**0.215**	**0.211**	**0.106**	**0.078**	**0.073**	**0.035**	**0.210**
Language													
Arabic	0.637	0.268	0.224	0.117	0.002	0.000	0.064	0.000	0.000	0.006	0.000	0.000	0.319
Dutch	0.371	0.201	0.141	0.149	0.364	0.225	0.068	0.027	0.055	0.004	0.006	0.000	0.168
English	0.506	0.367	0.295	0.235	0.241	0.230	0.160	0.201	0.128	0.034	0.031	0.006	0.221
French	0.418	0.196	0.227	0.356	0.414	0.109	0.083	0.056	0.180	0.010	0.008	0.004	0.208
Hindi	0.443	0.717	0.103	0.067	0.027	0.007	0.025	0.016	0.010	0.002	0.010	0.000	0.310
Indonesian	0.442	0.339	0.188	0.393	0.218	0.065	0.073	0.053	0.073	0.002	0.027	0.001	0.203
Italian	0.430	0.119	0.273	0.144	0.439	0.205	0.168	0.220	0.074	0.031	0.071	0.007	0.181
Japanese	0.115	0.142	0.199	0.223	0.003	0.336	0.268	0.323	0.137	0.000	0.055	0.004	0.133
Portuguese	0.380	0.340	0.426	0.249	0.128	0.004	0.294	0.310	0.092	0.155	0.183	0.110	0.177
Russian	0.375	0.044	0.267	0.248	0.249	0.028	0.000	0.000	0.000	0.000	0.000	0.000	0.122
Spanish	0.388	0.305	0.381	0.254	0.423	0.090	0.185	0.183	0.142	0.087	0.073	0.065	0.170
Tagalog	0.509	0.225	0.247	0.293	0.174	0.051	0.154	0.070	0.035	0.035	0.002	0.019	0.208
Thai	0.271	0.022	0.124	0.208	0.000	0.042	0.009	0.023	0.012	0.000	0.000	0.000	0.078
Turkish	0.469	0.392	0.132	0.118	0.085	0.121	0.023	0.055	0.036	0.059	0.003	0.002	0.174
(∗) Undefined	0.485	0.103	0.127	0.042	0.003	0.010	0.083	0.030	0.041	0.008	0.042	0.000	0.171

Table 1: (*top*) F1 scores for the BERTmoticon-LL and BERTmoticon models on 12 selected emojis, and the Macro-F1 incorporating all 80 target emoticons. The full BERTmoticon model offers significantly better performance across all emoji categories. (*bottom*) Performance of the BERTmoticon model broken down by language on 15 selected languages. The Undefined language corresponds to tweets for which the Twitter API was not able to assign a language. Even for these tweets, which are either written in an unsupported language or do not a significant amount of text within them, the BERTmoticon model is able to get performance comparable to many officially supported languages.

bacteria, cdc, china, corona, coronavirus, cough, covid, covid-19, covid19, disease, doctor, epidemic, fever, flatten the curve, flu, lockdown, n95, ncov, nurse, outbreak, pandemic, sars-cov-2, sick, sinophobia, social distancing, trump, vaccine, virus, wuhan

Figure 5: The 29 English-language search terms we used to select tweets. These terms were translated using Bing Translate into 72 other languages as part of our multilingual tweet filtering process.

language uses emojis with different frequencies. Arabic language tweets, for example, use the "crying tears of joy" emoticon (😂) frequently, but rarely use the "smiling face with heart eyes" emoticon (😍). The model has therefore learned to favor predictions of this emoticon whenever these predictions are present in the tweet. As Figure 1 demonstrates, this causes the same text translated into different languages to receive different emoji labels. We believe that this is a strength of our model, as different cultures use emojis differently, and our model is able to capture this fact.

3   Coronavirus Case Study

We now apply the BERTmoticon model to understand the emotional response of Twitter users to news about the coronavirus. We first introduce our TwitterCOVID dataset, then we present an analysis of this dataset.

3.1   The TwitterCOVID Dataset

The goal of the TwitterCOVID dataset is to include any geolocated tweet that references COVID-19 in any language. There is currently no standard procedure for generating multilingual datasets of tweets about a topic, so we used the following four step procedure: (1) We generated a list of 29 English-language search terms related to the coronavirus, as shown in Figure 5. The choice of terms was inspired by the terms used in a dataset generated by Chen et al. (2020), but we also removed Twitterisms like "kungflu" which would not translate well into non-English languages. (We discuss in detail the full differences between our dataset and the dataset of Chen et al. (2020) below.) Our search terms include generic words like "china" and "trump" that are not necessarily about the coronavirus, but given the time period we searched over, many tweets including these terms will be about the coronavirus. (2) We then used Bing's translation API to translate each of these terms into the 72 languages supported by Bing

Afrikaans, Arabic, Armenian, Bulgarian, Catalan, Chinese, Croatian, Czech, Danish, Dutch, English, Estonian, Finnish, French, German, Greek, Gujarati, Hebrew, Hindi, Hungarian, Icelandic, Indonesian, Irish, Italian, Japanese, Kannada, Korean, Latvian, Lithuanian, Malayalam, Marathi, Norwegian Bokmål, Persian, Polish, Portuguese, Romanian, Russian, Serbian, Sinhala, Slovak, Slovenian, Spanish, Swedish, Tagalog, Tamil, Tatar, Telugu, Thai, Turkish, Ukrainian, Urdu, Vietnamese

Figure 6: The full list of 54 languages supported by all 3 tools in our processing pipeline (Bing translate, Spacy, and the Twitter API). Tweets in other languages are also included in our `TwitterCOVID` dataset, but the filtering step is less accurate for these unsupported languages.

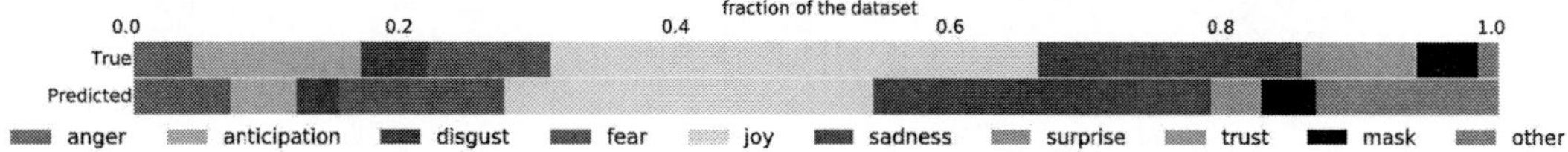

Figure 7: (*top*) The distribution of emotions in the subset of `TwitterCOVID` that contain emojis. (*bottom*) The distribution of emotions in the subset of `TwitterCOVID` that did not contain emojis, and that we used `BERTmoticon` to assign predictions for.

translate. (3) We used Python's `spaCy` library (Honnibal and Montani, 2017) to tokenize and lemmatize each of the 400 million geolocated tweets sent between January and June 2020. This is the same time period that we examined for the `TwitterEmoticon` dataset, and so we hope that the `BERTmoticon` model trained on the `TwitterEmoticon` dataset will transfer well to this `TwitterCOVID` dataset. `spaCy` supports tokenization in 58 different languages, and for each tweet we used the appropriate `spaCy` module for the language specified in the tweet's metadata. For languages not directly supported by `spaCy`, we tokenized on whitespace. (4) Finally, the `TwitterCOVID` dataset is constructed as the set of all tweets whose lemmatized text contains any of the search terms from the tweet's language or English. We include both languages in this filtering step because it is common for non-English tweets to use English words like "coronavirus" when referencing the virus. Figure 6 shows the full list of 54 languages that are supported by all 3 services. The `TwitterCOVID` dataset contains tweets in an unknown number of other languages, and the filtering procedure for these unsupported languages used language-agnostic steps, which likely results in less recall. In total, 16.2 million tweets meet the criteria to be included in the `TwitterCOVID` dataset.

The other significant dataset of coronavirus related tweets was introduced by Chen et al. (2020). There are two main differences between our dataset and theirs. First, we only include geolocated tweets, whereas they include non-geolocated tweets as well. This results in their dataset being about fifteen times larger than ours, with about 250 million tweets over the same time period. Because their data is not geolocated, however, it is not suitable for understanding how different countries have reacted emotionally to COVID-19. The second difference is that our dataset uses a more advanced language-aware filtering method. They only search for tweets that contain English keywords. Most languages, however, have few words in common with English, and non-Latin based languages frequently do not even use the word "coronavirus" to describe the virus. Chinese tweets, for example, commonly refer to COVID-19 with the string 病毒 , and Chinese-language tweets containing this string will get included in our dataset but not in their dataset. As a result of this more advanced processing, the fraction of non-English tweets is much larger in our dataset than theirs (48% versus 38%). Capturing as many non-English tweets as possible about COVID-19 is important for ensuring that our analysis is not unfairly skewed towards English-speaking countries.

3.2 Results

Only 15.11% percent of tweets in the `TwitterCOVID` dataset contain an emoticon. We used the `BERTmoticon` model to label the remaining tweets. Figure 7 shows the distribution of tweets present in the dataset vs those we predicted. The anticipation, disgust, joy, surprise, and trust emoticons appear less frequently in the predicted dataset, and the anger, sadness, and fear emotions appear more often in the predicted set. We hypothesize that this difference is due to the fact that more-formal Twitter accounts (such as for newspapers or government organizations) are less likely to use emoji in their tweets, and

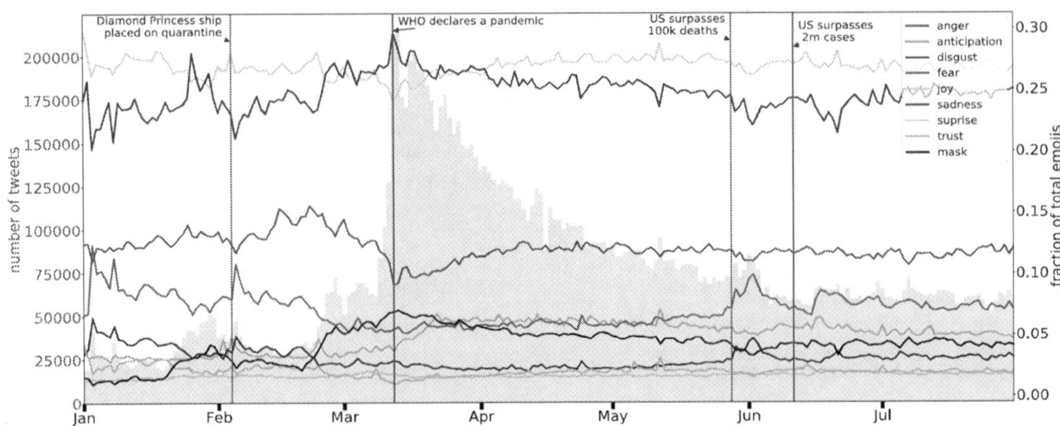

Figure 8: The emotional content of tweets in the `TwitterCOVID` dataset changes over time and reacts to major news events. The shaded bar plot in the background shows the total number of tweets in the `TwitterCOVID` dataset sent on a particular day (left y-axis scale), and the colored line charts show the fraction of tweets in a particular day that correspond to each emotion on the Plutchik wheel or the mask emoji (right y-axis scale). We can see clear emotional reactions to the news events labelled with vertical lines.

these formal accounts also tweet about different topics than more informal accounts of ordinary people.

Our main result is shown in Figure 8. For each day, we calculate the fraction of tweets that represent each emotion from the Plutchik wheel (see Figure 2), and we can observe a strong correlation between the emotional content of tweets and important COVID-19 news. For example, on March 11, the World Health Organization (WHO) declared COVID-19 a worldwide pandemic. At the same time, we can see a large spike in tweets about the coronavirus, and in particular we see an increase in sadness and a decrease in joy. Since sadness and joy are at opposite ends of the Plutchik wheel of emotions, it makes sense that a rise in one would cause a fall in the other. As another example, on May 28, the United States had its one hundred thousandth death to the coronavirus. At the same time, we see spikes in anger and disgust. The following tweet from this time period is a representative example:

> *How do we tolerate 3000 Americans dying everyday from #COVID19? THREE. THOUSAND. EVERY. DAY.*

This tweet was not originally sent with any emoticons, but our `BERTmoticon` model was able to label it with 😷, 😶, 😩, 😰. As another example, notice that the mask emoji usage increases in mid-January. Interestingly, at that time little information was available about COVID-19 and protecting yourself against it. Finally, in early February some important news-events that circulated in Twitter were the Diamond Princess Ship being placed under quarantine and the death of Doctor Li Wenliang (a Chinese doctor who issued a warning about the coronavirus before the pandemic was officially recognized). At that point we notice a spike in anger and disgust.

4 Conclusion

We introduced the `BERTmoticon` model for multilingual emoji prediction, and used this model to better understand how Twitter users responded emotionally to news about the coronavirus. In follow up studies, we hope to analyze how different countries and language communities reacted differently to events, and have designed our `TwitterCOVID` dataset and `BERTmoticon` model to facilitate these cross-sectional analyses. We also hope that the `BERTmoticon` model will prove useful for analyzing the emotions of text in other contexts outside of COVID-19, and we make the model available in an easy to use Python package to facilitate this process.

References

Francesco Barbieri, Miguel Ballesteros, and Horacio Saggion. Are emojis predictable? *arXiv preprint arXiv:1702.07285*, 2017.

Francesco Barbieri, Jose Camacho-Collados, Francesco Ronzano, Luis Espinosa Anke, Miguel Ballesteros, Valerio Basile, Viviana Patti, and Horacio Saggion. Semeval 2018 task 2: Multilingual emoji prediction. In *Proceedings of The 12th International Workshop on Semantic Evaluation*, pages 24–33, 2018.

Henna Budhwani and Ruoyan Sun. Creating covid-19 stigma by referencing the novel coronavirus as the "chinese virus" on twitter: Quantitative analysis of social media data. *Journal of Medical Internet Research*, 22(5):e19301, 2020.

Emily Chen, Kristina Lerman, and Emilio Ferrara. Tracking social media discourse about the covid-19 pandemic: Development of a public coronavirus twitter data set. *JMIR Public Health and Surveillance*, 6(2):e19273, 2020.

Marcel Danesi. *The semiotics of emoji: The rise of visual language in the age of the internet.* Bloomsbury Publishing, 2016.

Subasish Das and Anandi Dutta. Characterizing public emotions and sentiments in covid-19 environment: A case study of india. *Journal of Human Behavior in the Social Environment*, 0(0):1–14, 2020. doi: 10.1080/10911359.2020.1781015. URL https://doi.org/10.1080/10911359.2020.1781015.

Jacob Devlin, Ming-Wei Chang, Kenton Lee, and Kristina Toutanova. Bert: Pre-training of deep bidirectional transformers for language understanding, 2018.

Mohamed K Elhadad, Kin Fun Li, and Fayez Gebali. Covid-19-fakes: a twitter (arabic/english) dataset for detecting misleading information on covid-19. In *International Conference on Intelligent Networking and Collaborative Systems*, pages 256–268. Springer, 2020.

Bjarke Felbo, Alan Mislove, Anders Søgaard, Iyad Rahwan, and Sune Lehmann. Using millions of emoji occurrences to learn any-domain representations for detecting sentiment, emotion and sarcasm. *arXiv preprint arXiv:1708.00524*, 2017.

Fangxiaoyu Feng, Yinfei Yang, Daniel Cer, Naveen Arivazhagan, and Wei Wang. Language-agnostic bert sentence embedding. *arXiv preprint arXiv:2007.01852*, 2020.

Lichan Hong, Gregorio Convertino, and Ed H Chi. Language matters in twitter: A large scale study. In *ICWSM*, 2011.

Matthew Honnibal and Ines Montani. spaCy 2: Natural language understanding with Bloom embeddings, convolutional neural networks and incremental parsing. To appear, 2017.

Andrzej Jarynowski, Monika Wojta-Kempa, and Vitaly Belik. Perception of emergent epidemic of covid-2019/sars cov-2 on the polish internet. *Available at SSRN 3572662*, 2020.

Maria Renee Jimenez-Sotomayor, Carolina Gomez-Moreno, and Enrique Soto-Perez-de Celis. Coronavirus, ageism, and twitter: An evaluation of tweets about older adults and covid-19. *Journal of the American Geriatrics Society*, 2020.

Neel Kant, Raul Puri, Nikolai Yakovenko, and Bryan Catanzaro. Practical text classification with large pre-trained language models. *arXiv preprint arXiv:1812.01207*, 2018.

Diederik P Kingma and Jimmy Ba. Adam: A method for stochastic optimization. *arXiv preprint arXiv:1412.6980*, 2014.

Ramez Kouzy, Joseph Abi Jaoude, Afif Kraitem, Molly B El Alam, Basil Karam, Elio Adib, Jabra Zarka, Cindy Traboulsi, Elie W Akl, and Khalil Baddour. Coronavirus goes viral: quantifying the covid-19 misinformation epidemic on twitter. *Cureus*, 12(3), 2020.

Sebastian Kurten and Kathleen Beullens. # coronavirus: Monitoring the belgian twitter discourse on the severe acute respiratory syndrome coronavirus 2 pandemic. *Cyberpsychology, Behavior, and Social Networking*, 2020.

Chen Liu, Muhammad Osama, and Anderson De Andrade. Dens: a dataset for multi-class emotion analysis. *arXiv preprint arXiv:1910.11769*, 2019.

Telmo Pires, Eva Schlinger, and Dan Garrette. How multilingual is multilingual bert? *arXiv preprint arXiv:1906.01502*, 2019.

Robert Plutchik. *The emotions*. University Press of America, 1991.

Dr Prabhakar Kaila, Dr AV Prasad, et al. Informational flow on twitter–corona virus outbreak–topic modelling approach. *International Journal of Advanced Research in Engineering and Technology (IJARET)*, 11(3), 2020.

Nikhil Kumar Rajput, Bhavya Ahuja Grover, and Vipin Kumar Rathi. Word frequency and sentiment analysis of twitter messages during coronavirus pandemic. *arXiv preprint arXiv:2004.03925*, 2020.

Josimar E Chire Saire and Jimmy Frank Oblitas Cruz. Study of coronavirus impact on parisian population from april to june using twitter and text mining approach. *medRxiv*, 2020.

Leonard Schild, Chen Ling, Jeremy Blackburn, Gianluca Stringhini, Yang Zhang, and Savvas Zannettou. " go eat a bat, chang!": An early look on the emergence of sinophobic behavior on web communities in the face of covid-19. *arXiv preprint arXiv:2004.04046*, 2020.

Karishma Sharma, Sungyong Seo, Chuizheng Meng, Sirisha Rambhatla, Aastha Dua, and Yan Liu. Coronavirus on social media: Analyzing misinformation in twitter conversations. *arXiv preprint arXiv:2003.12309*, 2020.

Jared Suttles and Nancy Ide. Distant supervision for emotion classification with discrete binary values. In *International Conference on Intelligent Text Processing and Computational Linguistics*, pages 121–136. Springer, 2013.

The Unicode Consortium. The Unicode Standard. Technical Report Version 12.1.0, Unicode Consortium, 2019. URL http://www.unicode.org/versions/Unicode12.1.0/.

Shijie Wu, Alexis Conneau, Haoran Li, Luke Zettlemoyer, and Veselin Stoyanov. Emerging cross-lingual structure in pretrained language models. *arXiv preprint arXiv:1911.01464*, 2019.

Kai-Cheng Yang, Christopher Torres-Lugo, and Filippo Menczer. Prevalence of low-credibility information on twitter during the covid-19 outbreak. *arXiv preprint arXiv:2004.14484*, 2020.

Hui Yin, Shuiqiao Yang, and Jianxin Li. Detecting topic and sentiment dynamics due to covid-19 pandemic using social media. *arXiv preprint arXiv:2007.02304*, 2020.

Linrui Zhang, Yisheng Zhou, Yang Yu, and Dan Moldovan. Towards understanding creative language in tweets. *Journal of Software Engineering and Applications*, 12:447–459, 01 2019. doi: 10.4236/jsea.2019.1211028.

Experiencers, Stimuli, or Targets:
Which Semantic Roles Enable Machine Learning to Infer the Emotions?

Laura Oberländer, Kevin Reich, and **Roman Klinger**
Institut für Maschinelle Sprachverarbeitung, University of Stuttgart, Germany
`{firstname.lastname}@ims.uni-stuttgart.de`

Abstract

Emotion recognition is predominantly formulated as text classification in which textual units are assigned to an emotion from a predefined inventory (e.g., fear, joy, anger, disgust, sadness, surprise, trust, anticipation). More recently, semantic role labeling approaches have been developed to extract structures from the text to answer questions like: "who is described to feel the emotion?" (experiencer), "what causes this emotion?" (stimulus), and at which entity is it directed?" (target). Though it has been shown that jointly modeling stimulus and emotion category prediction is beneficial for both subtasks, it remains unclear which of these semantic roles enables a classifier to infer the emotion. Is it the experiencer, because the identity of a person is biased towards a particular emotion (X is always happy)? Is it a particular target (everybody loves X) or a stimulus (doing X makes everybody sad)? We answer these questions by training emotion classification models on five available datasets annotated with at least one semantic role by masking the fillers of these roles in the text in a controlled manner and find that across multiple corpora, stimuli and targets carry emotion information, while the experiencer might be considered a confounder. Further, we analyze if informing the model about the position of the role improves the classification decision. Particularly on literature corpora we find that the role information improves the emotion classification.

1 Introduction

Emotion analysis is now an established research area which finds application in a variety of different fields, including social media analysis (Purver and Battersby, 2012; Wang et al., 2012; Mohammad and Bravo-Marquez, 2017; Ying et al., 2019, i.a.), opinion mining (Choi et al., 2006, i.a.), and computational literary studies (Alm et al., 2005; Kim and Klinger, 2019a; Haider et al., 2020; Zehe et al., 2020, i.a.). The most prominent task in emotion analysis is emotion categorization, where text receives assignments from a predefined emotion inventory, such as the fundamental emotions of *fear, anger, joy, anticipation, trust, surprise, disgust,* and *sadness* which follow theories by Ekman (1999) or Plutchik (2001). Other tasks include the recognition of affect values, namely valence or arousal (Posner et al., 2005) or analyses of event appraisal (Hofmann et al., 2020; Scherer, 2005).

More recently, categorization (or regression) tasks have been complemented by more fine-grained analyses, namely emotion stimulus detection and role labeling, to detect which words denote the experiencer of an emotion, the emotion cue description, or the target of an emotion. These efforts lead to computational approaches of detecting stimulus clauses (Xia and Ding, 2019; Wei et al., 2020; Gao et al., 2017) and emotion role labeling and sequence labeling (Mohammad et al., 2014; Bostan et al., 2020; Kim and Klinger, 2018; Ghazi et al., 2015; Zehe et al., 2020), with different advantages and disadvantages we discuss in Oberländer and Klinger (2020).

Further, this work led to a rich set of corpora with annotations of different subsets of roles. An example of a sentence annotated with semantic role labels for emotion is "[John]$_{\text{EXPERIENCER}}$ [hates]$_{\text{CUE}}$ [cars]$_{\text{TARGET}}$ because they [pollute the environment]$_{\text{STIMULUS}}$." A number of English-language resources are available: Ghazi et al. (2015)

Proceedings of the Third Workshop on Computational Modeling of PEople's Opinions, PersonaLity, and Emotions in Social media, pages 119–128
Barcelona, Spain (Online), December 13, 2020.

Dataset	Whole Instance		Stimulus		Cue		Target		Exp.	
	#	∅len	#	∅len	#	∅len	#	∅len	#	∅len
Emotion-Stimulus, Ghazi et al. (2015)	2414	20.60	820	7.29	—	—	—	—	—	—
ElectoralTweets, Mohammad et al. (2014)	4056	19.14	2427	6.25	2930	5.08	2824	1.71	29	1.76
GoodNewsEveryone, Bostan et al. (2020)	5000	13.00	4798	7.29	4736	1.60	4474	4.86	3458	2.03
REMAN, Kim and Klinger (2018)	1720	72.03	609	9.33	1720	3.82	706	5.35	1050	2.04
Emotion Cause Analysis, Gao et al. (2017)	2558	62.24	2485	9.52	—	—	—	—	—	—

Table 1: Datasets with annotations of roles. # refers to the number of total instances. ∅len shows the average length of each role filler in each dataset in the number of tokens.

manually construct a dataset following FrameNet's emotion predicate and annotate the stimulus as its core argument. Mohammad et al. (2014) annotate Tweets for emotion cue phrases, emotion targets, and the emotion stimulus. In our previous work (Bostan et al., 2020) we publish news headlines annotated with the roles of emotion experiencer, cue, target, and stimulus. Kim and Klinger (2018) annotate sentence triples taken from literature for the same roles. A popular benchmark for emotion stimulus detection is the Mandarin corpus by Gui et al. (2016). Gao et al. (2017) annotate English and Mandarin texts in a comparable way on the clause level (*Emotion Cause Analysis*, ECA).

In this paper, we utilize role annotations to understand their influence on emotion classification. We evaluate which of the roles' contents enable an emotion classifier to infer the emotions. It is reasonable to assume that the roles' content carries different kinds of information regarding the emotion: One particular experiencer present in a corpus might always feel the same emotion; hence, be prone to a bias the model could pick up on. The target or stimulus might be independent of the experiencer and be sufficient to infer the emotion. The presence of a target might limit the set of emotions that can be triggered. Finally, as some of the corpora contain cue annotations, we assume that these are the most helpful to decide on the expressed emotion, as they typically have explicit references towards concrete emotion names.

2 Experimental Setting

In the following, we describe our experiments to understand which of the datasets' annotated roles contribute to the emotion classification performance.

Datasets. We base our experiments on five available datasets that are annotated for at least one of the roles of an experiencer, stimulus, target, or cue. The dataset by Ghazi et al. (2015) is one of the earliest we are aware of that contains stimulus annotations. They annotate based on FrameNet's *emotion-directed* frames that have a stimulus argument in the data (we refer to their corpus as *Emotion-Stimulus*, ES). Similarly early work is the Twitter corpus by Mohammad et al. (2014) (*ElectoralTweets*, ET). They also follow the emotion frame semantics definition but use data concerning the 2012 U.S. election. Therefore, their resource may be considered more diverse in language but more consistent in its domain than ES. More recently, Bostan et al. (2020) published an annotation of news headlines (*GoodNewsEveryone*, GNE). While they do not limit their corpus on a domain, they use a comparably narrow time window to retrieve the data and sample according to the inclusion of emotion words and popularity on social media. Kim and Klinger (2018, *REMAN*) and Gao et al. (2017, *Emotion Cause Analysis*, ECA) use literature data, which might be considered the most challenging for emotion analysis (for ECA, we use the English subset only).

As Table 1 shows, the literature data (REMAN, ECA) has the longest instances and also the longest stimulus annotations. The other resources have less than one third of their length in tokens, with GNE being the shortest. However, the overall annotation length does not differ dramatically. Cue, target, and experiencer annotations are only available in three out of five corpora (ET, REMAN, and GNE)[1].

Model Configuration. Our goal is to analyze the importance of different roles for the emotion classification. We use two different models, namely a bidirectional long short-term memory network (Hochreiter

---

[1]For ET, 90% of the annotated experiencers are the authors of the tweets without corresponding span annotation.

and Schmidhuber, 1997) with pretrained 300-dimensional GloVe embeddings[2] and a transformer-based model, RoBERTa (Liu et al., 2019). Both models take as input the text sequence and output the emotion class, where the concrete set of emotion labels depends on the dataset.

The models have different advantages and disadvantages in our experimental setting. The bi-LSTM with non-contextualized word embeddings might be more appropriate to be used in our setting in which we manipulate the input token sequence (see below). The transformer might benefit from the rich contextualized pretraining, which is particularly relevant given that the annotated corpora are of comparably limited size (in the context of deep learning)[3].

Setting and Hypotheses. We apply these models in several settings (illustrated in Table 2), which differ in the availability of information from the roles, namely (1), *As-Is*: This is the standard setting: The classifier has access to the whole text. (2), *Without* the text of the particular roles. (3), *Only* with the text of a particular role, masking the text that does not belong to it. Finally, (4), we keep the information available as is, but besides inform the model about the *Position* of the role. The latter is realized by adding positional indicators, inspired by Kim and Klinger (2019b) who showed the use of positional indicators for emotion relation classification[4].

Setting	Model Input							
As-Is	John	hates	cars	because	they	pollute	the	environment
Only Stim.	X	X	X	X	X	pollute	the	environment
Only Exp.	John	X	X	X	X	X	X	X
Only Tar.	X	X	cars	X	X	X	X	X
Without Stim.	John	hates	cars	because	they	X	X	X
Without Exp.	X	hates	cars	because	they	pollute	the	environment
Without Tar.	John	hates	X	because	they	pollute	the	environment
Pos. Stim.	John	hates	cars	because	they	⌊pollute	the	environment⌉
Pos. Exp.	⌊John⌉	hates	cars	because	they	pollute	the	environment
Pos. Tar.	John	hates	⌊cars⌉	because	they	pollute	the	environment

Table 2: Illustration of the experimental settings. X, ⌊, ⌉ denote special tokens added to the input according to each setting.

For roles that carry information relevant for emotion classification, we expect the *Without* setting to show a drop in performance compared to the *As-Is* setting. In such cases, the *Only* setting might show comparable performance, and the *Position* setting would show further improvements. When the role is a confounder, the performance in the *Without* setting is expected to be increased over the *As-Is* setting.

The label set depends on each of the datasets. For ES, we use the emotion labels *anger, disgust, fear, joy, no emotion, sadness,* and *surprise*; for ECA, we use *anger, sadness, disgust, joy, fear, surprise,* and *no emotion*. For GNE and ET, we merge the categories according to the rules described for ET by Bostan and Klinger (2018) and keep the primary emotions described in Plutchik's wheel. For REMAN, we group similarly and keep *anger, disgust, fear, joy, anticipation, surprise, sadness, trust,* and *no emotion*. ECA has a low number of instances annotated with multiple labels, which we ignore to keep all tasks as single-label classification. REMAN has emotion annotations only for the middle sentence in each triple. Thus we include only these middle segments in our experiments.

The results are based on a random split of each dataset into train, validation, and test (0.8, 0.1, 0.1). We report macro-averages across 10 runs for the bi-LSTM and 5 runs for RoBERTa.

3 Results

In the following, we discuss the results of the bi-LSTM model in detail and then point to differences to those of the transformer-based approach. Table 3 shows the results of our experiments for the bi-LSTM-

---

[2]We use 42B tokens, pretrained on CommonCrawl (Pennington et al., 2014), `https://nlp.stanford.edu/projects/glove/`

[3]The hyperparameters and details for the models are as follows. For the bi-LSTM, we set a dropout and recurrent dropout of 0.3 and optimize with Adam (Kingma and Ba, 2015), with a base learning rate of 0.0003, L2 regularization, on a batch size of 32, with early stopping with patience of 3, and initialization with Kaiming (He et al., 2015). We train for up to 100 epochs for the bi-LSTM model and 10 for the transformer-based model. Both models fine-tune their input representations during training. The hyperparameters of the model are optimized for ECA. For the bi-LSTM, we use AllenNLP (Gardner et al., 2018) and for the transformer the Hugging Face library (Wolf et al., 2019) (following the training procedure described by Devlin et al. (2019)). The code of our project is available at `http://www.ims.uni-stuttgart.de/data/emotion-classification-roles`.

[4]We experimented with adding two channels in the input embeddings which mark the tokens outside a role annotation with a 1 in one channel and the tokens which belong to the role annotation with a 1 in a second channel. The results were inferior to using positional indicators.

Dataset	Role	As-Is			Without			Only			Position		
		P	R	F_1	P	R	F_1	P	R	F_1	P	R	F_1
ECA	Stimulus	41	39	39	**48**	**48**	**48**	30	25	23	**52**	**51**	**51**
ES	Stimulus	93	89	90	**94**	89	90	65	23	18	**95**	**90**	**92**
REMAN	Cue	47	27	25	**61**	14	8	**53**	14	8	42	23	19
	Stimulus				41	22	19	**91**	11	4	44	14	12
	Experiencer				29	23	19	**60**	11	6	32	25	21
	Target				19	12	9	**57**	10	3	31	23	21
ET	Cue	51	26	25	**63**	23	22	**79**	18	15	**62**	25	23
	Stimulus				50	23	21	**59**	15	11	**57**	**27**	**27**
	Experiencer				53	26	24	**80**	12	7	48	23	20
	Target				56	**27**	**26**	**64**	16	14	**65**	24	21
GNE	Cue	34	14	12	**62**	13	10	**93**	10	5	**64**	13	10
	Stimulus				**93**	10	5	**85**	11	7	**60**	13	9
	Experiencer				**55**	**18**	**15**	**93**	10	5	**63**	**15**	**13**
	Target				**86**	12	8	**93**	10	5	**62**	14	11

Table 3: Results of our bi-LSTM based model for emotion classification, with access to all tokens (*As-Is*), *Only* to the respective role, to all tokens *Without* the respective role, and all tokens together with the *Position*al indicators of the role added. All F_1 scores are macro averaged, the scores which are higher than in the As-Is setting are bold.

based model. Intuitively, we would expect the *As-Is* setting to outperform both the *Without* and *Only* settings because there is more information available to the model. Conversely, because information is added in *Position*, we expect it to outperform the *As-Is* setting. As we see in column *As-Is*, the scores for the emotion classification task differ substantially, even when all available information is shown to the model. In the *Without* setting, we see that removing information can sometimes help a model improve its decision. For instance, when we mask the labels of the respective role, we observe a performance increase for the experiencer role in GNE, which could potentially point to an unwanted bias for particular experiencers in this corpus. This is also the case for the stimulus role in ECA and the target role in ET.

As expected, an important role for emotion classification is the cue. In REMAN, the performance drops the most when the classifier does not see the cue span and gains the most when only the cue is available. For all other corpora, the cue role is not as important, but performance still shows a drop when it is not available (*Without*). Similarly, for all datasets except ECA, the performance drops when the stimulus is not shown. On the other hand, the stimulus alone is insufficient to infer the emotion with competitive performance. Noteworthy here is the corpus ES, in which the performance drop is particularly high.

These results show that the information contained in different roles is of varying importance and depends on the data's source and domain. In the setting *Position*, we leave all information accessible to the model but add positional indicators for the investigated role to the input for emotion classification. We see improvements in most cases, except REMAN, for which adding the positional information hurts the classification for all roles. This result could be because REMAN has very long annotation spans. Both ECA and ES show an improvement for their annotated role (stimulus). For ET, an increase in performance is shown when additional knowledge about the stimulus position is given, and for GNE, a slight improvement is shown when the model is given the experiencer's position information.

Table 4 shows the results of the transformer-based model evaluated in the same settings. As expected, the model shows performance improvements across all datasets in comparison to the bi-LSTM model. In the *As-Is* setting, we see a substantial increase in performance for REMAN. This result can be explained by the fact that the pretrained large language model has seen more literary English than the embeddings used as pretrained input to the bi-LSTM. GNE and ET scores are also improved across the roles. In the *Without* setting, we do not see the same patterns as for the bi-LSTM based model; the scores when hiding the stimulus for ECA, the target for ET, and experiencer for GNE do not increase over the scores of the *As-Is* setting.

This might have two reasons: On one hand, it is less likely to improve upon already high values

Dataset	Role	As-Is			Without			Only			Position		
		P	R	F$_1$	P	R	F$_1$	P	R	F$_1$	P	R	F$_1$
ECA	Stimulus	68	70	68	4	17	7	4	17	7	**73**	**73**	**73**
ES	Stimulus	99	98	98	99	**99**	**99**	3	14	5	99	97	98
REMAN	Cue				3	12	5	3	12	5	**79**	**77**	**78**
	Stimulus	67	60	66	45	54	47	2	11	4	43	47	43
	Experiencer				60	60	56	2	11	4	62	56	56
	Target				46	42	42	2	11	3	44	45	42
ET	Cue				32	29	30	5	12	7	31	30	30
	Stimulus	34	33	34	**37**	33	34	9	15	11	33	32	32
	Experiencer				34	**34**	34	5	12	7	34	**34**	34
	Target				**35**	**34**	34	5	12	7	**35**	33	33
GNE	Cue				32	27	27	3	10	5	29	28	28
	Stimulus	32	31	31	7	11	7	24	23	23	**35**	**33**	**34**
	Experiencer				31	30	30	3	10	5	**35**	32	**33**
	Target				3	10	5	3	10	5	**35**	31	**32**

Table 4: Results of our transformer based model (RoBERTa) for emotion classification.

when changing the model configuration. On the other hand, and more interestingly, it might be that the contextualized embeddings compensate for missing information. Interestingly for the *Position* setting, the results are improving on all datasets, and REMAN gains from the cue's positional indicators. The dataset that stands out in this setting is ET, for which we see a slight decrease in performance across all roles available. The *Only* setting shows that the stimulus captures most of the emotion information for GNE and ET. The result for GNE is due to the particularly lengthy stimuli spans that sometimes stretch over the whole instance.

4 Conclusion and Future Work

Our experiments show that the importance of semantic roles for emotion classification differs between datasets and roles: The stimulus and cue are critical for classification, which correspond to the direct report of a feeling and the description that triggered an emotion. This result is shown in the drop in performance when removing these roles. This information is not redundantly available outside of these arguments.

It is particularly beneficial for the model's performance to have access to the position of cues and stimuli. This suggests that the classifier learns to tackle the problem differently when this information is available, especially so for ECA and ES – the cases in which literature has been annotated and the instances are comparably long.

The bi-LSTM model indicates that the experiencer role is a confounder in GNE. The performance can be increased when the model does not have access to its content. Similar results are observed for ET, in which the target role is a confounder. However, these results should be taken with a grain of salt given that they are not confirmed while switching to the transformer-based model. The differences in results between the bi-LSTM and the transformer also motivate further research, as they suggest that the contextualized representation might compensate for missing information, and is, therefore, more robust.

Finally, our results across both models and multiple datasets indicate that emotion classification approaches indeed benefit from semantic roles' information by adding the positional information. Similarly to targeted and aspect-based sentiment analysis, this motivates future work, in which emotion classification and role labeling should be modelled jointly. In this case, it can also be interesting to investigate what happens when the positional indicators are added to all roles jointly.

Acknowledgements

This work was supported by Deutsche Forschungsgemeinschaft (project SEAT, KL 2869/1-1). We thank Enrica Troiano and Heike Adel for fruitful discussions and the anonymous reviewers for helpful comments.

References

Cecilia Ovesdotter Alm, Dan Roth, and Richard Sproat. 2005. Emotions from text: Machine learning for text-based emotion prediction. In *Proceedings of Human Language Technology Conference and Conference on Empirical Methods in Natural Language Processing*, pages 579–586, Vancouver, British Columbia, Canada. Association for Computational Linguistics.

Laura-Ana-Maria Bostan and Roman Klinger. 2018. An analysis of annotated corpora for emotion classification in text. In *Proceedings of the 27th International Conference on Computational Linguistics*, pages 2104–2119, Santa Fe, New Mexico, USA. Association for Computational Linguistics.

Laura Ana Maria Bostan, Evgeny Kim, and Roman Klinger. 2020. GoodNewsEveryone: A corpus of news headlines annotated with emotions, semantic roles, and reader perception. In Nicoletta Calzolari, Khalid Choukri, Thierry Declerck, Hrafn Loftsson, Bente Maegaard, Joseph Mariani, Asuncion Moreno, Jan Odijk, and Stelios Piperidis, editors, *Proceedings of the 12th International Conference on Language Resources and Evaluation (LREC'20)*, Marseille, France. European Language Resources Association (ELRA).

Yejin Choi, Eric Breck, and Claire Cardie. 2006. Joint extraction of entities and relations for opinion recognition. In *Proceedings of the 2006 Conference on Empirical Methods in Natural Language Processing*, pages 431–439, Sydney, Australia, July. Association for Computational Linguistics.

Jacob Devlin, Ming-Wei Chang, Kenton Lee, and Kristina Toutanova. 2019. BERT: Pre-training of deep bidirectional transformers for language understanding. In *Proceedings of the 2019 Conference of the North American Chapter of the Association for Computational Linguistics: Human Language Technologies, Volume 1 (Long and Short Papers)*, pages 4171–4186, Minneapolis, Minnesota, June. Association for Computational Linguistics.

Paul Ekman. 1999. Basic emotions. In Tim Dalgleish and Mick J. Power, editors, *Handbook of Cognition and Emotion*. John Wiley & Sons, Sussex, UK.

Qinghong Gao, Jiannan Hu, Ruifeng Xu, Gui Lin, Yulan He, Qin Lu, and Kam-Fai Wong. 2017. Overview of NTCIR-13 ECA task. In *Proceedings of the 13th NTCIR Conference on Evaluation of Information Access Technologies*, pages 361–366, Tokyo, Japan, December.

Matt Gardner, Joel Grus, Mark Neumann, Oyvind Tafjord, Pradeep Dasigi, Nelson F. Liu, Matthew Peters, Michael Schmitz, and Luke Zettlemoyer. 2018. AllenNLP: A deep semantic natural language processing platform. In *Proceedings of Workshop for NLP Open Source Software (NLP-OSS)*, pages 1–6, Melbourne, Australia, July. Association for Computational Linguistics.

Diman Ghazi, Diana Inkpen, and Stan Szpakowicz. 2015. Detecting emotion stimuli in emotion-bearing sentences. In *International Conference on Intelligent Text Processing and Computational Linguistics*, pages 152–165. Springer.

Lin Gui, Dongyin Wu, Ruifeng Xu, Qin Lu, and Yu Zhou. 2016. Event-driven emotion cause extraction with corpus construction. In *Proceedings of the 2016 Conference on Empirical Methods in Natural Language Processing*, pages 1639–1649, Austin, Texas, November. Association for Computational Linguistics.

Thomas Haider, Steffen Eger, Evgeny Kim, Roman Klinger, and Winfried Menninghaus. 2020. PO-EMO: Conceptualization, annotation, and modeling of aesthetic emotions in German and English poetry. In *Proceedings of the 12th Language Resources and Evaluation Conference*, pages 1652–1663, Marseille, France, May. European Language Resources Association.

K. He, X. Zhang, S. Ren, and J. Sun. 2015. Delving deep into rectifiers: Surpassing human-level performance on imagenet classification. In *2015 IEEE International Conference on Computer Vision (ICCV)*, pages 1026–1034.

Sepp Hochreiter and Jürgen Schmidhuber. 1997. Long short-term memory. *Neural Comput.*, 9(8):1735–1780, November.

Jan Hofmann, Enrica Troiano, Kai Sassenberg, and Roman Klinger. 2020. Appraisal theories for emotion classification in text. In *Proceedings of the 28th International Conference on Computational Linguistics*.

Evgeny Kim and Roman Klinger. 2018. Who feels what and why? annotation of a literature corpus with semantic roles of emotions. In *Proceedings of the 27th International Conference on Computational Linguistics*, pages 1345–1359. Association for Computational Linguistics.

Evgeny Kim and Roman Klinger. 2019a. An analysis of emotion communication channels in fan-fiction: Towards emotional storytelling. In *Proceedings of the Second Workshop on Storytelling*, pages 56–64, Florence, Italy, August. Association for Computational Linguistics.

Evgeny Kim and Roman Klinger. 2019b. Frowning Frodo, wincing Leia, and a seriously great friendship: Learning to classify emotional relationships of fictional characters. In *Proceedings of the 2019 Conference of the North American Chapter of the Association for Computational Linguistics: Human Language Technologies, Volume 1 (Long and Short Papers)*, pages 647–653, Minneapolis, Minnesota, June. Association for Computational Linguistics.

Diederik P. Kingma and Jimmy Ba. 2015. Adam: A method for stochastic optimization. In *3rd International Conference on Learning Representations, ICLR 2015, San Diego, CA, USA, May 7-9, 2015*.

Yinhan Liu, Myle Ott, Naman Goyal, Jingfei Du, Mandar Joshi, Danqi Chen, Omer Levy, Mike Lewis, Luke Zettlemoyer, and Veselin Stoyanov. 2019. Roberta: A robustly optimized bert pretraining approach. *arXiv preprint arXiv:1907.11692*.

Saif Mohammad and Felipe Bravo-Marquez. 2017. WASSA-2017 shared task on emotion intensity. In *Proceedings of the 8th Workshop on Computational Approaches to Subjectivity, Sentiment and Social Media Analysis*, pages 34–49, Copenhagen, Denmark. Association for Computational Linguistics.

Saif Mohammad, Xiaodan Zhu, and Joel Martin. 2014. Semantic role labeling of emotions in tweets. In *Proceedings of the 5th Workshop on Computational Approaches to Subjectivity, Sentiment and Social Media Analysis*, pages 32–41, Baltimore, Maryland, June. Association for Computational Linguistics.

Laura Oberländer and Roman Klinger. 2020. Token sequence labeling vs. clause classification for english emotion stimulus detection. In *Proceedings of the 9th Joint Conference on Lexical and Computational Semantics (*SEM 2020)*, Barcelona, Spain, December. Association for Computational Linguistics.

Jeffrey Pennington, Richard Socher, and Christopher Manning. 2014. Glove: Global vectors for word representation. In *Proceedings of the 2014 Conference on Empirical Methods in Natural Language Processing (EMNLP)*, pages 1532–1543, Doha, Qatar. Association for Computational Linguistics.

Robert Plutchik. 2001. The nature of emotions human emotions have deep evolutionary roots, a fact that may explain their complexity and provide tools for clinical practice. *American Scientist*, 89(4):344–350.

Jonathan Posner, James A. Russell, and Bradley S. Peterson. 2005. The circumplex model of affect: an integrative approach to affective neuroscience, cognitive development, and psychopathology. *Development and Psychopathology*, 17(3):715–734.

Matthew Purver and Stuart Battersby. 2012. Experimenting with distant supervision for emotion classification. In *Proceedings of the 13th Conference of the European Chapter of the Association for Computational Linguistics*, pages 482–491, Avignon, France, April. Association for Computational Linguistics.

Klaus R. Scherer. 2005. What are emotions? And how can they be measured? *Social Science Information*, 44(4):695–729.

Wenbo Wang, Lu Chen, Krishnaprasad Thirunarayan, and Amit P. Sheth. 2012. Harnessing twitter "big data" for automatic emotion identification. In *SocialCom/PASSAT*, pages 587–592. IEEE.

Penghui Wei, Jiahao Zhao, and Wenji Mao. 2020. Effective inter-clause modeling for end-to-end emotion-cause pair extraction. In *Proceedings of the 58th Annual Meeting of the Association for Computational Linguistics*, pages 3171–3181, Online, July. Association for Computational Linguistics.

Thomas Wolf, Lysandre Debut, Victor Sanh, Julien Chaumond, Clement Delangue, Anthony Moi, Pierric Cistac, Tim Rault, Rémi Louf, Morgan Funtowicz, Joe Davison, Sam Shleifer, Patrick von Platen, Clara Ma, Yacine Jernite, Julien Plu, Canwen Xu, Teven Le Scao, Sylvain Gugger, Mariama Drame, Quentin Lhoest, and Alexander M. Rush. 2019. Huggingface's transformers: State-of-the-art natural language processing. *ArXiv*, abs/1910.03771.

Rui Xia and Zixiang Ding. 2019. Emotion-cause pair extraction: A new task to emotion analysis in texts. In *Proceedings of the 57th Annual Meeting of the Association for Computational Linguistics*, pages 1003–1012, Florence, Italy, July. Association for Computational Linguistics.

Wenhao Ying, Rong Xiang, and Qin Lu. 2019. Improving multi-label emotion classification by integrating both general and domain-specific knowledge. In *Proceedings of the 5th Workshop on Noisy User-generated Text (W-NUT 2019)*, pages 316–321, Hong Kong, China, November. Association for Computational Linguistics.

Albin Zehe, Julia Arns, Lena Hettinger, and Andreas Hotho. 2020. Harrymotions – classifying relationships in harry potter based on emotion analysis. In *5th SwissText & 16th KONVENS Joint Conference*.

Appendix

Qualitative Discussion of Examples

We analyze a subset of interesting cases from the results section in the following, to better understand why removing stimuli from ECA improves the results and further why the same can be observed on ET for targets.

We show examples for these cases in Table 5. We observe in instances correctly classified in the *Without* setting that removing the stimulus makes the classification task easier by removing potential sources for overfitting: The remaining tokens contain the explicit cue, even though they are not explicitly annotated for ECA. For instance, in "[his angry outbreak]$_{STIMULUS}$ [saddened]$_{CUE}$ [me]$_{EXPERIENCER}$", we see that removing the stimulus which also contains a reference to another emotion, the task of picking the most dominant emotion from the remaining tokens is more straight-forward.

This holds similarly for other examples in ECA, in which the stimulus describes an event that could also be evaluated as scary; however, the experiencer mentions that he is surprised ("To my surprise").

| Dataset | Gold | All | without | | | | Text |
			Stim.	Exp.	Cue	Targ.	
GNE	**J**	Su	**J**	Su	Su	Su	[Djokovic]$_{EXPERIENCER}$ [happy]$_{CUE}$ [to carry on cruising]$_{STIMULUS}$
GNE	**J**	Su	**J**	Su	A	Su	[Trump]$_{EXPERIENCER}$ [upbeat]$_{CUE}$ [on potential for US-Japan trade deal.]$_{STIMULUS}$
ECA	**J**	F	**J**	–	–	–	["Michie Reetchie"]$_{STIMULUS}$, said Xavier, and again he burst into laughter that choked further speech. He controlled himself and laid his finger on his vein.
ECA	**Su**	F	**Su**	–	–	–	One morning Pop sent me down to the river to catch some fish for breakfast. To my surprise [there was a canoe in the water and there was no one in]$_{STIMULUS}$. Immediately I jumped into the river and brought the canoe to the side.
ECA	**F**	S	**F**	–	–	–	I did not answer, fearing [to tell him that I had been awake watching him]$_{STIMULUS}$
ECA	**A**	S	**A**	–	–	–	A massy stone and shook the ranks of Troy, as when in anger [against long - screaming cranes]$_{STIMULUS}$ a watcher of the field leaps from the ground in swift hand whirling round his head the sling and speeds the stone against them scattering.
ECA	**D**	A	**D**	–	–	–	[A year after being fired from his job]$_{STIMULUS}$ he has a lot of resentment towards his former boss.
ET	**D**	T	D	T	S	**D**	Three words to describe the entire [#GOP convention]$_{TARGET}$ [Mean and demeaning.]$_{CUE}$
ET	**A**	D	D	D	D	**A**	[#Republicans]$_{TARGET}$ are a joke . [Clint Eastwood]$_{STIMULUS}$ is their mascot ! America is in trouble if [these idiots]$_{CUE}$ win ! #RNC
ET	**J**	T	T	J	T	**J**	[Obama Voter]$_{TARGET}$ [Says Vote for Obama]$_{STIMULUS}$ [YES WE CAN AGAIN !]$_{CUE}$
ET	**J**	Ant	T	T	T	**J**	[So excited]$_{CUE}$ to vote this upcoming [election]$_{TARGET}$ [finally exercising my right to choose our next president]$_{STIMULUS}$ #Obama
ET	**D**	A	A	A	A	**D**	[Romney]$_{TARGET}$ is gonna put The Onion out of business . [#TheStench]$_{CUE}$
REMAN	**J**	noemo	noemo	**J**	noemo	–	And [she]$_{EXPERIENCER}$ returned the quiet but jubilant kiss that he laid upon her lips.

Table 5: Examples in which the prediction is incorrect when the model is applied on the whole instance, but it is correct when the respective role is removed. The correct prediction is marked in bold face. J: Joy, T: Trust, Su: Surprise, Ant: Anticipation, D: Disgust, F: Fear, A: Anger, S: Sadness

Detailed Results for Additional Positional Information

We have seen in the results that adding position information of the semantic roles increases the performance for both datasets which contain examples drawn from literature. This is particularly interesting for future research on jointly modelling roles and classification. Therefore, we show details per emotion class in Table 6 (only for the bi-LSTM model).

We see for the ECA dataset, that when the positional information is made accessible to the model, the classifier learns better to predict all emotion classes with a substantial improvement for anger and disgust. Similarly, ES improves over all emotions with the exception of disgust and sadness.

Data	Emotion	All			Stimulus Position		
		P	R	F_1	P	R	F_1
ECA	Anger	15	11	13	**36**	**44**	**40**
	Disgust	25	06	09	11	**11**	**11**
	Fear	56	56	56	**78**	**70**	**74**
	Joy	57	58	57	**65**	58	**61**
	Sadness	50	67	57	**57**	**72**	**64**
	Surprise	40	38	39	**63**	**53**	**58**
	Macro	40	39	38	**52**	**51**	**51**
ES	Anger	90	97	94	**92**	**98**	**95**
	Disgust	85	54	67	**100**	45	63
	Fear	97	88	93	95	**95**	**95**
	Joy	93	92	92	**100**	92	**96**
	Sadness	94	99	97	90	96	93
	Shame	100	94	97	100	**100**	**100**
	Surprise	91	95	93	88	**100**	**94**
	Macro	93	89	90	**95**	**90**	**91**

Table 6: Results per emotion for ECA and ES with and without positional stimuli information. Bold numbers indicate that their value is greater than in the As-Is setting.

Analysis of Content of Roles

Table 7 shows the most frequent tokens marked as *cue, stimulus, experiencer* or *target* over each dataset. They differ substantially per dataset and reflect well the respective source. The counts suggest a Zipfian distribution for *ElectoralTweets* (stimulus and target) and *GoodNewsEveryone* (experiencer, stimulus). This could explain the results obtained in the *Without* setting by the bi-LSTM-based model. The most common tokens annotated with the *target* role in *ElectoralTweets* also show the polarized nature of those who tweeted about the election.

Figure 1 shows the distribution of the most frequent tokens (across all roles) for the most frequent emotions of ET and GNE. The plots marked with "overall" show the prior distribution of emotions in the respective dataset. We see that for the emotion *admiration*, "president" stands out. Further we note that "Romney" is associated with *dislike* in this corpus.

For GNE we observe that the most frequent tokens are occurring less in instances annotated with *positive surprise* than overall, and more in instances annotated with *anger* (except for "Biden") showing that these tokens could be biased towards more negative emotions. This shows a bias of the dataset towards negative emotion when it comes to the most prominent tokens.

	Role	Tokens
ECA	Stim.	see (80), like (49), man (49), go (43), life (43), father (43), time (42), day (34), came (33), son (32)
ES	Stim.	see (36), way (12), find (11), left (9), people (9), prospect (8), thought (8), like (8), losing (8), work (7)
REMAN	Cue	love (32), suddenly (31), afraid (15), smile (12), beautiful (11), trust (11), pleasure (10), ugly (7), things (7), wish (6)
	Stim.	little (10), another (8), face (8), got (7), lord (7), left (7), great (7), wife (7), men (6), life (6)
	Exp.	man (23), woman (12), boy (7), old (7), isabel (6), people (6), god (5), father (5), heart (5), henry (5)
	Target	man (22), little (9), things (8), woman (8), see (8), old (7), god (6), wife (6), another (6), true (5)
ET	Cue	Obama (136), Romney (105), vote (89), like (65), Mitt (56), people (53), get (52), president (50), really (49), excited (49)
	Stim.	Obama (249), Romney (211), vote (108), Mitt (87), Barack (74), president (66), people (51), speech (40), like (40), get (35)
	Exp.	gop, anyone, presidency, clint
	Target	Obama (446), Romney (420), Mitt (146), Barack (112), People (53), president (40), election (20), debate (19), Michelle (19), Clinton (15)
GNE	Cue	killed (38), crisis (33), attacks (33), death (26), war (25), arrested (24), racist (24), help (22), new (20), fight (19)
	Stim.	Trump (279), border (68), Mueller (58), back (57), report (56), Iran (57), report (56), war (55), people (55), deal (55)
	Exp.	Trump (401), Donald (66), man (46), democrats (44), Biden (40), House (37), woman (36), police (35), Mueller (34), Sanders (33)
	Target	Trump (345), new (94), Mueller (54), House (44), border (43), people (42), democrats (41), deal (36), report (36), president (35)

Table 7: Most frequent 10 tokens with frequencies for each role and dataset.

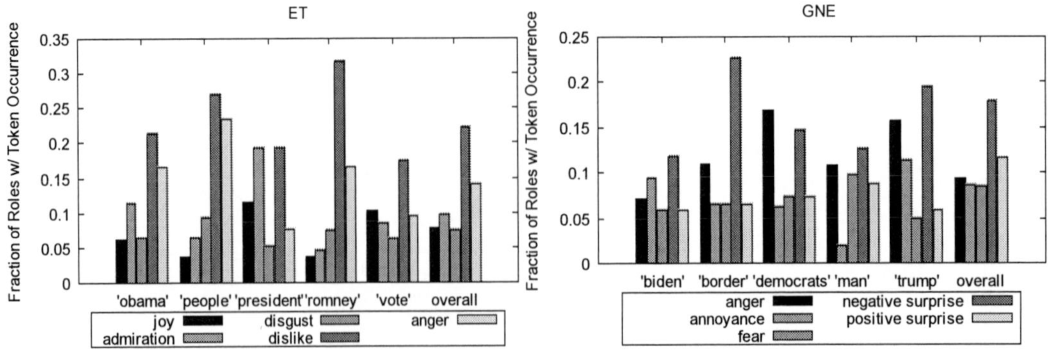

Figure 1: Emotion distribution of instances containing the respective tokens (% for the top-5 most frequent emotions for each dataset). "overall" represents the emotion distribution for those emotions across all instances.

Learning Emotion from 100 Observations: Unexpected Robustness of Deep Learning under Strong Data Limitations

Sven Buechel[*]
Friedrich-Schiller-Universität Jena
`sven.buechel@uni-jena.de`

João Sedoc
New York University
`jsedoc@stern.nyu.edu`

H. Andrew Schwartz
Stony Brook University
`has@cs.stonybrook.edu`

Lyle Ungar
University of Pennsylvania
`ungar@cis.upenn.edu`

Abstract

One of the major downsides of Deep Learning is its supposed need for vast amounts of training data. As such, these techniques appear ill-suited for NLP areas where annotated data is limited, such as less-resourced languages or emotion analysis, with its many nuanced and hard-to-acquire annotation formats. We conduct a questionnaire study indicating that indeed the vast majority of researchers in emotion analysis deems neural models inferior to traditional machine learning when training data is limited. In stark contrast to those survey results, we provide empirical evidence for English, Polish, and Portuguese that commonly used neural architectures can be trained on surprisingly few observations, outperforming n-gram based ridge regression on only 100 data points. Our analysis suggests that high-quality, pre-trained word embeddings are a main factor for achieving those results.

1 Introduction

Deep Learning (DL) has radically changed the rules of the game in NLP by boosting performance figures in almost all application areas. Yet in contrast to more conventional techniques, such as n-gram based linear models, *neural* methodologies seem to rely on vast amounts of training data, as is obvious in areas such as machine translation (Vaswani et al., 2017) or representation learning for individual words (Mikolov et al., 2013; Pennington et al., 2014) or contextualized word sequences (Devlin et al., 2019; Yang et al., 2019; Joshi et al., 2020).

With this profile, DL seems ill-suited for many prediction tasks in sentiment and subjectivity analysis (Balahur et al., 2014). For the widely studied problem of polarity prediction (distinguishing only between *positive* and *negative* emotion), training data is relatively abundant especially for the social media domain (Rosenthal et al., 2017). However, in recent years, there has been a growing interest in more nuanced and informative annotation formats for affective states (Bostan and Klinger, 2018; De Bruyne et al., 2019). Such annotation schemes often follow distinct psychological theories such as the dimensional approach to emotion representation (Bradley and Lang, 1994) or basic emotions (Ekman, 1992). Yet, annotating for more complex representations of affective states seems to be significantly harder in terms of both time consumption and inter-annotator agreement (IAA) (Strapparava and Mihalcea, 2007). Adding even more complexity, computational work following this trend often uses numerical scores as target variables making, emotion analysis a regression, rather than a classification problem (Buechel and Hahn, 2016; Mohammad et al., 2018). What makes this situation even worse is that, first, we currently have a situation where there is no community-wide consensus on how emotion should be represented. That is, different ways of annotating emotion (see, e.g., Table 2) compete with each other, leading to decreased inter-operability of language resources and provoking additional data sparsity (Buechel and Hahn, 2018b). And, second, especially large-scale annotated corpora are almost exclusively available for English, leaving most of the world's languages with little or no gold data at all.

[*] Work partially conducted at the University of Pennsylvania.

Proceedings of the Third Workshop on Computational Modeling of PEople's Opinions, PersonaLity, and Emotions in Social media, pages 129–139
Barcelona, Spain (Online), December 13, 2020.

> **Data Requirements for Deep Learning in Emotion Analysis**
> We're interested in your beliefs about what training size is necessary for deep learning techniques. Your response will be used for academic research and stored anonymously. Thank you very much!
> Consider the task of fine-grained emotion analysis, using what you believe to be the best deep learning architecture (e.g., RNN, CNN, Self-Attention) with input from pre-trained word embeddings (e.g., word2vec, GloVe; NOT contextualized embeddings like ELMO or BERT):
>
> 1. How many training examples do you believe are necessary for deep learning to provide results in line with traditional discriminative learning (e.g. SVM, penalized linear regression, random forests)?
> 2. How many observations do you believe are necessary for deep learning approaches to provide a clear benefit over traditional discriminative learning?
>
> Thank you for completing the survey! Do you have any additional comments regarding this questionnaire?

Figure 1: Survey on expected data requirements of deep learning.

For the social media domain, this lack of gold data can be partly countered by (pre-)training with distant supervision using signals such as emojis or hashtags as a surrogate for manual annotation (Mohammad and Kiritchenko, 2015; Felbo et al., 2017; Abdul-Mageed and Ungar, 2017). Yet, this procedure is less viable for target domains other than social media, as well as for predicting other subjective phenomena such as empathy, uncertainty, or personality (Khanpour et al., 2017; Rubin, 2007; Liu et al., 2017). Besides pre-training the entirety of the model with distant supervision, an alternative strategy is pre-training word representations, only. This approach is feasible for a wide range of languages, including otherwise less-resourced ones, since raw text is much more readily available than gold data, e.g., through Wikipedia (Grave et al., 2018). Very recently, *contextualized* word representations generated by pre-trained language models have established themselves as a powerful alternative (Peters et al., 2018; Devlin et al., 2019).

In summary, deep learning supposedly depends on vast amounts of annotated data—and this seems particularly troublesome for the field of emotion analysis because such phenomena are intrinsically hard to annotate. However, we suspect that this *gold* data dependency may, for emotion analysis at least, be less severe than anticipated because large, pre-trained embedding models already seem to encode word-level emotion quite well (Du and Zhang, 2016; Li et al., 2017; Buechel and Hahn, 2018c), possibly allowing to fit sentence-level DL architectures on rather small datasets. If that was true, it would be the *reputation* of DL rather than its actual characteristics which prevent its wider application for emotion analysis in low-resource environments.

Contribution. We start by quantifying the expectations of the research community regarding the data requirements of DL. To this end, we first conduct a questionnaire study among NLP researchers in the field of emotion analysis finding that the median respondent expects DL to be viable only from 10,000 training examples onward. Next, we perform a series of experiments on English, Polish, and Portuguese emotion corpora. In contrast to the survey results, we show that commonly used architectures can be fitted on as little as 100 data points and still outperform supposedly more robust n-gram based approaches. We believe these findings potentially open up DL to many low-resource areas and, by extension, wider cross-lingual or cross-domain applications.

2   Survey

We conducted a short questionnaire study asking the research community about their beliefs regarding data requirements of deep learning in the context of emotion analysis. We included two questions, one asking for the number of training examples "necessary for deep learning to provide results *in line* with traditional discriminative learning" (question 1), the other asking for the number of examples necessary for "deep learning approaches to provide a *clear benefit* over traditional discriminative learning" (question 2). The full text of the questionnaire is given in Figure 1. Participants were instructed to focus on *non*-contextualized word representations (in line with our latter experiments; the use of contextualized word embeddings is left for future work) being used as input to the, from their view, most suitable model

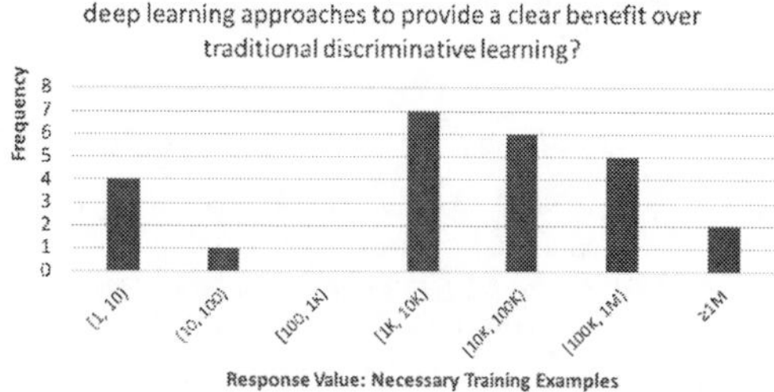

Figure 2: Responses to survey questions 1 (left) and 2 (right).

Corpus	Language	Size	Annotation	Emb. Alg.	Dims.	Emb. Data	Emb. Data Size
SE07	English	1000	BE6 $[1, 100]$	word2vec	300	Google News	100B tokens
WASSA	English	≤ 2252	BE4 $[0, 1]$	word2vec	400	Twitter	400M tweets
ANPST	Polish	718	VAD $[1, 9]$	FastText	300	Wikipedia	4B tokens
MAS	Portuguese	192	VAD $[1, 9]$ + BE5 $[1, 5]$	FastText	300	Wikipedia	4B tokens

Table 1: Annotated corpora and embedding models used for experiments; with language, number of instances, annotation format, embedding algorithm, embedding dimensions, and dataset (size) embeddings were trained on.

architecture.

To recruit participants, we queried the ACL Anthology for papers from between 2016 and 2018 using the keyword "emotion", we collected all email addresses in the author field of all retrieved PDFs (166 papers in total). Invitations to participate in the survey were sent to the resulting 391 email addresses on February 28, 2019. We received 26 responses within four weeks (6% response rate). One response (stating in the optional comment field that no numeric answer could be given) was excluded. Figure 2 shows the distribution of the 25 remaining responses on a logarithmic scale.

As can be seen, the responses to both questions clearly support the intuition that deep learning is thought of as being dependent on large amounts of training data by the scientific community. In both cases, the median response was 10,000. Perhaps surprisingly, a total of 5 participants stated that fewer than 100 instances are necessary for deep learning to show clear improvements over more traditional methods (compared to 20 who believed the opposite), whereas only 2 believed that less than 100 instances are enough to show results "in line with" traditional methods. Inspecting the individual responses, we found that this discrepancy stems from a minority of participants (4 of out 25) who indicated that traditional learning performs worse than DL on small datasets but may catch up as dataset sizes grow.

Another interesting, most likely related outcome is that the responses to question 2 show a bi-modal distribution: While a minority of 5 participants believed that DL approaches are superior below 100 observations, the vast majority of participants (20) states that 1,000 or more instances are necessary for that. Yet, no one responded with a number between 100 and 1,000.

While we do not validate the claim of this minority, the remainder of the paper provides strong evidence that the majority of the participants largely overestimated the data requirements of deep learning.

3 Data

For the following study, we selected four small (< 3000 instances) and typologically diverse datasets described below. Pre-trained, publicly available word2vec (Mikolov et al., 2013) and FastText vectors (Bojanowski et al., 2017) of matching language and target domain were used as model input. Table 1 summarizes the employed data. Illustrative examples of the particular styles and annotation formats of those corpora are provided in Table 2.

SE07: The test set of SemEval 2007 Task 14 (Strapparava and Mihalcea, 2007) comprises 1000 English news headlines that are annotated according to six Basic Emotions, joy, anger, sadness, fear, disgust,

Corpus	Text	Val	Aro	Dom	Joy	Ang	Sad	Fea	Dis	Sur
SE07	*Inter Milan set Serie A win record*	-	-	-	50	2	0	0	0	9
	TBS to pay $2M fine for ad campaign bomb scare	-	-	-	11	25	28	45	32	43
WASSA	*@TheRevAl please tell us why 'protesting' injustice requires #burning #beating and #looting terrible optics #toussaintromain is true leader!*	-	-	-	-	.73	-	-	-	-
	@TauDeltaPhiDK THANK YOU FOR MY OBAMA CUT OUT!!!!!! I am elated that he's back home	-	-	-	.83	-	-	-	-	-
ANPST	*Decyzje podjęte w przeszłość i kształtują naszą teraźniejszość.* 'Decisions made in the past shape our present.'	4.9	4.1	5.8	-	-	-	-	-	-
	Dopóki walczysz i podejmujesz starania, jesteś zwycięzcą. 'As long as you fight and keep trying, you are a winner.'	7.3	5.3	7.4	-	-	-	-	-	-
MAS	*A praia é espetacular.* 'The beach is spectacular.'	8.0	4.0	6.7	4.2	1.0	1.0	1.0	1.0	-
	A tinta é azul. 'The ink is blue.'	5.0	3.9	5.5	1.3	1.0	1.0	1.0	1.0	-

Table 2: Exemplary entries from our four datasets illustrating differences in linguistic characteristics and emotion annotation scheme. Emotion variables: valence, arousal, dominance, joy, anger, sadness, fear, disgust, and surprise. English translations for ANPST and MAS were provided by the respective dataset creators.

and surprise on a $[0, 100]$-scale (BE6 annotation format). The news headlines are quite short and rather objective, being written by professional journalists. However, they may still elicit strong emotional reactions in readers as illustrated in Table 2. For this corpus, we used the word2vec embeddings trained on Google News.[1]

WASSA: The English Twitter dataset of the WASSA 2017 shared task (Mohammad and Bravo-Marquez, 2017b) contains four subsets, one for each of the first four basic emotions, annotated on a $[0, 1]$ scale (BE4 format). Their sizes vary between 1533 and 2252 samples (union of the respective train, dev, and test set). Being a Twitter corpus, these data display features typical for the social media domain, e.g., extensive use of colloquialism, emojis, and explicit language, as well as platform-specific phenomena such as hashtags ('#') and user mentions ('@'). Note that different from other corpora, here each individual instance is annotated according to only one emotion variable, whereas in SE07, ANPST, and MAS every instance is annotated for all variables covered by the respective dataset. Here, we used Twitter word2vec embeddings by Godin et al. (2015).

ANPST: The Affective Norms for Polish Short Texts (Imbir, 2017) is a dataset designed as stimulus in psychological experiments. It is annotated according to valence, arousal, and dominance on a $[1, 9]$-scale (VAD). ANPST comprises sentences of various genres (such as proverbs, jokes, literature quotes, or newswire material) from a wide range of sources (Imbir, 2017). The resulting selection of raw data seems often quite complex and ambiguous in terms of the elicited emotion (see examples in Table 2). We used the FastText embeddings by Grave et al. (2018) trained on the Polish Wikipedia.

MAS: Like ANPST, the Minho Affective Sentences (Pinheiro et al., 2017) is a dataset designed by psychologists, also being annotated according to valence, arousal, and dominance on a $[1, 9]$-scale (VAD). Yet, additionally, MAS is also annotated according to the first five Basic Emotions (omitting 'surprise') on a $[1, 5]$-scale (BE5). It consists of very short situation descriptions in the third person in European Portuguese (Pinheiro et al., 2017). Those sentences were purposefully constructed by psychologists to be simple in language and familiar in content for a large proportion of the population. This was done to make the dataset more widely applicable as experimental stimulus, yet also resulted in a slightly ar-

---

[1]`code.google.com/archive/p/word2vec/`

Model	Description
Ridge$_{\text{ngram}}$	n-gram features with $n \in \{1,2,3\}$; feature normalization; automatically chosen regularization coefficient from $\{10^{-4}, 10^{-3}, .., 10^{4}\}$
Ridge$_{\text{BV}}$	*bag of vectors*-features; regularization coefficient chosen as in 'Ridge$_{\text{ngram}}$'
FFN	*bag of vectors*-features; two dense layers (256 and 128 units)
CNN	one conv. layer (filter size 3, 128 channels), max-pooling layer with .5 dropout; dense layer (128 units)
GRU	recurrent layer (128 units, uni-directional); last timestep receives .5 vertical dropout and is fed into a dense layer (128 units)
LSTM	identical to 'GRU'
CNN-LSTM	conv. layer as in 'CNN'; max-pooling layer (pool size 2, stride size 1) with .5 dropout; LSTM identical to 'GRU'

Table 3: Model-specific design choices.

tificial style. MAS is the smallest dataset considered, having only 192 instances. We used the FastText embeddings by Grave et al. (2018), trained on the Portuguese Wikipedia.

4 Methods

We provide two distinct linear baseline models which both rely on Ridge regression, an ℓ^2-regularized version of linear regression. The first one, Ridge$_{\text{ngram}}$, is based on n-gram features where we use $n \in \{1,2,3\}$. The second one, Ridge$_{\text{BV}}$ uses *bag-of-vectors* features, i.e., the pointwise mean of the embeddings of the words in a text. Regarding the deep learning approaches, we compare Feed-Forward Networks (FFN), Gated Recurrent Unit Networks (GRU), Long Short-Term Memory Networks (LSTM), Convolutional Neural Networks (CNN), as well as a combination of the latter two (CNN-LSTM) (Cho et al., 2014; Hochreiter and Schmidhuber, 1997; Kalchbrenner et al., 2014).

Since holding out a dev set from the already limited training data does not seem feasible for some of the datasets (see Table 1), we decided to instead use constant hyperparameter settings across all corpora. We also keep most hyperparameters constant between models. Hence, hyperparameter choices followed well-established recommendations described in the next paragraph.

The input to the DL models is based on pre-trained word vectors. ReLu activation was used everywhere except in recurrent layers. Dropout is used for regularization with a probability of .2 for embedding layers and .5 for dense layers following the recommendations by Srivastava et al. (2014). We use .5 dropout also on other types of layers where it would conventionally be considered too high (e.g. on max pooling layers). Our models are trained for 200 epochs using the Adam optimizer (Kingma and Ba, 2015) with a fixed learning rate of .001 and a batch size of 32. Word embeddings were not updated during training. Since, in compliance with our gold data, we treat emotion analysis as a regression problem (Buechel and Hahn, 2016), the output layers of our models consist of an affine transformation, i.e., a dense layer without non-linearity. To reduce the risk of overfitting on such small data sets, we used relatively simple models both in terms of the number of layers and units in them (mostly 2 and 128, respectively). An overview of our models and details about their *individual* hyperparameter settings are provided in Table 3. `Keras.io` and `scikit-learn.org` (Pedregosa et al., 2011) were used for the implementation.

	SE07	WASSA	ANPST	MAS	Mean
$Ridge_{ngram}$	.53	.67	.32	.16	.42
$Ridge_{BV}$	.62	.64	.52	.62	.60
CNN-LSTM	.66	.69	.50	.63	.62
CNN	**.67**	.70	.47	.61	.62
FFN	.67	.69	.50	.65	.63
LSTM	.65	.73	.52	.65	.64
GRU	.67	**.73**	**.54**	**.66**	**.65**

Table 4: Comparative results of the 10×10-cross-validation in Pearson's r; averaged over all variables of the respective annotation format.

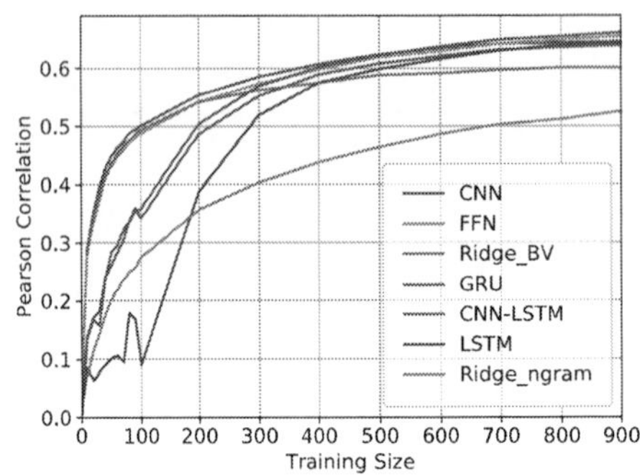

Figure 3: Comparison of model performance vs. training size on the SE07 dataset in Pearson's r.

5 Experimental Results

5.1 Repeated Cross-Validation

Given our small datasets, conventional 10-fold cross-validation (CV) would lead to very small test splits (only 19 instances in the case of MAS) thus causing high variance between the individual splits and, ultimately, even regarding the average of all 10 runs. Therefore, we *repeat 10-fold CV ten times* (10×10-CV) with different data splits, then averaging the results (Dietterich, 1998). Performance is measured as Pearson correlation r between predicted and human gold ratings. To further increase reliability, identical data splits were used for each of the approaches under comparison. Results are given in Table 4.

All DL approaches (FFN, CNN, GRU, LSTM, CNN-LSTM) yield a satisfying performance of $r >$ .6 on average over all corpora, despite the small data sizes. Each one of them clearly outperforms $Ridge_{ngram}$, representing more conventional learning techniques, on every single dataset. This stands in sharp contrast to our survey results where the median respondent indicated that DL would need at least 10,000 instances to provide a clear benefit over conventional techniques—the datasets we employed are between 4 and 50 times smaller.

Overall, the GRU performs best. However, differences between the DL models are quite small on average. (We emphasize that our primary concern is to compare deep vs. conventional learning techniques under data limitations whereas comparisons within the group of DL architectures are secondary.) Perhaps surprisingly, $Ridge_{BV}$, which takes a middle ground between DL and conventional approaches, also performs very competitively. Given its low computational cost, our results indicate that this model may constitute an excellent baseline.

Observe that $Ridge_{BV}$ and FFN rely solely on lexical information—their inputs are computed by mere averaging of word embeddings whereas CNN, LSTM, GRU, and CNN-LSTM learn their own composition functions from gold data. Still, the former two both display satisfying performance. This suggests that the quality of the pre-trained embeddings may be a key factor for their strong results.

	FFN	CNN	GRU	LSTM	CNN-LSTM	Mean
Learned	.24	.23	.38	.26	.30	.28
Tuned	.59	.55	.59	.59	.57	.58
Frozen	**.63**	**.62**	**.65**	**.64**	**.62**	**.63**

Table 5: Comparison of embedding training strategies (average Pearson's r over all datasets).

5.2 Embedding Training Strategies

To further examine this conjecture, we repeated the above experiment two more times, altering the training strategy of the embeddings (only applicable to DL models). Instead of using pre-trained vectors without updating them (**Frozen**), we looked at embeddings which were either randomly initialized and updated (**Learned**) or pre-trained and updated (**Tuned**). As can be seen from Table 5, both strategies involving pre-trained vectors (frozen and tuned) outperform learned word embeddings by a large margin (about 30%-points on average). Frozen embeddings yield the highest performance, even outperforming fine-tuned vectors (5%-point margin on average), a possible reason being that the large increase in the number of parameters leads to overfitting.

5.3 Training Size vs. Model Performance

We will now continue to explore the unexpected behavior of DL architectures by further limiting the available training data. For each number $N \in \{1, 10, 20, ..., 100, 200, ..., 900\}$, we randomly sampled N instances from the SE07 corpus for training and tested on the held-out data. This procedure was repeated 100 times for each of the training data sizes before averaging the results. Each of the models was evaluated with identical data splits. The outcome of this experiment is depicted in Figure 3. As can be seen, recurrent models suffer only a moderate loss of performance down to a third of the original training data (about 300 observations). The CNN, FFN, and Ridge$_{BV}$ models remain stable even longer—their performance only begins to decline rapidly at about 100 instances. In contrast, Ridge$_{ngram}$ declines more steadily yet its overall performance is much lower as well. Most notably, all DL models but the LSTM *always* performed better than the conventional Ridge$_{ngram}$ baseline no matter how little training data was used.

	Joy	Anger	Sadness	Fear	Disgust	Surprise	Mean
WINNER	.23	.32	.41	.45	.13	.17	.28
IAA	.60	.50	.68	.64	.45	.36	.54
BECK	.59	.65	.70	.74	.54	.47	.62
GRU	**.60**	**.70**	**.75**	**.77**	**.61**	**.53**	**.66**

Table 6: Comparison of previously reported results, human performance (IAA), and our proposed GRU model on the SE07 dataset in Pearson's r.

Official Rank	Team/System	Joy	Anger	Sadness	Fear	Mean
1	Prayas	.762	.765	.732	.732	.747
2	IMS	.726	.767	.690	.705	.722
3	SeeNet	.698	.745	.715	.676	.708
–	**Our Work**	.658	.668	.724	.717	.692
4	UWaterloo	.699	.703	.693	.643	.685

Table 7: Comparison against official WASSA 2017 shared task results (in Pearson's r).

5.4 Comparison against Previous Work

The above experiments have shown that our DL models perform robustly under strong data limitations, beating a conventional baseline in the vast majority of cases. Yet, perhaps this was achieved by designing overly simple network architectures, thus trading an excessive amount of performance for robustness in low-data scenarios. To rule out this possibility, we will now move forward and compare our findings against previous work.

SemEval 2007 Affective Text First, we compare our best performing model, the GRU, against previously reported results for the SE07 corpus. Table 6 provides the performance of the winning system of the original shared task (WINNER; Chaumartin (2007)), the inter-annotator agreement (IAA) as given by the organizers (Strapparava and Mihalcea, 2007), the performance by Beck (2017), the highest one reported for this dataset so far (BECK), as well as the results for our GRU from the 10×10-CV set-up.

As can be seen, the GRU established a new state-of-the-art surpassing the previous one by about 4%-points on average over all emotion categories. The difference is statistically significant (two-tailed one-sample t-test comparing the results of the 10 cross-validation runs against the reported performance by Beck (2017); $p < .001$). Our GRU also outperforms IAA, as already did BECK. This may sound improbable at first glance. However, Strapparava and Mihalcea (2007) employ a rather weak notion of human performance which is—broadly speaking—based on the reliability of a single human rater.[2] Interestingly, the GRU shows particularly large improvements over human performance for categories where the IAA is low (anger, disgust, and surprise).

WASSA 2017 Shared Task Data Table 7 displays the official results of the four best systems (out of 21 submissions) of the WASSA 2017 shared task (Mohammad and Bravo-Marquez, 2017b) as well as the performance our GRU achieved. For this experiment, we deviated from the above 10×10-CV set-up but instead used the official train-dev-test split for comparability. As for all experiments in this paper, hyperparameters were kept constant and were not adjusted to this dataset. Consequently, train and dev sets were combined for training. Training and testing were repeated ten times with different random seeds but otherwise identical configuration following the recommendation by Reimers and Gurevych (2018). Table 7 shows our *average* performance over those ten runs.

As can be seen, our GRU performs very competitively and would have been ranked fourth place, outperforming 18 out of 21 submissions. The difference to the next lower-performing system (UWaterloo) is statistically significant (two-tailed one-sample t-test comparing our ten runs against their official results; $p < .001$).

6 Conclusion

Annotating emotion is necessarily subjective thus making gold data in this area particularly rare. As such, applying DL may seem ill-advised since supposedly large amounts of training data are required. But is this really the case? We started our investigation by conducting a survey among researchers in emotion analysis. 80% of the respondents believed that DL is superior to traditional machine learning techniques only when at least 1,000 training examples are available. Half of the participants even believed that 10,000 or more examples are necessary. Putting this popular notion to the test, we provided the first examination of neural emotion analysis under severe data constraints, featuring five distinct neural architectures and three typologically diverse languages. In stark contrast to the survey results, we found that *all* architectures could be fitted on datasets comprising as little as 200 observations, CNNs and FFNs even being robust on 100 observations. A subsequent analysis indicated that high-quality, pre-trained word embeddings are a key factor in achieving those results. In the future, we would like to extend this work to *contextualized* word representations, e.g., by ELMo or BERT (Peters et al., 2018; Devlin et al., 2019).

---

[2]Instead, other approaches to IAA computation for numerical values, such as split-half or inter-study reliability, constitute a more challenging comparison since they are based on the reliability of *many* raters, not one (Mohammad and Bravo-Marquez, 2017a; Buechel and Hahn, 2018a).

Acknowledgements

We thank the anonymous reviewers for their helpful suggestions and comments. Sven Buechel thanks his doctoral advisor Udo Hahn, JULIE Lab, for funding his research visit at the University of Pennsylvania.

References

Muhammad Abdul-Mageed and Lyle Ungar. 2017. EmoNet: Fine-grained emotion detection with gated recurrent neural networks. In *Proceedings of the 55th Annual Meeting of the Association for Computational Linguistics (Volume 1: Long Papers)*, pages 718–728.

Alexandra Balahur, Rada Mihalcea, and Andrés Montoyo. 2014. Computational approaches to subjectivity and sentiment analysis: Present and envisaged methods and applications. *Computer Speech & Language*, 28(1):1–6.

Daniel Beck. 2017. Modelling representation noise in emotion analysis using gaussian processes. In *Proceedings of the 8th International Joint Conference on Natural Language Processing (Volume 2: Short Papers)*, pages 140–145.

Piotr Bojanowski, Edouard Grave, Armand Joulin, and Tomáš Mikolov. 2017. Enriching word vectors with subword information. *Transactions of the Association for Computational Linguistics*, 5(1):135–146.

Laura-Ana-Maria Bostan and Roman Klinger. 2018. An analysis of annotated corpora for emotion classification in text. In *Proceedings of the 27th International Conference on Computational Linguistics*, pages 2104–2119.

Margaret M. Bradley and Peter J. Lang. 1994. Measuring emotion: The Self-Assessment Manikin and the semantic differential. *Journal of Behavior Therapy and Experimental Psychiatry*, 25(1):49–59.

Sven Buechel and Udo Hahn. 2016. Emotion analysis as a regression problem: Dimensional models and their implications on emotion representation and metrical evaluation. In *Proceedings of the 22nd European Conference on Artificial Intelligence*, pages 1114–1122.

Sven Buechel and Udo Hahn. 2018a. Emotion representation mapping for automatic lexicon construction (mostly) performs on human level. In *Proceedings of the 27th International Conference on Computational Linguistics*, pages 2892–2904.

Sven Buechel and Udo Hahn. 2018b. Representation mapping: A novel approach to generate high-quality multilingual emotion lexicons. In *Proceedings of the 11th International Conference on Language Resources and Evaluation*, pages 184–191.

Sven Buechel and Udo Hahn. 2018c. Word emotion induction for multiple languages as a deep multi-task learning problem. In *Proceedings of the 2018 Conference of the North American Chapter of the Association for Computational Linguistics: Human Language Technologies, Volume 1 (Long Papers)*, pages 1907–1918.

François-Régis Chaumartin. 2007. UPAR7: A knowledge-based system for headline sentiment tagging. In *Proceedings of the 4th International Workshop on Semantic Evaluations*, pages 422–425.

Kyunghyun Cho, Bart van Merrienboer, Dzmitry Bahdanau, and Yoshua Bengio. 2014. On the properties of neural machine translation: Encoder–decoder approaches. In *Proceedings of SSST-8, 8th Workshop on Syntax, Semantics and Structure in Statistical Translation*, pages 103–111.

Luna De Bruyne, Pepa Atanasova, and Isabelle Augenstein. 2019. Joint emotion label space modelling for affect lexica. *arXiv:1911.08782 [cs.CL]*.

Jacob Devlin, Ming-Wei Chang, Kenton Lee, and Kristina Toutanova. 2019. BERT: Pre-training of deep bidirectional transformers for language understanding. In *Proceedings of the 2019 Conference of the North American Chapter of the Association for Computational Linguistics: Human Language Technologies, Volume 1 (Long and Short Papers)*, pages 4171–4186.

Thomas G Dietterich. 1998. Approximate statistical tests for comparing supervised classification learning algorithms. *Neural Computation*, 10(7):1895–1923.

Steven Du and Xi Zhang. 2016. Aicyber's system for IALP 2016 Shared Task: Character-enhanced word vectors and boosted neural networks. In *Proceedings of the 2016 International Conference on Asian Language Processing*, pages 161–163.

Paul Ekman. 1992. An argument for basic emotions. *Cognition & Emotion*, 6(3-4):169–200.

Bjarke Felbo, Alan Mislove, Anders Søgaard, Iyad Rahwan, and Sune Lehmann. 2017. Using millions of emoji occurrences to learn any-domain representations for detecting sentiment, emotion and sarcasm. In *Proceedings of the 2017 Conference on Empirical Methods in Natural Language Processing*, pages 1615–1625.

Fréderic Godin, Baptist Vandersmissen, Wesley De Neve, and Rik Van de Walle. 2015. Multimedia Lab @ ACL WNUT NER Shared Task: Named entity recognition for Twitter microposts using distributed word representations. In *Proceedings of the Workshop on Noisy User-generated Text*, pages 146–153.

Edouard Grave, Piotr Bojanowski, Prakhar Gupta, Armand Joulin, and Tomas Mikolov. 2018. Learning word vectors for 157 languages. In *Proceedings of the 11th International Conference on Language Resources and Evaluation*, pages 3483–3487.

Sepp Hochreiter and Jürgen Schmidhuber. 1997. Long short-term memory. *Neural Computation*, 9(8):1735–1780.

Kamil K Imbir. 2017. The affective norms for polish short texts (ANPST) database properties and impact of participants' population and sex on affective ratings. *Frontiers in Psychology*, 8:855.

Mandar Joshi, Danqi Chen, Yinhan Liu, Daniel S. Weld, Luke Zettlemoyer, and Omer Levy. 2020. SpanBERT: Improving pre-training by representing and predicting spans. *Transactions of the Association for Computational Linguistics*, 8:64–77.

Nal Kalchbrenner, Edward Grefenstette, and Phil Blunsom. 2014. A convolutional neural network for modelling sentences. In *Proceedings of the 52nd Annual Meeting of the Association for Computational Linguistics (Volume 1: Long Papers)*, pages 655–665.

Hamed Khanpour, Cornelia Caragea, and Prakhar Biyani. 2017. Identifying empathetic messages in online health communities. In *Proceedings of the 8th International Joint Conference on Natural Language Processing (Volume 2: Short Papers)*, pages 246–251.

Diederik P. Kingma and Jimmy Ba. 2015. Adam: A method for stochastic optimization. In *Proceedings of the 3rd International Conference on Learning Representations*.

Minglei Li, Qin Lu, Yunfei Long, and Lin Gui. 2017. Inferring affective meanings of words from word embedding. *IEEE Transactions on Affective Computing*, 8(4):443–456.

Fei Liu, Julien Perez, and Scott Nowson. 2017. A language-independent and compositional model for personality trait recognition from short texts. In *Proceedings of the 15th Conference of the European Chapter of the Association for Computational Linguistics: Volume 1, Long Papers*, pages 754–764.

Tomas Mikolov, Ilya Sutskever, Kai Chen, Greg S Corrado, and Jeff Dean. 2013. Distributed representations of words and phrases and their compositionality. In C. J. C. Burges, L. Bottou, M. Welling, Z. Ghahramani, and K. Q. Weinberger, editors, *Advances in Neural Information Processing Systems 26*, pages 3111–3119. Curran Associates, Inc.

Saif Mohammad and Felipe Bravo-Marquez. 2017a. Emotion intensities in tweets. In *Proceedings of the 6th Joint Conference on Lexical and Computational Semantics*, pages 65–77.

Saif Mohammad and Felipe Bravo-Marquez. 2017b. WASSA-2017 shared task on emotion intensity. In *Proceedings of the 8th Workshop on Computational Approaches to Subjectivity, Sentiment and Social Media Analysis*, pages 34–49.

Saif M Mohammad and Svetlana Kiritchenko. 2015. Using hashtags to capture fine emotion categories from tweets. *Computational Intelligence*, 31(2):301–326.

Saif Mohammad, Felipe Bravo-Marquez, Mohammad Salameh, and Svetlana Kiritchenko. 2018. SemEval-2018 Task 1: Affect in tweets. In *Proceedings of the 12th International Workshop on Semantic Evaluation*, pages 1–17.

Fabian Pedregosa, Gaël Varoquaux, Alexandre Gramfort, Vincent Michel, Bertrand Thirion, Olivier Grisel, Mathieu Blondel, Peter Prettenhofer, Ron Weiss, Vincent Dubourg, and others. 2011. Scikit-learn: Machine learning in Python. *Journal of Machine Learning Research*, 12:2825–2830.

Jeffrey Pennington, Richard Socher, and Christopher D. Manning. 2014. GloVe: Global vectors for word representation. In *Proceedings of the 2014 Conference on Empirical Methods in Natural Language Processing*, pages 1532–1543.

Matthew Peters, Mark Neumann, Mohit Iyyer, Matt Gardner, Christopher Clark, Kenton Lee, and Luke Zettle-moyer. 2018. Deep contextualized word representations. In *Proceedings of the 2018 Conference of the North American Chapter of the Association for Computational Linguistics: Human Language Technologies, Volume 1 (Long Papers)*, pages 2227–2237.

Ana P. Pinheiro, Marcelo Dias, João Pedrosa, and Ana P. Soares. 2017. Minho Affective Sentences (MAS): Probing the roles of sex, mood, and empathy in affective ratings of verbal stimuli. *Behavior Research Methods*, 49(2):698–716.

Nils Reimers and Iryna Gurevych. 2018. Why comparing single performance scores does not allow to draw conclusions about machine learning approaches. *arXiv:1803.09578 [cs.LG]*.

Sara Rosenthal, Noura Farra, and Preslav Nakov. 2017. SemEval-2017 Task 4: Sentiment analysis in Twitter. In *Proceedings of the 11th International Workshop on Semantic Evaluation*, pages 502–518.

Victoria L. Rubin. 2007. Stating with certainty or stating with doubt: Intercoder reliability results for manual annotation of epistemically modalized statements. In *Human Language Technologies 2007: The Conference of the North American Chapter of the Association for Computational Linguistics; Companion Volume, Short Papers*, pages 141–144.

Nitish Srivastava, Geoffrey E Hinton, Alex Krizhevsky, Ilya Sutskever, and Ruslan Salakhutdinov. 2014. Dropout: A simple way to prevent neural networks from overfitting. *Journal of Machine Learning Research*, 15(1):1929–1958.

Carlo Strapparava and Rada Mihalcea. 2007. SemEval-2007 Task 14: Affective text. In *Proceedings of the 4th International Workshop on Semantic Evaluations*, pages 70–74.

Ashish Vaswani, Noam Shazeer, Niki Parmar, Jakob Uszkoreit, Llion Jones, Aidan N Gomez, Łukasz Kaiser, and Illia Polosukhin. 2017. Attention is all you need. In I. Guyon, U. V. Luxburg, S. Bengio, H. Wallach, R. Fergus, S. Vishwanathan, and R. Garnett, editors, *Advances in Neural Information Processing Systems 30*, pages 5998–6008. Curran Associates, Inc.

Zhilin Yang, Zihang Dai, Yiming Yang, Jaime Carbonell, Russ R Salakhutdinov, and Quoc V Le. 2019. XLNet: Generalized autoregressive pretraining for language understanding. In H. Wallach, H. Larochelle, A. Beygelz-imer, F. d' Alché-Buc, E. Fox, and R. Garnett, editors, *Advances in Neural Information Processing Systems 32*, pages 5753–5763. Curran Associates, Inc.

Cross-lingual Emotion Intensity Prediction

Irean Navas Alejo
Expert System
irean.navas@gmail.com

Toni Badia
Universitat Pompeu Fabra
tbadia@upf.edu

Jeremy Barnes
University of Oslo
jeremycb@ifi.uio.no

Abstract

Emotion intensity prediction determines the degree or intensity of an emotion that the author expresses in a text, extending previous categorical approaches to emotion detection. While most previous work on this topic has concentrated on English texts, other languages would also benefit from fine-grained emotion classification, preferably without having to recreate the amount of annotated data available in English in each new language. Consequently, we explore cross-lingual transfer approaches for fine-grained emotion detection in Spanish and Catalan tweets. To this end we annotate a test set of Spanish and Catalan tweets using Best-Worst scaling. We compare six cross-lingual approaches, e.g., machine translation and cross-lingual embeddings, which have varying requirements for parallel data – from millions of parallel sentences to completely unsupervised. The results show that on this data, methods with low parallel-data requirements perform surprisingly better than methods that use more parallel data, which we explain through an in-depth error analysis. We make the dataset and the code available at https://github.com/jerbarnes/fine-grained_cross-lingual_emotion.

1 Introduction

Emotion analysis within natural language processing attempts to identify the private states (Wiebe et al., 2005) expressed in written text, which in many cases are only implicitly available. Research often classifies these emotions into discrete categories (Ekman, 1999; Plutchik, 2001), such as *anger*, *fear*, *joy*, or *sadness*. This *discrete* approach to emotion has been applied to fairy tales (Alm et al., 2005), headlines (Strapparava and Mihalcea, 2007), and more recently micro-blogging services, such as twitter (Mohammad et al., 2015; Schuff et al., 2017). However, people can express emotion in ways that require a more fine-grained approach than the basic discrete version. Take the following two sentences:

(1) I am not feeling particularly happy today

(2) I feel like I am the most miserable person on earth

Both of these examples would be labelled with the emotion *sadness*. However, it is clear that the second sentence expresses a larger degree of sadness than the first, which categorical approaches to emotion analysis would not be able to identify. This motivates the need to move to a more fine-grained approach to emotion analysis. *Emotion intensity prediction* (Mohammad and Bravo-Marquez, 2017) does just this by extending emotion prediction from a classification task to a regression task. Given a text, the goal is to determine a real-valued number between -1 and 1 representing the *intensity* of the emotion present. This approach allows to capture more subtle differences between expressions of emotion.

Current state-of-the-art approaches to emotion intensity are based on supervised machine learning approaches, which combine several sources of annotated corpora, emotion and sentiment lexicons in order to achieve the best performance. However, the combination of all of these necessary resources is only

Proceedings of the Third Workshop on Computational Modeling of PEople's Opinions, PersonaLity, and Emotions in Social media, pages 140–152
Barcelona, Spain (Online), December 13, 2020.

available in a few high-resource languages, with English easily having the largest number. Collecting a similar set of resources for all other languages is prohibitively expensive and would require years of work. Therefore, it would be preferable to find a way to use the available resources in English to perform emotion intensity prediction in other languages.

Cross-lingual methods – either translation or cross-lingual embedding approaches – offer a possible solution to the lack of labeled data and have shown promise for sentiment analysis at document-level (Chen et al., 2018; Chen et al., 2019), sentence-level (Barnes et al., 2018; Feng and Wan, 2019), and fine-grained (Hangya et al., 2018; Barnes and Klinger, 2019). However, the greater number of classes in emotion classification and the difficulty of the regression task means that it is not obvious that the cross-lingual approaches that work well for sentiment analysis will necessarily work for cross-lingual emotion intensity prediction.

In this work, we provide the first attempt at cross-lingual emotion intensity prediction, by comparing methods which rely on cross-lingual embeddings, machine translation, and unsupervised machine translation to transfer resources from English to predict the emotion in languages that do not have large available datasets or lexicon resources. For testing, we additionally annotate a dataset of tweets in Spanish and Catalan. Our results show that surprisingly unsupervised machine translation is able to outperform both supervised machine translation and cross-lingual embedding methods on these datasets. We additionally perform detailed quantitative and qualitative error analyses of the supervised and unsupervised translation approaches, concluding that while the overall translation quality of the supervised system is better than the unsupervised system, it often does not translate hashtags, which are an important source of emotion information for this task.

In the rest of the paper we discuss related work (Section 2) and provide a description of the datasets (Section 3) and models (Section 4) used for the experiments. We then discuss the results (Section 5) and provide an in-depth analysis of why certain models perform better (Section 6).

2   Related Work

Emotion detection attempts to identify explicitly or implicitly mentioned emotions in a text, either by following a proposed set of basic emotion categories (Plutchik, 1980; Ekman, 1992; Ekman, 1999) or through valence-arousal approaches (Russell, 2003). However, in contrast to other tasks which also attempt to detect evaluative language, such as subjectivity or sentiment analysis, there are relatively few annotated resources, and most of these resources are found only in English (Alm et al., 2005; Aman and Szpakowicz, 2007; Strapparava and Mihalcea, 2007; Schuff et al., 2017). A notable exception is the deISEAR dataset (Troiano et al., 2019), which crowdsources descriptions of emotional events in German.

Annotating categorical emotion is a subjective and complicated task, which often leads to low inter-annotator agreement (Schuff et al., 2017). However, Best-worst scaling has shown to improve overall agreement scores when annotating tweets (Mohammad and Bravo-Marquez, 2017; Mohammad et al., 2018). In this approach, annotators are shown n items ($n > 1$, normally 4) and they must choose only the items that are *best* and *worst*, *i. e.* those that most and least represent the phenomena under question. Despite these advances in annotating, for most languages in the world, there exists no annotated emotion dataset which could enable supervised emotion classification.

On English data, previous approaches to classifying emotion have used word and character n-gram features (Mohammad, 2012), sentiment and emotion lexicon features (Mohammad and Kiritchenko, 2015), as well as a variety of neural networks (Köper et al., 2017; Felbo et al., 2017; Bostan and Klinger, 2019). Typically, strong emotion classification systems use a combination of these features to get the strongest performance.

2.1   Emotion intensity prediction

Emotion intensity proposes a more fine-grained view of emotion classification. Specifically, given a tweet and an emotion X, the goal is to determine the intensity or degree of emotion X expressed in the text – a real-valued score between 0 and 1. This task has already been the topic of two shared tasks (Mohammad and Bravo-Marquez, 2017; Mohammad et al., 2018), which attracted many participants.

Given the complexity of the task and the relatively small amount of annotated training data available, it is perhaps unsurprising that state-of-the-art methods incorporate information from external sources, either in the form of specialized word embeddings (Goel et al., 2017), lexicon features (Köper et al., 2017; Duppada and Hiray, 2017), or transfer learning methods (Felbo et al., 2017).

Additionally, in contrast to related tasks, such as sentiment analysis where end-to-end neural methods often give state-of-the-art results (Barnes et al., 2017; Ambartsoumian and Popowich, 2018), for emotion intensity prediction n-grams, character n-grams, word embedding features, and lexicon features play a more important role (Mohammad and Bravo-Marquez, 2017; Köper et al., 2017; Duppada and Hiray, 2017). However, it is not clear if the same features are equally important when performing this task crosslingually.

2.2 Cross-lingual approaches

For other tasks which classify affective text, such as sentiment analysis, cross-lingual approaches have shown promise for classifying a low-resource target language by leveraging labeled data from high-resource source languages, such as English (Barnes et al., 2018; Chen et al., 2019).

We divide cross-lingual approaches into machine translation (MT) techniques and word embedding techniques, as they generally have different data requirements and different models. MT approaches can either be supervised, which requires parallel corpora, or unsupervised, relying only on monolingual corpora) approaches. While most MT research has focused on resource-rich languages where Neural MT (NMT) has indeed displaced Statistical MT, a recent line of work has managed to train a NMT system without any supervision, relying on monolingual corpora alone (Artetxe et al., 2018). This would be particularly useful for low-resource languages if the translation quality proved good enough to enable a classifier to reliable predict the emotion.

Cross-lingual embedding methods instead require large monolingual corpora, and small amounts of bilingual signal, often only small bilingual lexica. Barnes et al. (2018) uses monolingual embeddings, bilingual lexicons and jointly learns cross-lingual embeddings while training an sentiment classifier. The bilingual sentiment embeddings (BLSE) method predicts sentiment of source sentences projecting the vector of the source embeddings into the joint space and repeats the process for the target language using the target embeddings, meaning the original datasets and not the translations, and projecting them into the joint space to obtain the prediction.

More recently, cross-lingual methods have resorted to multilingual language modelling (Devlin et al., 2019; Conneau et al., 2020) based on pretraining large transformer models (Vaswani et al., 2017) on unlabeled text. These models do not explicitly model inter-language representations, but they give surprising cross-lingual performance on many tasks (Wu and Dredze, 2019).

3 Datasets

For training the emotion intensity classifiers, we use the English data from the WASSA 2017 shared task on emotion intensity prediction (Mohammad and Bravo-Marquez, 2017). The authors collected tweets and used crowd-annotation to achieve real-valued labels for four emotions (*anger*, *fear*, *joy*, and *sadness*). We use their predefined splits (statistics are shown in Table 3).

3.1 Annotation of test data

For testing in the two target languages (Spanish and Catalan) we create two annotated datasets following the methodology of Mohammad and Bravo-Marquez (2017). We gather tweets (342 Spanish tweets and 280 Catalan tweets) which contained one of the six emotion terms[1] *anger, disgust, fear, joy, sadness* and *surprise*). This original download leads to between 385-600 tweets per emotion, totalling 3279 Spanish and 2941 Catalan tweets. These tweets are then filtered and normalized in order to delete the retweets, mentions and links, as well as adverts and tweets that only contained images, resulting in 342 tweets in Spanish and 280 in Catalan.

---

[1] We used the following translations of the emotion terms to gather tweets: *felicidad, enfadado, tristeza, asco, miedo, sorpresa* for Spanish and *felicitat, enfadat, tristesa, fàstic, por, sorpresa* in Catalan.

1.	Que lindo fue volver a meterse a nadar hoy
2.	Hoy estoy triste....
3.	le acabo de romper una pata a la araña y se me subio a la mano
4.	estoy tan enfadado.... gracias a dios que nadie me entiende.

Table 1: An example 4-tuple for the Spanish data for *sadness*.

	Catalan		Spanish	
	Pearson	Spearman	Pearson	Spearman
anger	0.68 (0.02)	0.66 (0.03)	0.77 (0.02)	0.78 (0.02)
disgust	0.71 (0.02)	0.70 (0.02)	0.76 (0.02)	0.77 (0.02)
fear	0.69 (0.02)	0.67 (0.02)	0.74 (0.02)	0.74 (0.02)
joy	0.66 (0.02)	0.64 (0.02)	0.76 (0.02)	0.76 (0.02)
sadness	0.65 (0.02)	0.64 (0.02)	0.74 (0.02)	0.75 (0.02)
surprise	0.44 (0.03)	0.44 (0.04)	0.65 (0.02)	0.62 (0.02)

Table 2: Split-half reliability (as measured by Pearson and Spearman rank correlation) for *anger*, *disgust*, *fear*, *joy*, *sadness*, and *surprise* annotations of tweets in the Tweet Emotion Intensity Dataset.

Following the methodology set out in Best-Worst Scaling (BWS), each annotator is given four items (4-tuple) and is asked which item is the *best* (highest in terms of the property of interest) and which is the *worst* (least in terms of the property of interest) (Kiritchenko and Mohammad, 2016). The annotator must then choose which one of those 4 tweets represents each emotion the most and which represents it the least. Given the small number of tweets, we include all in the annotation of each emotion. An example of the annotation process in Spanish is shown in Table 1.

This annotation task presents a number of challenges. For example, annotators cannot simply rely on keywords in the tweet to identify the intensity of an emotion, given that many times the authors of tweets use emotional hashtags ironically. Additionally, differentiating between four tweets that all have relatively low intensities of an emotion can be difficult. Finally, inferring the emotion conveyed in a short text is known to be subjective and challenging on its own (Schuff et al., 2017).

3.2 Inter-annotator agreement

After annotating the tuples, we use split-half correlation to determine inter-annotator agreement (shown in Table 2). We report Pearson correlation, which is a number between -1 and 1 that indicates the extent to which two variables are linearly related, and Spearman correlation, which measures the strength and direction of association between two ranked variables. As shown in Table 2, we obtain strong correlations (> 0.6) for all emotions except for *surprise*. We find a higher correlation score in Spanish than in Catalan for all emotions. The lower correlation for the Catalan tweets could be due to the fact that there are fewer tweets referring to *joy* and *surprise*, which made the annotation task harder. It is important to point out that *surprise* has the lowest scores, which is known to be a difficult emotion to classify (Schuff et al., 2017), and has even been split into positive and negative surprise (Alm et al., 2005). In fact, we disregard *surprise* and *disgust* for the rest of the experiments, as we have no English annotated data for these emotions. However, the data will be made available with all annotations.

4 Experimental Setup

In order to determine how much bilingual signal is required to predict crosslingual emotion intensity, we compare four methods with differing data needs. In the following, we describe these methods from those that require the largest amount of bilingual signal (MT) to those that require the least (UNSUP).

	EN_{train}	EN_{dev}	EN_{test}	CA_{test}	ES_{test}
anger	857	84	760	280	342
fear	1147	110	995	280	342
joy	823	79	714	280	342
sadness	786	74	673	280	342

Table 3: Statistics of the English train (EN_{train}), development (EN_{dev}), and Catalan (CA_{test}) and Spanish (ES_{test}) test sets used in the experiments.

Each model is trained on EN_{train} and then tested on EN_{test}, CA_{test}, and ES_{test}. EN_{dev} is only used for hyperparameter optimization.

Supervised Machine Translation (MT):   We use GoogleTranslate[2], which makes use of large amounts of parallel data, to translate the test samples to English. We then train a Support Vector Regression model[3] on bag of words representations (MT-BOW) and a second model with a number of additional features (MT-FULL). For the MT-FULL model, we include n-gram features (1-4), character n-grams (3-5), embedding features created by averaging the embeddings of all the tokens in the tweet, and finally features from the following lexicons: NRC Hashtag Sentiment Lexicon (Mohammad et al., 2013), NRC hashtag emotion association lexicon (Mohammad, 2012; Mohammad and Kiritchenko, 2015) and the NRC Word-Emotion Association Lexicon (Mohammad and Turney, 2013), where each feature is a real valued number which represents how much each word is associated to a polarity or emotion. The final representation of each tweet using the MT-FULL method is therefore a 65860 dimensional vector. Finally, we train the SVR model using the following settings (linear kernel, $C = 100$) on the original English training data and test on the translated test set.

Cross-lingual Word Embeddings (CWE):   We create 300 dimensional monolingual word2vec embeddings for source and target languages by training on Wikipedia corpora (see UNSUP for more information on the corpora) and then use VecMap (Artetxe et al., 2017) to learn an orthogonal projection of the word embeddings to a joint shared embedding space using a small bilingual lexicon[4] as supervision (5749 and 5310 translation pairs for EN-ES and EN-CA, respectively). Finally, we train a Support Vector Regression model on the source language (EN) using only the crosslingual embeddings as features using the following settings (linear kernel, $C = 100$) and test it on the target languages (ES, CA). It is important to highlight that this method does not use the translations but the original texts.

Bilingual Sentiment Embeddings (BLSE):   Like CWE, this model uses a bilingual lexicon to learn a mapping from both original vector spaces to a shared bilingual space, but instead jointly learns to predict the sentiment and employs two linear projection matrices. This allows the model to infuse the target embedding space with sentiment information by updating the source space for sentiment and requiring that the target space resemble it as much as possible, using the bilingual dictionary to anchor terms. In this work, we adapt the model to predict emotion intensity by replacing the cross-entropy loss with mean-squared error. We train the model on the English training data and the same bilingual lexicons as for CWE, optimizing with Adam (Kingma and Ba, 2014) for 100 epochs with an α of 0.001. We keep the model with the best performance on the source language development set, and finally test on the target test set. As with CWE, we highlight that this method does not use the translations but the original texts.

Unsupervised Statistical Machine Translation (UNSUP)   We train an unsupervised statistical machine translation model (Artetxe et al., 2018) on Wikipedia corpora for both English-Spanish and

---

[2]Available at `https://translate.google.com`.
[3]We use the version available in the Sklearn toolkit (Pedregosa et al., 2011).
[4]We use the lexicons made available from Barnes et al. (2018).

| | Monolingual | | | | | Cross-lingual | | | | | | | | | |
| | English | | | | | Catalan | | | | | Spanish | | | | |
	anger	fear	joy	sadness	avg.	anger	fear	joy	sadness	avg.	anger	fear	joy	sadness	avg.
CWE	0.17	0.30	0.22	0.28	0.24	0.04	-0.02	0.13	0.03	0.05	0.03	-0.04	0.16	0.00	0.04
BLSE	0.35	0.27	0.46	0.39	0.37	0.24	-0.06	0.03	0.06	0.07	0.14	0.09	0.24	**0.12**	0.15
MT-BOW	0.41	0.51	0.48	0.47	0.47	0.28	0.10	0.19	0.02	0.15	0.14	0.06	0.17	-0.11	0.07
UNSUP-BOW	0.41	0.51	0.48	0.47	0.47	0.21	-0.03	0.17	0.03	0.10	0.14	0.01	0.13	-0.10	0.05
MT-FULL	**0.60**	0.60	**0.64**	**0.62**	**0.62**	0.37	0.35	**0.46**	0.17	0.34	0.33	0.24	0.43	0.05	0.26
UNSUP-FULL	**0.60**	0.60	**0.64**	**0.62**	**0.62**	**0.42**	0.40	0.45	0.21	**0.37**	**0.42**	**0.31**	**0.43**	0.10	**0.32**
MBERT	0.20	0.27	0.33	0.31	0.27	-0.05	0.06	0.03	-0.15	-0.03	0.12	0.13	0.05	0.0	0.08
XLM-ROBERTA	0.44	**0.61**	0.54	0.58	0.54	0.35	**0.42**	0.39	**0.25**	0.35	0.34	0.29	**0.43**	**0.12**	0.30

Table 4: Pearson results of monolingual English-English experiments, as well as cross-lingual English-Catalan and English-Spanish for each emotion and each model. Average column added and best results are shown in **bold**.

English-Catalan. The model first creates monolingual embeddings, then learns to project them to a bilingual space by selecting identical strings as pivots, which serve as a noisy bilingual lexicon, which is improved iteratively. Next, the model induces a noisy phrase table for the SMT model, which is again improved iteratively.

We extract cleaned corpora[5] from Wikipedia dumps and sentence and word tokenize them, resulting in 89~/29~/10~ million sentences for English, Spanish, and Catalan, respectively. We train the UNSUP model using the default settings (removing sentences with fewer than 3 and more than 80 tokens, 5-gram language model, 300 dimensional embeddings, 10 rounds of unsupervised tuning for the SMT and 3 rounds of backtranslation). We then translate the test data to English using the UNSUP system. Finally, we use bag-of-words representations (UNSUP-BOW) and additional n-gram, character n-gram, embedding, and lexicon information (UNSUP-FULL) and train a Support Vector Regression model using the following settings (linear kernel, $C = 100$), as we do with the MT models.

Multi-lingual Language Models We use pretrained MBERT and XLM-ROBERTA models to extract features for each example by taking the final [CLS] embedding as the representation for the example. These features are then used to train an SVR model, as with the other experiments. We additionally experimented with adding a linear layer after the final LM layer and fine-tuning the full model, only fine-tuning the linear layer, and using a max pooled representation instead of the [CLS] embedding, but found that these approaches did not perform as well.

5 Results

The Pearson correlation results are summarized for all models in Table 4 for Spanish and Catalan. We report the individual scores for *anger, fear, joy*, and *sadness*, as well as the averaged Pearson score of all emotions.

The approach that obtains the highest overall Pearson correlation across all emotions on both languages is UNSUP-FULL, averaging 0.37 on Catalan and 0.32 on Spanish. In addition, it is the best performing model on 4 of the 8 tasks, except for Catalan *joy*, where MT-FULL is 0.01 percentage points (pp.) better, reaching 0.46 and Catalan *sadness* (XLM-ROBERTA is 0.04 pp. better, at 0.25) and Catalan *fear* (XLM-ROBERTA is 0.02 pp. better, at 0.42) and Spanish *sadness* (BLSE is 0.02 pp. better, reaching 0.12). XLM-ROBERTA is the second best model, averaging 0.35 and 0.30 on Catalan and Spanish, respectively, while MT-FULL is slightly worse (0.34 and 0.26). MT-BOW and UNSUP-BOW perform much worse (0.15/0.07 and 0.10/0.05), and the cross-lingual embedding methods are the worst by far (0.04/0.03 for CWE and 0.07/0.15 for BLSE).

---

[5]We use the wikiextractor tool available at `https://github.com/attardi/wikiextractor`.

		hashtags	lexical	insert.	delet.	untrans.	slang	names	nums.	Total
CA	MT	**90**	53	2	18	17	26	5	2	213
	UNSUP	60	**67**	**7**	**14**	**168**	29	**81**	**9**	**435**
ES	MT	**62**	37	0	4	12	68	0	0	183
	UNSUP	35	**142**	**13**	**43**	**84**	**101**	**49**	**16**	**467**

Table 5: Error analysis of the the machine translation used in MT and UNSUP approaches. The error categories include incorrectly translated hashtags, lexical errors, insertions, deletions, untranslated segments, translation errors of slang and non-standard language, mistranslated names and numbers. Number refer to the number of tweets where these errors are found, rather than the number of errors.

It is clear that the additional features (character n-grams, embedding features, and lexicon features) are essential. MT-FULL performs an average of 0.19 pp. Pearson better than MT-BOW, while UNSUP-FULL leads to 0.28 pp. improvement over UNSUP-BOW. We further confirm this in Section 6.2.

Regarding the cross-lingual embedding models, it seems evident that these do not contain enough information to accurately predict emotion intensity in the target language. BLSE does outperform CWE on both Catalan and Spanish (an average of 0.03 pp. and 0.12 pp., respectively) and both MT-BOW and UNSUP-BOW on Catalan (0.08 pp. and 0.10 pp.), but the overall performance is still poor. These models are also the poorest performers monolingually.

There is large performance gap between XLM-ROBERTA and MBERT, on both the monolingual (0.27 pp.) and cross-lingual tasks (0.38/0.22 pp.), as MBERT is the weakest cross-lingual model and XLM-ROBERTA the second best.

Additionally, there is a divergence between *sadness* and the rest of the emotions analyzed, with no model achieving more than 0.21 or 0.12 in Catalan and Spanish. This seems to indicate that sadness may be harder to classify cross-lingually, as monolingually this class is has the best classification results (Mohammad and Bravo-Marquez, 2017; Köper et al., 2017). This class also has the fewest training and development examples in English, which may indicate that the good previous results monolingually may have been due to overfitting to the data. It is also possible that the particulars of the target language test data are the reason for this difference, although the inter-annotator agreement scores suggest that *sadness* is not more difficult than the other classes.

6 Analysis

In this section we compare both quantitatively and qualitatively the differences in translation quality between MT and UNSUP. Furthermore, we perform an ablation study to determine which features are the most important for MONO, MT-FULL, and UNSUP-FULL.

6.1 Differences in translation quality

Given that twitter is a social network where people express their emotions and opinions on a large variety of topics – social or personal events, news, and politics – the translation task is made more difficult. Additionally, relevant information to emotion classification in tweets is often contained in hashtags (Mohammad et al., 2013), which are known to be difficult to translate (Gotti et al., 2014). Therefore, cross-lingual approaches to fine-grained emotion detection in twitter are particularly challenging since the language used in twitter usually contains abbreviations, acronyms, emoticons, unusual orthographic elements, slang, and misspellings (Liew and Turtle, 2016). All of these phenomena are difficult for both translation- and projection-based cross-lingual approaches.

We manually examine the MT and UNSUP translations of the Catalan and Spanish tweets for translation errors. For each tweet, we determine if there has been an error regarding the hashtags, any lexical errors, insertions, deletions, untranslated segments, errors with non-standard language, errors translating

original	#*DiosLosCríaYEllosSeJuntan* L'advocat de Camacho en el cas Método 3
	va redactar la sentència de Puig Antich link
MT	# *DiosLosCríaYesLocated* The Camacho lawyer in the case Method 3
	wrote the sentence of Puig Antich link
UNSUP	# *DiosLosCríaYEllosSeJuntan* l'advocat of camacho in the case história 3
	drafted the verdict of abu-jamal link
manual trans.	#*BirdsOfAFeatherFlockTogether* Camacho's lawyer in the Método 3 case
	is the one who sentenced Puig Antich link

Table 6: An example of a tweet in Catalan (original), its translations using the two machine translation systems (MT, UNSUP), as well as a manual translation. *Untranslated tokens* are highlighted in red, while *entity errors* are highlighted in blue.

original	Harto de la situación en #*Cataluña*. Votamos mayoritariamente a delincuentes
	y tenemos lo que merecemos. No hay solución #*verguenza*
MT	Fed up of the situation in # *Catalonia* . We vote mostly criminals and we have
	what we deserve. There is no solution # *verguenzak*
UNSUP	Fed up with the situation in # *catalonia* . They voted overwhelmingly to criminals
	and we have what they deserve no solution # disgrace
manual trans.	Tired of the situation in #*Catalonia*. We mainly vote for criminals
	and get what we deserve. There's no solution. #*shame*

Table 7: An example of tweet in Spanish (original) and its translation using the two machine translations systems (MT, UNSUP). *Hashtag translation errors* are highlighted in grey and *lexical errors* are highlighted in green.

names and errors translating number and show the results in Table 5. MT has fewer errors overall compared to UNSUP (213/183 compared to 435/467, respectively) and has fewer of all error types, except for hashtags. For the task of predicting emotion intensity in tweets, the hashtags are often the most informative source, which explains why UNSUP-FULL performs better than MT-FULL in our experiments.

The Spanish translation models generally perform better than the Catalan ones. This is likely due to the larger amount of training data available. However, the Spanish data also contains more use of non-standard language, which is reflected in the *slang* errors. In these cases, MT generally performs much better than UNSUP. Interestingly, UNSUP tends to mistranslate named entities. Specifically, the model often replaces a named entity with a *similar* entity in the target language. For example, mentions of the Catalan freedom fighter Salvador Puig i Antich are consistently translated to Mumia Abu-Jamal, an American journalist (see Table 6). Both were accused of killing a police officer and sentenced to death, which lead to large protests. This is likely due to the nearest neighbor search used to create the original phrase tables.

Besides the mistranlation of named entities, in Table 6 we can also see that the multiword hashtag, which contains information necessary to properly interpret the emotional content of the tweet, has not been translated by MT or UNSUP. Note that although this problem could be improved by properly segmenting the hashtags in a previous step (Declerck and Lendvai, 2015; Çelebi and Özgür, 2016), translation would still likely lead to a loss of information (Gotti et al., 2014) important for emotion classification.

Table 7, instead, shows an example from the Spanish dataset where, even though the MT version better preserves the semantics of the original tweet, it did not correctly translate the emotional hashtag, while UNSUP did. On the other hand, for cases where MT-FULL has better performance, translation quality tends to be the main factor. Specifically, UNSUP-FULL tends to leave many words untranslated.

		ALL	-ngrams	-char	-embs	-hashtag	-emo	-sent	-all lex
	MONO	0.60	**-0.31**	-0.04	-0.01	-0.06	-0.01	-0.01	-0.06
anger	MT-FULL	0.37	**-0.30**	-0.00	-0.00	-0.02	-0.00	-0.02	-0.07
	UNSUP-FULL	0.42	**-0.23**	-0.05	-0.00	-0.02	-0.01	-0.05	-0.11
	MONO	0.60	**-0.30**	-0.01	-0.00	-0.01	-0.00	-0.01	-0.04
fear	MT-FULL	0.35	**-0.31**	+0.06	-0.00	-0.02	-0.01	-0.05	-0.14
	UNSUP-FULL	0.40	**-0.26**	+0.03	-0.00	-0.01	-0.01	-0.08	-0.21
	MONO	0.64	-0.03	-0.03	-0.00	-0.00	-0.02	-0.03	**-0.06**
joy	MT-FULL	0.46	-0.07	-0.02	-0.00	-0.01	-0.02	-0.02	**-0.11**
	UNSUP-FULL	0.45	-0.05	-0.03	-0.00	-0.01	-0.02	-0.04	**-0.16**
	MONO	0.62	-0.01	-0.02	-0.00	-0.00	-0.00	-0.01	**-0.04**
sadness	MT-FULL	0.17	-0.01	-0.01	-0.00	-0.01	-0.00	-0.09	**-0.15**
	UNSUP-FULL	0.21	-0.02	+0.05	-0.00	-0.02	-0.02	-0.06	**-0.20**

Table 8: Ablation study of MONO (used to show an informative monolingual baseline), MT-FULL and UNSUP-FULL on the Catalan dataset, where we show the drop in performance (Pearson correlation) when we remove only a single feature at a time (except for -all lex, where all lexicon features are removed). We show the largest drop in **bold** and the second largest underlined. On most emotions (*anger, fear joy*), removing the n-gram feature leads to the largest drop both mono- and cross-lingually. For *sadness*, however, the NRC sentiment lexicon features (sent) are most decisive.

6.2 Ablation study

In order to determine which features are most predictive for emotion intensity, we perform an ablation study of MONO, MT-FULL, and UNSUP-FULL on the Catalan test data[6]. Specifically, we remove a single feature at at time, except for -all lex, where all lexicon features are removed. We include MONO as an upper-bound to determine what features are most important for the task, given enough monolingual data, but note that the test data is different for MT-FULL and UNSUP-FULL, so the exact results are therefore not strictly comparable. The results are shown in Table 8.

In general, the cross-lingual models exhibit the same relationship to the features as the monolingual model, although with generally lower performance. Token n-grams are the most important feature for *anger* and *fear*, although less important for *joy* and *sadness*. Word embedding features seem to contribute nothing to the performance. Character n-gram features, on the other hand, contribute little, or even hurt the performance (removing them actually improves the results for MT-FULL and UNSUP-FULL on *fear*, and for MONO and UNSUP-FULL on *sadness*). Finally, the lexicon features are important for all emotions.

For *joy*, removing any one set of features does not lead to large drops in performance. Given the good performance of all models on this emotion, it seems to indicate that this class is the easiest to predict, and that the features are relatively redundant. However for UNSUP-FULL, removing all lexicon features still leads to a drop of 0.16 pp.

Sadness is the most difficult emotion, with the cross-lingual models performing on par with MONO. The lexicon features are the most informative for all models, specifically the NRC sentiment lexicon features (-sent). This effect is even stronger cross-lingually, where without them, the models perform at chance level.

---

[6]The ablation study results for the Spanish data are similar.

7 Conclusion

In this paper, we provided the first attempt at cross-lingual emotion intensity prediction, by comparing methods which rely on differing amounts of cross-lingual signal, ranging from millions of parallel sentences (MT), small bilingual dictionaries (cross-lingual embeddings), to no explicit cross-lingual signal at all (UNSUP). We compare these methods on two target languages, Spanish and Catalan, which do not have large available emotion datasets or lexicon resources. In order to test the models, we additionally annotated a small dataset of tweets in Spanish and Catalan.

Our results show that translation methods outperform embedding-based methods for almost all emotions and achieve reasonable average results, although there is still a noticeable gap to reach monolingual levels. Surprisingly, unsupervised translation is the best performing cross-lingual method, largely due to the fact that it more accurately translates hashtags. XLM-ROBERTA performs nearly as well, but unfortunately cannot be combined with sentiment and emotion lexicons available in English, as it processes the original target-language data. These results may not hold for other domains, such as literature or opinion pieces, where emotional information is not concentrated in a similar way.

In the future, it would be interesting to perform experiments on various domains, in order to determine whether unsupervised machine translation for cross-lingual emotion is robust to domain shift. Theoretically, this is simpler for unsupervised MT rather than supervised MT, which could motivate further research in this direction. As lexicon information has proven so useful for this task, it could be interesting to look into approaches that use this information to improve pretrained multilingual language models. Additionally, given the importance of hashtags for emotion detection in tweets, it would be important for future work in cross-lingual emotion detection to concentrate on achieving better translations of hashtags.

Finally, we contemplate promising research on emotion detection and classification using the newly annotated data in Catalan and Spanish we introduce here. We expect that this will contribute to furthering research on these two languages.

References

Cecilia Ovesdotter Alm, Dan Roth, and Richard Sproat. 2005. Emotions from text: Machine learning for text-based emotion prediction. In *Proceedings of Human Language Technology Conference and Conference on Empirical Methods in Natural Language Processing*, pages 579–586, Vancouver, BC, Canada, October.

Saima Aman and Stan Szpakowicz. 2007. Identifying expressions of emotion in text. In *Text, Speech and Dialogue: 10th International Conference, TSD 2007, Pilsen, Czech Republic, September 3-7, 2007. Proceedings*, pages 196–205. Springer.

Artaches Ambartsoumian and Fred Popowich. 2018. Self-attention: A better building block for sentiment analysis neural network classifiers. In *Proceedings of the 9th Workshop on Computational Approaches to Subjectivity, Sentiment and Social Media Analysis*, pages 130–139, Brussels, Belgium, October.

Mikel Artetxe, Gorka Labaka, and Eneko Agirre. 2017. Learning bilingual word embeddings with (almost) no bilingual data. In *Proceedings of the 55th Annual Meeting of the Association for Computational Linguistics (Volume 1: Long Papers)*, pages 451–462, Vancouver, Canada, July. Association for Computational Linguistics.

Mikel Artetxe, Gorka Labaka, and Eneko Agirre. 2018. Unsupervised statistical machine translation. In *Proceedings of the 2018 Conference on Empirical Methods in Natural Language Processing*, pages 3632–3642, Brussels, Belgium, October-November. Association for Computational Linguistics.

Jeremy Barnes and Roman Klinger. 2019. Embedding projection for targeted cross-lingual sentiment: Model comparisons and a real-world study. *Journal of Artificial Intelligence Research*, 66:691–742.

Jeremy Barnes, Roman Klinger, and Sabine Schulte im Walde. 2017. Assessing State-of-the-Art Sentiment Models on State-of-the-Art Sentiment Datasets. In *Proceedings of the 8th Workshop on Computational Approaches to Subjectivity, Sentiment and Social Media Analysis*, pages 2–12, Copenhagen, Denmark, September.

Jeremy Barnes, Roman Klinger, and Sabine Schulte im Walde. 2018. Bilingual sentiment embeddings: Joint projection of sentiment across languages. In *Proceedings of the 56th Annual Meeting of the Association for Computational Linguistics (Volume 1: Long Papers)*, pages 2483–2493, Melbourne, Australia, July. Association for Computational Linguistics.

Laura Ana Maria Bostan and Roman Klinger. 2019. Exploring fine-tuned embeddings that model intensifiers for emotion analysis. In *Proceedings of the Tenth Workshop on Computational Approaches to Subjectivity, Sentiment and Social Media Analysis*, pages 25–34, Minneapolis, USA, June. Association for Computational Linguistics.

Arda Çelebi and Arzucan Özgür. 2016. Segmenting hashtags using automatically created training data. In *Proceedings of the Tenth International Conference on Language Resources and Evaluation (LREC'16)*, pages 2981–2985, Portorož, Slovenia, May. European Language Resources Association (ELRA).

Xilun Chen, Yu Sun, Ben Athiwaratkun, Claire Cardie, and Kilian Weinberger. 2018. Adversarial deep averaging networks for cross-lingual sentiment classification. *Transactions of the Association for Computational Linguistics*, 6:557–570.

Xilun Chen, Ahmed Hassan Awadallah, Hany Hassan, Wei Wang, and Claire Cardie. 2019. Multi-source cross-lingual model transfer: Learning what to share. In *Proceedings of the 57th Annual Meeting of the Association for Computational Linguistics*, pages 3098–3112, Florence, Italy, July. Association for Computational Linguistics.

Alexis Conneau, Kartikay Khandelwal, Naman Goyal, Vishrav Chaudhary, Guillaume Wenzek, Francisco Guzmán, Edouard Grave, Myle Ott, Luke Zettlemoyer, and Veselin Stoyanov. 2020. Unsupervised cross-lingual representation learning at scale. In *Proceedings of the 58th Annual Meeting of the Association for Computational Linguistics*, pages 8440–8451, Online, July. Association for Computational Linguistics.

Thierry Declerck and Piroska Lendvai. 2015. Processing and normalizing hashtags. In *Proceedings of the International Conference Recent Advances in Natural Language Processing*, pages 104–109, Hissar, Bulgaria, September. INCOMA Ltd. Shoumen, BULGARIA.

Jacob Devlin, Ming-Wei Chang, Kenton Lee, and Kristina Toutanova. 2019. BERT: Pre-training of deep bidirectional transformers for language understanding. In *Proceedings of the 2019 Conference of the North American Chapter of the Association for Computational Linguistics: Human Language Technologies, Volume 1 (Long and Short Papers)*, pages 4171–4186, Minneapolis, Minnesota, June. Association for Computational Linguistics.

Venkatesh Duppada and Sushant Hiray. 2017. Seernet at EmoInt-2017: Tweet emotion intensity estimator. In *Proceedings of the 8th Workshop on Computational Approaches to Subjectivity, Sentiment and Social Media Analysis*, pages 205–211, Copenhagen, Denmark, September. Association for Computational Linguistics.

Paul Ekman. 1992. An argument for basic emotions. *Cognition and Emotion*, pages 169–200.

Paul Ekman. 1999. Basic emotions. In Tim Dalgleish and M. J. Powers, editors, *Handbook of Cognition and Emotion*. Wiley.

Bjarke Felbo, Alan Mislove, Anders Søgaard, Iyad Rahwan, and Sune Lehmann. 2017. Using millions of emoji occurrences to learn any-domain representations for detecting sentiment, emotion and sarcasm. In *Proceedings of the 2017 Conference on Empirical Methods in Natural Language Processing*, pages 1615–1625, Copenhagen, Denmark, September. Association for Computational Linguistics.

Yanlin Feng and Xiaojun Wan. 2019. Learning bilingual sentiment-specific word embeddings without cross-lingual supervision. In *Proceedings of the 2019 Conference of the North American Chapter of the Association for Computational Linguistics: Human Language Technologies, Volume 1 (Long and Short Papers)*, pages 420–429, Minneapolis, Minnesota, June. Association for Computational Linguistics.

Pranav Goel, Devang Kulshreshtha, Prayas Jain, and Kaushal Kumar Shukla. 2017. Prayas at EmoInt 2017: An ensemble of deep neural architectures for emotion intensity prediction in tweets. In *Proceedings of the 8th Workshop on Computational Approaches to Subjectivity, Sentiment and Social Media Analysis*, pages 58–65, Copenhagen, Denmark, September. Association for Computational Linguistics.

Fabrizio Gotti, Phillippe Langlais, and Atefeh Farzindar. 2014. Hashtag occurrences, layout and translation: A corpus-driven analysis of tweets published by the Canadian government. In *Proceedings of the Ninth International Conference on Language Resources and Evaluation (LREC'14)*, pages 2254–2261, Reykjavik, Iceland, May. European Language Resources Association (ELRA).

Viktor Hangya, Fabienne Braune, Alexander Fraser, and Hinrich Schütze. 2018. Two methods for domain adaptation of bilingual tasks: Delightfully simple and broadly applicable. In *Proceedings of the 56th Annual Meeting of the Association for Computational Linguistics (Volume 1: Long Papers)*, pages 810–820, Melbourne, Australia, July. Association for Computational Linguistics.

Diederik Kingma and Jimmy Ba. 2014. Adam: A method for stochastic optimization. *Proceedings of the 3rd International Conference on Learning Representations (ICLR)*, dec.

Svetlana Kiritchenko and Saif M. Mohammad. 2016. Capturing reliable fine-grained sentiment associations by crowdsourcing and best–worst scaling. In *Proceedings of the 2016 Conference of the North American Chapter of the Association for Computational Linguistics: Human Language Technologies*, pages 811–817, San Diego, California, June. Association for Computational Linguistics.

Maximilian Köper, Evgeny Kim, and Roman Klinger. 2017. IMS at EmoInt-2017: Emotion intensity prediction with affective norms, automatically extended resources and deep learning. In *Proceedings of the 8th Workshop on Computational Approaches to Subjectivity, Sentiment and Social Media Analysis*, pages 50–57, Copenhagen, Denmark, September.

Jasy Suet Yan Liew and Howard R. Turtle. 2016. Exploring fine-grained emotion detection in tweets. In *Proceedings of the NAACL Student Research Workshop*, pages 73–80, San Diego, California, June. Association for Computational Linguistics.

Saif Mohammad and Felipe Bravo-Marquez. 2017. WASSA-2017 shared task on emotion intensity. In *Proceedings of the 8th Workshop on Computational Approaches to Subjectivity, Sentiment and Social Media Analysis*, pages 34–49, Copenhagen, Denmark, September.

Saif M. Mohammad and Svetlana Kiritchenko. 2015. Using hashtags to capture fine emotion categories from tweets. *Computational Intelligence*, 31(2):301–326.

Saif M. Mohammad and Peter D. Turney. 2013. Crowdsourcing a word–emotion association lexicon. *Computational Intelligence*, 29(3):436–465.

Saif Mohammad, Svetlana Kiritchenko, and Xiaodan Zhu. 2013. NRC-canada: Building the state-of-the-art in sentiment analysis of tweets. In *Second Joint Conference on Lexical and Computational Semantics (*SEM), Volume 2: Proceedings of the Seventh International Workshop on Semantic Evaluation (SemEval 2013)*, pages 321–327, Atlanta, Georgia, USA, June. Association for Computational Linguistics.

Saif M. Mohammad, Xiaodan Zhu, Svetlana Kiritchenko, and Joel Martin. 2015. Sentiment, emotion, purpose, and style in electoral tweets. *Information Processing Management*, 51(4):480 – 499.

Saif Mohammad, Felipe Bravo-Marquez, Mohammad Salameh, and Svetlana Kiritchenko. 2018. SemEval-2018 task 1: Affect in tweets. In *Proceedings of The 12th International Workshop on Semantic Evaluation*, pages 1–17, New Orleans, Louisiana, June. Association for Computational Linguistics.

Saif Mohammad. 2012. #emotional tweets. In **SEM 2012: The First Joint Conference on Lexical and Computational Semantics – Volume 1: Proceedings of the main conference and the shared task, and Volume 2: Proceedings of the Sixth International Workshop on Semantic Evaluation (SemEval 2012)*, pages 246–255, Montréal, Canada, 7-8 June. Association for Computational Linguistics.

Fabian Pedregosa, Gaël Varoquaux, Alexandre Gramfort, Vincent Michel, Bertrand Thirion, Olivier Grisel, Mathieu Blondel, Peter Prettenhofer, Ron Weiss, Vincent Dubourg, Jake Vanderplas, Alexandre Passos, David Cournapeau, Matthieu Brucher, Matthieu Perrot, and Édouard Duchesnay. 2011. Scikit-learn: Machine learning in python. *J. Mach. Learn. Res.*, 12:2825–2830, November.

Robert Plutchik. 1980. A general psychoevolutionary theory of emotion. *Emotion: Theory, research, and experience*, 1(3):3–33.

Robert Plutchik. 2001. The nature of emotions. *American Scientist*, 89(July-August):344–350.

James A. Russell. 2003. Core affect and the psychological construction of emotion. *Psychological review*, 110(1):1–145.

Hendrik Schuff, Jeremy Barnes, Julian Mohme, Sebastian Padó, and Roman Klinger. 2017. Annotation, modelling and analysis of fine-grained emotions on a stance and sentiment detection corpus. In *Proceedings of the 8th Workshop on Computational Approaches to Subjectivity, Sentiment and Social Media Analysis*, pages 13–23, Copenhagen, Denmark, September. Association for Computational Linguistics.

Carlo Strapparava and Rada Mihalcea. 2007. SemEval-2007 Task 14: Affective Text. In *Proceedings of the Fourth International Workshop on Semantic Evaluations (SemEval-2007)*, pages 70–74, Prague, Czech Republic, June.

Enrica Troiano, Sebastian Padó, and Roman Klinger. 2019. Crowdsourcing and validating event-focused emotion corpora for German and English. In *Proceedings of the 57th Annual Meeting of the Association for Computational Linguistics*, pages 4005–4011, Florence, Italy, July. Association for Computational Linguistics.

Ashish Vaswani, Noam Shazeer, Niki Parmar, Jakob Uszkoreit, Llion Jones, Aidan N Gomez, Ł ukasz Kaiser, and Illia Polosukhin. 2017. Attention is all you need. In I. Guyon, U. V. Luxburg, S. Bengio, H. Wallach, R. Fergus, S. Vishwanathan, and R. Garnett, editors, *Advances in Neural Information Processing Systems 30*, pages 5998–6008. Curran Associates, Inc.

Janyce Wiebe, Theresa Wilson, and Claire Cardie. 2005. Annotating expressions of opinions and emotions in language. *Language Resources and Evaluation*, 39(2-3):165–210.

Shijie Wu and Mark Dredze. 2019. Beto, bentz, becas: The surprising cross-lingual effectiveness of BERT. In *Proceedings of the 2019 Conference on Empirical Methods in Natural Language Processing and the 9th International Joint Conference on Natural Language Processing (EMNLP-IJCNLP)*, pages 833–844, Hong Kong, China, November. Association for Computational Linguistics.

The LiLaH Emotion Lexicon of Croatian, Dutch and Slovene

Nikola Ljubešić
Dept. of Language Technologies
Jožef Stefan Institute, Slovenia
`nikola.ljubesic@ijs.si`

Ilia Markov
CLIPS Research Center
University of Antwerp, Belgium
`ilia.markov@uantwerpen.be`

Darja Fišer
Faculty of Arts
University of Ljubljana, Slovenia
`darja.fiser@ff.uni-lj.si`

Walter Daelemans
CLIPS Research Center
University of Antwerp, Belgium
`walter.daelemans@uantwerpen.be`

Abstract

In this paper, we present emotion lexicons of Croatian, Dutch and Slovene, based on manually corrected automatic translations of the English NRC Emotion lexicon. We evaluate the impact of the translation changes by measuring the change in supervised classification results of socially unacceptable utterances when lexicon information is used for feature construction. We further showcase the usage of the lexicons by calculating the difference in emotion distributions in texts containing and not containing socially unacceptable discourse, comparing them across four languages (English, Croatian, Dutch, Slovene) and two topics (migrants and LGBT). We show significant and consistent improvements in automatic classification across all languages and topics, as well as consistent (and expected) emotion distributions across all languages and topics, proving for the manually corrected lexicons to be a useful addition to the severely lacking area of emotion lexicons, the crucial resource for emotive analysis of text.

1 Introduction

Emotion lexicons are rather scarce resources for most languages (Buechel et al., 2020), although they are a very important ingredient for robust emotion detection in text (Mohammad et al., 2018). They are mostly differentiated between depending on the way they encode emotions – either via continuous or discrete representations (Calvo and Mac Kim, 2013). In this work, we present emotion lexicons for three languages – Croatian, Dutch and Slovene, developed by manually correcting automatic translations that are part of the NRC Emotion Lexicon (Mohammad and Turney, 2013). In that lexicon, sentiment (positive or negative) and a discrete model of emotion covering *anger*, *anticipation*, *disgust*, *fear*, *joy*, *sadness*, *surprise* and *trust*, are encoded via a binary variable for each emotion. The size of the lexicon is 14,182 entries, and automatic translations of that lexicon were performed by the authors in 2017 via Google Translate.

The three languages in question are generally not covered well with emotional lexicons. The first lexical dataset encoding emotion for Croatian was published recently (Ćoso et al., 2019), encoding valence and arousal for 3,022 words. For Dutch two resources exist – the LIWC (Tausczik and Pennebaker, 2010) translation into Dutch (Boot et al., 2017) covering around 4,500 entries, and the norms for 4,300 Dutch words for dominance, valence and arousal (Moors et al., 2013). There are no available emotion lexicons for the Slovene language except the automatic translation of the NRC lexicon.

Just recently, an automatic approach to building emotion lexicons for many languages beyond mere translation has emerged (Buechel et al., 2020) and its results cover all three languages in question, showing reasonable correlations with the available small psychological norms in various languages.

2 The Lexicon Translation Procedure

We base our approach to building reliable emotion lexicons for the three languages in question on a very simple approach – we manually correct automatic translations of an existing English emotion lexicon.

Proceedings of the Third Workshop on Computational Modeling of PEople's Opinions, PersonaLity, and Emotions in Social media, pages 153–157
Barcelona, Spain (Online), December 13, 2020.

These automatic translations consist to the greatest part of single-word translations, only rare entries being translated with short phrases.

We used different translators for each language as our aim was for the translations to be performed by native speakers. We used a uniform translation methodology across the three languages, ensuring comparability between the resulting lexicons. The guidelines presented to the translators were the following:

- While translating, the sentiment and emotion labels should be taken into account by the translator.

- If a source word is polysemous, we translate only those senses that relate to the given sentiment and emotion.

- We include all target synonyms of the source word that are frequent and that are not polysemous or homonymous with target words of a different sentiment and emotion association.[1]

- Given that the original lexicon was not part-of-speech encoded, we do not encode it in the translations either. We add translations in multiple parts-of-speech if this follows the guidelines above.

While we decided to correct translations of all entries for Croatian and Slovene, for Dutch we only corrected those entries that were marked for emotion, i.e., they had at least one positive value among the two sentiment and eight binary variables encoded in the lexicon. The reason for this decision was the limited availability of the Dutch translator and the fact that the emotion-marked part of the lexicon is most useful for various applications. Given this decision, the resulting lexicons of Croatian and Slovene have 14,182 entries, while the Dutch version has only 6,468 entries.

Translating the lexicons resulted in a different level of modifications in each of the three languages. In Table 1, we present the distribution of emotion-marked (left) and emotion-empty (right) entries regarding whether (1) the original translation was kept, (2) the original was extended with additional translations, or (3) the entry was fully modified. Among the marked entries the fewest interventions were necessary in the Dutch lexicon. This might be due to two facts: (1) the English-Dutch automatic translation is performing in general better than the English-Croatian and English-Slovene one, and (2) the Dutch inflectional system is closer to the English one than that of Croatian and Slovene, the latter both being (South) Slavic languages. For the emotion-empty entries that were translated to Croatian and Slovene only, these have required overall less intervention when compared to emotion-full entries. A higher number of emotion-empty entries was kept in their original state and a lower number of these entries was fully modified. This phenomenon might derive from the fact that emotion-marked words are to some level culture-specific (Jackson et al., 2019; Markov et al., 2018), but even more to our intuition that emotion-marked words are harder to machine-translate than those that are emotion-empty.

	marked			empty		
	original	extended	fully modified	original	extended	fully modified
Croatian	45.9%	22.7%	31.5%	54.8%	16.5%	28.7%
Dutch	68.2%	19.1%	12.7%	-	-	-
Slovene	31.0%	7.8%	61.2%	35.9%	7.2%	56.9%

Table 1: The per-language distribution of emotion-loaded (left) and empty (right) entries that were kept untouched, were only extended, or were fully modified during the manual correction process.

3   Analyses

In this section, we present two types of analyses of the manually corrected LiLaH emotion lexicons – one based on machine learning that compares the original automatically translated NRC and the manually corrected LiLaH lexicon, and another based on descriptive statistics, exploiting only the LiLaH emotion lexicon.

---

[1] The percentage of entries translated into more than a single translation is the following by language: Croatian has 27% of such translations, Dutch 24%, and Slovene 24%.

In the first analysis, we measure the impact of the corrections performed in the lexicon on the task of supervised classification of messages potentially containing socially unacceptable discourse (SUD; hate speech being one type of SUD).

In the second analysis, we perform a descriptive analysis of emotion difference between socially unacceptable and socially acceptable discourse (SUD and non-SUD onwards), showcasing the potential of the new lexicon for data analysis.

We perform both analyses on the same set of datasets with manual annotations of SUD - the FRENK Croatian, English and Slovene datasets and the LiLaH Dutch dataset. All four datasets consist of comment threads of mainstream media Facebook posts in Croatia, Great Britain, Slovenia and Flanders. The comment threads in the datasets belong to two topics: migrants and LGBT. The size of the datasets varies, per language and topic, between 3836 and 6941 comments. Each comment in a thread is annotated with an annotation schema encoding the type and target of SUD (Ljubešić et al., 2019). In this work, we only use the basic information whether a comment contains SUD or not. The percentage of SUD comments in the datasets lies between 32% (Dutch LGBT) and 64% (Croatian LGBT).

3.1 Machine Learning Experiments

For our machine learning experiments we transform each text in the datasets in a frequency distribution of emotion associations (or their lack thereof). Let us assume that we discriminate only between two emotions, *anger* and *joy*. For a textual instance "I am so happy", which we lemmatize into a sequence "I be so happy", in our lexicon we cover only the word "happy" with *joy* associated, but not *anger*. We represent this utterance, given that there are four words in the utterance, as $\{\texttt{anger\_yes:0}, \texttt{anger\_no:4}, \texttt{joy\_yes:1}, \texttt{joy\_no:3}\}$.[2]

We perform our experiments by training a binary SVM classifier with an RBF kernel over the textual data transformed with (1) the automatic NRC lexicon and (2) the manually corrected LiLaH lexicon. In Table 2, we present the results of the classification experiments over the three languages of the LiLaH lexicon, and the two topics, migrants and LGBT. We evaluate each system via macro F1 by cross-validating. As a lower bound we use the stratified random baseline. We finally calculate the Δ as the percentage of error reduction that was obtained by manually correcting the machine translated lexicon, considering the random baseline results as our lower bound. All bold results are statistically significantly higher than their counterpart given the McNemar test (McNemar, 1947) at a significance level of $p < 0.0001$.

topic	lang	random	automatic	manual	Δ
migrants	sl	0.495	0.614	**0.639**	4.9%
lgbt	sl	0.500	0.581	**0.636**	11.0%
migrants	nl	0.501	0.601	**0.646**	9.0%
lgbt	nl	0.503	0.617	**0.648**	6.2%
migrants	hr	0.501	0.625	**0.648**	4.6%
lgbt	hr	0.498	0.619	**0.636**	3.4%

Table 2: The macro F1 results of the binary supervised classification experiments on using the automatically translated lexicon or the manually corrected one.

The results show that the manually corrected lexicons improve over the system using automatic translation in each of the six (three languages, two topics) cases, all the improvements being statistically significant. The percentage of the error reduction obtained by moving from the automatically translated lexicon to the manually corrected one, using the random baseline as a lower bound, lies between 3.4% and 11%. These results show that the manually corrected lexicons contain more signal than the automatically translated ones for the task at hand. One has keep in mind that machine learning was used here not to obtain best possible results on the task, but just to measure the impact of the improvements of the lexicon on the formal description of the task at hand, and thereby on other similar problems.

---

[2]Different representations of the data, e.g., recording only positive associations, not negative ones, resulted in slightly lower results, but yielding the same conclusions.

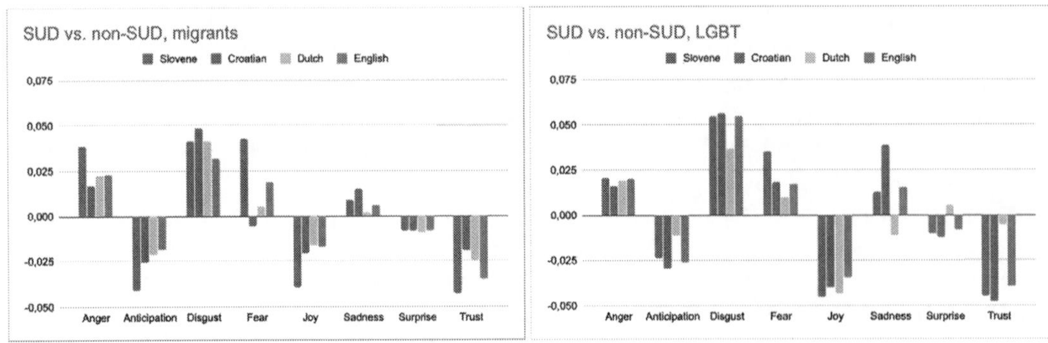

Figure 1: Difference in emotion distribution between texts containing socially unacceptable discourse and not containing such discourse, across the two topics (migrants left, LGBT right) throughout the four languages.

3.2 Emotion Difference Analysis

In this subsection, we do not focus on the difference between the automatically translated and the manually corrected lexicon, but simply apply the manually corrected lexicon over the FRENK and LiLaH datasets to showcase both its usefulness and robustness. Given that in this analysis we are not interested in the difference between the automatically and manually translated lexicon, we are able to include English into this analysis and perform it on all four languages.

We measure the emotion difference between the text containing and not containing SUD as the difference in their probability distribution of emotion associations. For each of the two categories we count the number or tokens that are associated with a specific emotion, and then calculate the probability distribution over the eight emotions. Finally, we simply subtract the distribution calculated on texts not containing SUD from the distribution calculated on texts containing SUD. By doing so we discard the problem of some emotions being more represented in the underlying lexicons than others. The resulting emotion differences are presented in Figure 1 separately for the topic of migrants and LGBT throughout the four languages.

The results show in the first place a high consistency between the four languages. Overall, on both topics, *anger*, *disgust*, *fear* and *sadness* are more prevalent in SUD texts, while the remaining four emotions are more prevalent in non-SUD texts.

The most prominent differences between the four languages can be observed on the emotion of *fear* for the topic of migrants, with Croatian expressing an even higher level of *fear* among the non-SUD texts, which is probably due to a very hardlined discussion of the topic. Another notable difference on the series of emotions can be observed on the topic of LGBT for the Dutch language, which contains an overall less aggressive discussion on that topic in comparison to the three other languages.

Regarding the differences between the two topics, SUD texts on the LGBT topic seem to contain more *disgust* and *sadness* and less *joy*, while SUD texts on the topic of migrants are imbued with more *anger*.

4 Conclusion

In this paper, we presented the LiLaH emotion lexicons – manually corrected automatic translations of the NRC Emotion Lexicon into Croatian, Dutch and Slovene. We have shown that the manually corrected lexicons are more potent in a supervised learning scenario where the lexicon information is used for data representation. We have additionally showcased a usage scenario of the LiLaH lexicons for emotion text analysis – we analysed emotional differences between texts containing socially acceptable and unacceptable discourse, showing a large amount of consistency across languages and topics, with some interesting peculiarities. The presented lexicons are available for download at `http://hdl.handle.net/11356/1318` (Daelemans et al., 2020).

Acknowledgement

This work has been supported by the Slovenian Research Agency and the Flemish Research Foundation through the bilateral research project ARRS N6-0099 and FWO G070619N "The linguistic landscape of hate speech on social media", the Slovenian Research Agency research core funding No. P6-0411 "Language resources and technologies for Slovene language", and the European Union's Rights, Equality and Citizenship Programme (2014-2020) project IMSyPP (grant no. 875263).

References

Peter Boot, Hanna Zijlstra, and Rinie Geenen. 2017. The Dutch translation of the Linguistic Inquiry and Word Count (LIWC) 2007 dictionary. *Dutch Journal of Applied Linguistics*, 6(1):65–76.

Sven Buechel, Susanna Rücker, and Udo Hahn. 2020. Learning and Evaluating Emotion Lexicons for 91 Languages. In *Proceedings of the 58th Annual Meeting of the Association for Computational Linguistics*, pages 1202–1217, Online, July. Association for Computational Linguistics.

Rafael A Calvo and Sunghwan Mac Kim. 2013. Emotions in text: dimensional and categorical models. *Computational Intelligence*, 29(3):527–543.

Bojana Ćoso, Marc Guasch, Pilar Ferré, and José Antonio Hinojosa. 2019. Affective and concreteness norms for 3,022 Croatian words. *Quarterly Journal of Experimental Psychology*, 72(9):2302–2312.

Walter Daelemans, Darja Fišer, Jasmin Franza, Denis Kranjčić, Jens Lemmens, Nikola Ljubešić, Ilia Markov, and Damjan Popič. 2020. The LiLaH Emotion Lexicon of Croatian, Dutch and Slovene. Slovenian language resource repository CLARIN.SI.

Joshua Conrad Jackson, Joseph Watts, Teague R Henry, Johann-Mattis List, Robert Forkel, Peter J Mucha, Simon J Greenhill, Russell D Gray, and Kristen A Lindquist. 2019. Emotion semantics show both cultural variation and universal structure. *Science*, 366(6472):1517–1522.

Nikola Ljubešić, Darja Fišer, and Tomaž Erjavec. 2019. The FRENK Datasets of Socially Unacceptable Discourse in Slovene and English. In *International Conference on Text, Speech, and Dialogue*, pages 103–114. Springer.

Ilia Markov, Vivi Nastase, Carlo Strapparava, and Grigori Sidorov. 2018. The role of emotions in native language identification. In *Proceedings of the 9th Workshop on Computational Approaches to Subjectivity, Sentiment and Social Media Analysis*, pages 123–129, Brussels, Belgium. Association for Computational Linguistics.

Quinn McNemar. 1947. Note on the sampling error of the difference between correlated proportions or percentages. *Psychometrika*, 12(2):153–157.

Saif M Mohammad and Peter D Turney. 2013. Crowdsourcing a word–emotion association lexicon. *Computational Intelligence*, 29(3):436–465.

Saif Mohammad, Felipe Bravo-Marquez, Mohammad Salameh, and Svetlana Kiritchenko. 2018. Semeval-2018 task 1: Affect in tweets. In *Proceedings of the 12th international workshop on semantic evaluation*, pages 1–17.

Agnes Moors, Jan De Houwer, Dirk Hermans, Sabine Wanmaker, Kevin Van Schie, Anne-Laura Van Harmelen, Maarten De Schryver, Jeffrey De Winne, and Marc Brysbaert. 2013. Norms of valence, arousal, dominance, and age of acquisition for 4,300 Dutch words. *Behavior research methods*, 45(1):169–177.

Yla R Tausczik and James W Pennebaker. 2010. The psychological meaning of words: LIWC and computerized text analysis methods. *Journal of language and social psychology*, 29(1):24–54.